Arnold Wesker Revisited

Twayne's English Authors Series

Kinley E. Roby, Editor
Northeastern University

TEAS 506

ARNOLD WESKER
Photograph by Erich Stering/Pressens Bild

Arnold Wesker Revisited

Reade W. Dornan

University of Michigan–Flint

Twayne Publishers • New York
Maxwell Macmillan Canada • Toronto
Maxwell Macmillan International • New York Oxford Singapore Sydney

Arnold Wesker Revisited
Reade W. Dornan

Copyright © 1994 by Twayne Publishers
All rights reserved. No part of this book may be reproduced or transmitted in any form or by any means, electronic or mechanical, including photocopying, recording, or by any information storage and retrieval system, without permission in writing from the Publisher.

Twayne Publishers
Macmillan Publishing Company
866 Third Avenue
New York, New York 10022

Maxwell Macmillan Canada, Inc.
1200 Eglinton Avenue East
Suite 200
Don Mills, Ontario M3C 3N1

Library of Congress Cataloging-in-Publication Data
Dornan, Reade W.
Arnold Wesker revisited / by Reade W. Dornan.
p. cm.— (Twayne's English authors series; TEAS 506)
Includes bibliographical references and index.
ISBN 0-8057-7031-3 (alk. paper)
1. Wesker, Arnold—Criticism and interpretation. I. Title. II. Series.
PR6073.E75Z63 1994
822'.14—dc20
94-1771
CIP

The paper used in this publication meets the minimum requirements of American National Standard for Information Sciences—Permanence of Paper for Printed Library Materials. ANSI Z39.48-1984.∞ ™

10 9 8 7 6 5 4 3 2 1

Printed in the United States of America.

To Tom—Wherever You Are

Contents

Preface   ix
Acknowledgments   xiii
Chronology   xv

> *Chapter One*
> Discovery as an Angry Young Man   1
>
> *Chapter Two*
> Debts to the Court   20
>
> *Chapter Three*
> Theatre, Why?   42
>
> *Chapter Four*
> Distinctions, Intimidations, and Hysteria   69
>
> *Chapter Five*
> Two Roots of Judaism   90
>
> *Chapter Six*
> The Women in Wesker's Writing   113
>
> *Chapter Seven*
> A Sense of What Should Follow   139

Notes and References   153
Selected Bibliography   159
Index   165

Preface

In the late 1950s, when Arnold Wesker's first play was mounted at London's Royal Court Theatre, it reminded critics of John Osborne's *Look Back in Anger* (1956), which had recently played to record audiences. Unlike other plays of its time, *Look Back in Anger* had openly confronted the harsh realities of deprivation and frustration felt by many in postwar Britain. If Wesker's plays initially attracted attention on the coattails of Osborne's popularity, they held audiences on their own merit. Britons welcomed in them a hope, not found in Osborne's plays, that social reform was possible. Tempering the bitterness of Wesker's characters was a reassertion of nineteenth-century socialist values—fairness to the common man, education, and a resistance to technocracy—and these idealistic values brought optimism to his audiences. In Wesker's message was an almost naive refusal to retreat to private concerns and a moral commitment to his own age—rare for an Angry Young Man.

Wesker's early plays became the fashion for several seasons in London between 1960 and 1965. For a while, much was made of Wesker's working-class background. As a pastry cook turned playwright, his was a Cinderella story rarely found in postwar Britain. And London's theater circles responded particularly to his trilogy—*Chicken Soup with Barley, Roots,* and *I'm Talking about Jerusalem,* produced collectively in 1960—because the plays offered a window on working-class life.

Wesker enjoyed his sudden success, but he could also foresee that it would probably be short-lived, so he joined forces with a number of young working-class artists to form Centre 42, a cooperative enterprise for playwrights, producers, directors, and actors. Their purpose was to provide an outlet for nontraditional artists, writers, and directors who wished to wrest control of their own productive means from commercial interests. Their leaders were largely socialist activists who envisioned a vehicle for a more revolutionary message and an alliance with trade unions. Espousing a common goal in socialism, Wesker joined the others in calling for an organization that would minimize the monetary and competitive aspects of life and seek ways in which artists could take control of their own means of expression. Wesker became their co-director.

The effect of Centre 42 was to draw even more attention to Wesker as a personality. Many critics, who had found him fresh and exciting as a working-class playwright, were equally intrigued by his sympathy for socialist causes. He made news for their columns when he spoke about affordable arts for the working classes, and, once again, stories about his idealism filled their columns when he was arrested with Sir Bertrand Russell while marching against nuclear armaments. His plays continued to draw large audiences, but they were often overshadowed by the internal politics of Centre 42. With the debates came an irreconcilable schism in the administration. As a leftist, Wesker was regarded as interesting by the press and public, but not commercial material. And yet he was considered too centrist by his colleagues. Pushed more and more to the margins by leftists in control of Britain's alternative theater movement of the 1970s, he found himself locked out of the decision-making processes after the collapse of Centre 42. It became increasingly difficult to mount a production in London's alternative theaters.

Wesker has struggled ever since the late 1960s to regain his standing in London. After a decade of conflict with his colleagues, the press, and the board of directors of Centre 42, Wesker closed the Centre's doors in 1970. He was initially bewildered by events, but in 1985 he confessed in an interview with me that, in retrospect, he was probably not politically aligned with the socialists as much as he once imagined, at least not in the "strictly doctrinaire, political sense" of his radical contemporaries. Wesker repeated the revelation in a 1986 television interview. He believes now he has found his voice as a humanist, as a champion of individual rights and human values, while defending the causes of the dispossessed—the aged, isolated women, and Jews. It is not, therefore, his political alignment as much as a Jewish humanist philosophy that shapes his thoughts.

Since identifying his ideology, Wesker has learned the unpopularity of his choice. Humanism, with its idealism and neo-romantic roots in individualism, lost ground several decades ago to hardened realists who recognized in it aspects of failure. "A humanist," Colin Wilson wrote in *The Outsider* (1956), is "the most irritating of the human lice . . . with his puffed-up pride in Reason and his ignorance of his own silliness." Regarded a socialist or a working-class writer of the 1960s, Wesker was newsworthy; as a humanist of the 1970s and 1980s, a period when such lofty ideals were considered pretentious, he has been ignored by theater critics and other journalists who have either not understood the nature of what seemed to them an ideological shift or who are embarrassed by the strength of his passions and his willingness to lay open his ideas to further attack. Moreover, he has fought his critics, answering their reviews and debating their assertions in the press, often when it would have served him best to remain quiet.

Although many of his recent plays are interesting for their insights into human nature and rich in their complexity, they are frequently discounted by theater reviewers, who are disappointed with the topics Wesker has chosen in his later works. In January 1992 Wesker spent two weeks in Chicago to observe rehearsals for the premiere of his play *Three Women Talking*, and I had the opportunity to attend these rehearsals. Since short scenes were still being added here and there, lines were being fine-tuned, and director Russell Vandenbroucke was negotiating the additions and deletions with the actors, the atmosphere was quite intense. The cast was expected to give polished performances each night to their preview audiences, regardless of the complex changes that were made earlier in the afternoon.

Despite the demands of these rehearsals, Wesker was periodically called away for interviews—with local newspapers, the local public radio station, a Yiddish newspaper. He also stopped work now and again to spend some time with old friends who had come some distance to be with him. Perhaps Wesker is accustomed to that sort of schedule, but those days were as intellectually stimulating and rich with activity as any I have ever experienced. Curious to find out what the writer in Wesker would remember from this period, I asked him what he would take away with him. "I shall recall the story about the aunt who scolded her nephew for not reading the newspaper," he said. I was baffled. That was some trivial story I had told him while we were walking in the rain, gaping at Chicago's skyscrapers.

Because Wesker is known variously as one of Britain's Angry Young Men or as a socialist or Jewish writer, or perhaps as a working-class writer, it is easy to forget what focus *he* finds most important. Beyond ideological considerations, Wesker fixes on the human condition. He is fascinated by human beings and their familial relationships—their hopes, desires, failures. The everyday exchanges that most of us take for granted are the stuff of his plays. He leaves the glamour and dazzle for journalists to write about, history for academics to record, and religion and politics to debate in editorial columns. Although topical issues condition his plays, and these are evident in the long set speeches given by central characters, it is precisely the human beings and their interactions with each other that govern all else.

For a better understanding of Wesker's writings, particularly those written since 1970, I provide a needed reexamination of the Wesker canon with some clarification of what the author calls his "old-fashioned humanism" and with a special emphasis on how Judaism influences his thinking. It is not difficult to guess the source of his plays, because he makes the point again and again that they come out of his own experience. To write his "Miniautobiography" he even used scenes and lines from his plays to explain his history. Since most of his plays are by his own admission strongly autobiographical, I draw on them to sort out the patterns of his artistic development. Wesker's essays are often probes for his plays, so each chapter of this study contains a detailed discussion of both the fictional pieces and their companion essays, some of them written about the same time. I also use published journal entries, unpublished letters written by Wesker to friends and colleagues, the minutes from Centre 42's meetings, and informal discussions I had with Arnold Wesker. In the end, I demonstrate that his plays bear less resemblance to Osborne's existential frame of reference than the critics once thought and establish him as a thoughtful writer who has stubbornly defied this and other pigeon-holing to carve out his own place in British theater.

Acknowledgments

This book would not have been possible without the kindness of Arnold Wesker, Clive Barker, and John McGrath, who gave me copies of unpublished manuscripts and Centre 42 documents. Interviews with each of them also helped this Yankee understand the dynamics of British theater. Their generosity, patience, and concern for getting it right continue to impress me and leave me deeply indebted to them.

Special thanks also go to Professor Herbert Greenberg of Michigan State University and colleague Julie Colish at the University of Michigan–Flint for reading various chapters of the manuscript. Their remarks were particularly helpful at a crucial point in the writing.

Finally, my gratitude and love to David Dornan, who cooked many a good meal to assure completion of this project.

Chronology

1932	Arnold Wesker born 26 May in Stepney, East London, the second child of Joseph Wesker, a tailor, and Leah (née Cecile Leah Perlmutter).
1936–1948	Is evacuated to various places in England and Wales during the war.
1943–1948	Attends Upton House Technical School in Hackney, East London.
1948	Is accepted by the Royal Academy of Dramatic Arts but does not attend for lack of tuition.
1948–1952	Works as a pastry cook, furniture maker, bookseller's assistant, and plumber's mate; does two years' national service in the Royal Air Force.
1957	Writes *The Kitchen*.
1958	*Chicken Soup with Barley* premieres at the Belgrade Theatre, Coventry, and is transferred to London's Royal Court Theatre; is awarded an Arts Council grant of £300, which Wesker uses to marry Doreen (Dusty) Bicker.
1959	*Roots* premieres at the Belgrade Theatre (later staged at the Royal Court Theatre and in the West End). First son, Lindsay Joe, is born.
1960	*I'm Talking about Jerusalem* premieres as part of Wesker's trilogy at the Royal Court Theatre.
1961	*The Kitchen* is staged at the Belgrade Theatre and is transferred to the Royal Court Theatre (film version is also released). Daughter, Tanya Jo, is born.
1962	*Chips with Everything* premieres at the Royal Court Theatre and is voted Best Play of 1962; runs successfully in the West End. Second son, Daniel, is born.
1963	*Menace* is aired on BBC television. *Chips with Everything* premieres on Broadway.
1964	*Their Very Own and Golden City* premieres at Belgian National Theatre and is awarded the Italian Premio Marzotto prize of £3,000.

1965 *The Four Seasons* premieres at the Belgrade Theatre.

1966 *Their Very Own and Golden City* is staged at the Royal Court Theatre.

1970 *The Friends* premieres at Centre 42. Wesker resigns as its artistic director in December. *Fears of Fragmentation*, an essay collection mostly about Centre 42.

1971 *Six Sundays in January*.

1972 *The Journalists* is written but not performed because of an actors' revolt. *The Old Ones* premieres at the Royal Court Theatre.

1974 *The Wedding Feast* premieres in Stockholm at the Stadtsteater (British premiere is at the Leeds Playhouse in 1977). *Love Letters on Blue Paper*, short story collection.

1976 Television production of *Love Letters on Blue Paper*. *The Merchant* (now called *Shylock*) premieres in Stockholm. *Words—as Definitions of Experience*, with an afterword by Richard Appignanesi.

1977 *One More Ride on the Merry-Go-Round* is written but not performed until 1985 at the Phoenix Arts in Leicester. The English version of *Shylock* premieres on Broadway (not staged in England until 1978, in Birmingham).

1978 *Said the Old Man to the Young Man*, short story collection.

1979 *Chicken Soup with Barley* wins a gold medal for best foreign play. *The Journalists: A Triptych*, a collection with journal entries and a personal essay.

1980 *Lady Othello* is written as a film script.

1981 *Caritas* premieres at the Cottesloe, National Theatre. *The Journalists* premieres in Wilhelmshaven, Germany.

1982 *Four Portraits—of Mothers* premieres in Tokyo (first U.K. performance is at Edinburgh Festival in 1984; first London performance is at the Half Moon Theater in 1987).

1983 *Annie Wobbler* is heard as a radio play on Germany's Suddeutscher Rundfunk (staged in London in 1984 at the Fortune Theatre).

1984 *Yardsale* is broadcast by BBC Radio 3 (staged at the Edinburgh Festival in 1985).
1985 *Distinctions*.
1986 *When God Wanted a Son* is written.
1987 *Yardsale* and *Whatever Happened to Betty Lemon?* are staged together at the Lyric Theatre Studio, Hammersmith. *Badenheim 1939* is adapted from an Appelfeld novel. *Lady Othello* is adapted as a play.
1988 Wesker writes *The Mistress* and *Beorhtel's Hill*, a community play that celebrates the fortieth anniversary of Basildon, a New Town in England. *Caritas* is adapted into a libretto.
1990 *Three Women Talking* is written (premieres at Chicago's Northlight Theatre in 1992).
1991 *The Mistress* premieres at Rome's Teatro Flaiano (world premiere is at the Teatro Petrach, Arezzo, Italy).
1992 *Letter to a Daughter* premieres in Milan at the Piccolo Teatro in a production sponsored by the British Council. *Wild Spring* is written. *Blood Libel* (originally titled *William of Norwich*) is adapted from a historical account by Thomas of Monmouth for a theater opening in Norwich.
1994 Wesker begins his autobiography for Century Publishers, *As Much as I Dare*. The trilogy is mounted as a co-production of four theaters in France and is revived in London.

Chapter One

Discovery as an Angry Young Man

Arnold Wesker came into prominence in Great Britain with the success of his play *Chicken Soup with Barley* in 1958 at the Belgrade Theatre, Coventry, and the Royal Court Theatre, London. *Roots* and *I'm Talking about Jerusalem* followed in 1959 and 1960, respectively. With the trilogy, Wesker became a celebrated playwright whose works have never left the public's view in one way or another. At least one of his plays has been staged somewhere in the world just about every day since the early 1970s. Today his early plays in particular have become standards in secondary school syllabi and are often revived in university settings or regional theaters. His later plays, however, are staged abroad more often than they are in England; in fact, few of these plays, although staged elsewhere and published, have been produced in a major London venue.

Wesker's works enjoyed that measure of early success in part because those first plays closely followed the overnight sensation of John Osborne's *Look Back in Anger*. Once that association was made, Wesker's name was understandably thrown among those of the Angry Young Men. These were the novelists—Colin Wilson, Kingsley Amis, and John Braine—who were generally dissatisfied with society, especially with the class structure. These were the playwrights of the postwar generation—Arnold Wesker, Shelagh Delaney, Bernard Kops, John Arden, and Margaretta D'Arcy—who injured England's national pride by charging that they had been sold out by a postwar government that had falsely promised a future for them. They felt unjustly crushed by the British class system. Cheated out of their hopes, they despaired of change. The label of Angry Young Man fits Wesker in many significant ways. As a working-class pastry cook who never attended college, he was certainly writing from outside the staid literary establishment, filled with indignation about injustices in the system. Like the others, he wrote about young people who voiced a cause, and he did so to effect change.

The Angry Young Men of the late 1950s gained importance when, as forerunners of the 1960s protesters, they marked a turning point in

Britain's politics, and they refashioned theater circles as well. Suddenly their brand of protest drama created a general dissatisfaction with the traditional fare in London, which up to that time had consisted of anemic drawing room comedy, gentle revues, comfortable musicals, and conventional, middle-class plays. For Wesker there was one significant difference: his voice was not as acrimonious as the others'. Osborne's bitter style, which attacked social malaise and endorsed the legitimacy of alienation, shook London's theater at its foundations when it also destroyed several myths about bourgeois gentility. Tacitly Osborne was questioning British producers and directors about who should occupy the audiences, what constitutes appropriate subject matter, and how much theater should be shaped by middle-class tastes.

Despite their less aggressive tone, Wesker's first four plays (the trilogy plus *The Kitchen*) were marked as *Look Back in Anger*'s successors, largely because they were inspired by Osborne's model and articulated the disgust felt by many young playwrights of the time. Furthermore, Wesker accompanied his plays with a number of angry articles sent to key publications like the *New Statesman*. Acting as footnotes to his plays and sounding as though they were written by Osborne's Jimmy Porter, the articles challenged the government to a more inclusive educational system, issued provocative statements about the need for greater access to the arts by the working classes, and recommended various changes for a utopian socialist system. Fractious and sometimes naive, these letters irritated people in government and in theater circles, but Wesker's excesses were forgiven as long as his plays were popular. Onstage, his best spokesperson for these concerns was his protagonist Ronnie, the angry young man of the trilogy who, like Jimmy Porter, contended that Britain's class structure excluded the working classes even when they had the opportunity to be educated. Through Ronnie, Wesker stood for a classless society, expressed openly a concern about humanity and humaneness, and attempted to establish a new aesthetic environment for ordinary people, particularly the working classes.

Wesker's plays were also linked to Osborne's because they ran at the Royal Court Theatre, the home of *Look Back in Anger* and London's alternative and experimental drama. In 1956 George Devine of the English Stage Company at the Court was looking for a box office success when he stumbled on *Look Back in Anger* while testing the market with Britain's first run of Arthur Miller's *The Crucible*. *Anger* turned out to be such a money-maker that it underwrote later productions of Bertolt Brecht's *The Good Woman of Setzuan*, Eugène Ionesco's *The Lesson*, as well as Samuel Beckett's *Fin de Partie* and *Acts without Words I*. Until Devine was willing to take a chance on them, plays like these were virtually unavailable to the public anywhere in the United Kingdom. Osborne's success likewise opened the way at the Court to a string of new locally grown dramas that were considered comparable. Devine probably hoped to luck into another blockbuster. *Chicken Soup with Barley* and *Roots* were two of the beneficiaries, even though Wesker's plays did not have the groundbreaking structure of Beckett's or the attendance-record-breaking capacity of Osborne's.

Kitchen-Sink Dramatist

The working-class context of Osborne's and Wesker's plays had wide appeal as a fresh, new perspective for London's audiences. Wesker himself was a novelty since it was rare for anyone who had not attended Oxford or Cambridge—least of all for one who had failed his O-level exams—to be taken seriously in London's closed literary circles. Wesker's success as a playwright created a sensation in the media, in part because he stood for the open society Britons wanted to create in the postwar era and for hope at a time when Britons needed to read about successes.

Wesker was not trying to be a novelty, however. He was merely doing what he did best—writing autobiographically by drawing heavily on his experiences in a Jewish family, with a communist mother and socialist friends. He wrote stories about his wife, his working-class neighborhood in London's East End, and his trade union aunts who fought the good fight for political causes. Because his plays seemed solidly centered on his working-class home life, some critics—John Elsom, Richard Findlater, and Walter Allen—tagged Wesker and others, including Shelagh Delaney and John Arden, as the "kitchen-sink dramatists." They borrowed the trendy expression from an art movement in the 1950s centered in North England and known for its realistic depiction of domestic, working-class scenes. The term is catchy but not entirely appropriate, as it applies primarily to Wesker's earliest plays. Wesker is among the few playwrights to have explored the particulars of a Jewish working-class family—a perspective that is still uncommon for the British stage—and he used the topos because these were the people he knew. Even more to the point, he wrote about them to call attention to the injustices done to them rather than to give an insider's perspective on this community.

The working-class theme suddenly became popular after *Look Back in Anger* gave it currency in 1956. Although Osborne himself does not come from a working-class family, his hero, Jimmy Porter, seethes with class resentment against his wife and her privileged family. Wesker's early characters do have origins in the working class and express this class's discontent, and so they do not glorify young rebels who are alienated and disaffected without knowing why. Unlike Osborne's Jimmy Porter, who is a "disconcerting mixture of sincerity and cheerful malice, of tenderness and freebooting cruelty,"[1] Wesker's Ronnie Kahn is simply frustrated and rebellious. He is more of a traditional hero, fed up with a stultifying system and ready to throw it over for something new. Jimmy complains about women who "bleed us to death" and nihilistically believes "there aren't any good, brave causes left. If the big bang does come, and we all get killed off, it won't be in aid of the old-fashioned, grand design. It'll be for the Brave New-nothing-very-much-thank-you" (Osborne, 140–41). Ronnie, on the other hand, believes he can empower his girlfriend, Beatie Bryant, by inspiring her to become an activist. He is clearly more idealistic and optimistic than Jimmy Porter, albeit frustrated and angry.

Even without the sardonic Jimmy Porter, Wesker's working-class characters were embraced by many Britons of the 1950s as a metaphor for their own class discontents. The postwar economy had been massively disappointing. Jobs had not materialized as expected, and the Americans were pouring their money into the reconstruction of Germany through the Marshall Plan; consequently capital resources for retooling in England were limited. Competition from the European markets was keener than expected, the influx of immigrants from the colonies, the burden of war taxes, and the loss of the Suez Canal were more of a humiliation than the government of Harold Wilson would concede. Even though their emphasis was on the complaints of the working-class community and would seem to play successfully to popular audiences, Wesker's plays were more readily adopted by university and college students, teachers and technocrats—an increasingly large group of the disaffected seeking a voice for the counterculture. Recognizing and embracing the leftist themes, especially his campaign to ameliorate the working-class condition, many young intellectuals began linking Wesker's plays to the trendy socialist theater of the time.

Socialist Writer

Tantalized by the innovative theater of Beckett, Miller, and Osborne, London audiences and critics had high expectations for more interesting theater to follow. They were ready for the likes of Wesker because he pursued not only new themes but seemed to suggest hope for a discouraged, postwar-weary Britain. Expectations for a theatrical revolution rested all the more on Wesker's shoulders because he was a vocal, self-avowed socialist who imagined a role for the artist in the formation of a new state. Many of his socialist ideals were passed on to him at the knee of his mother, who was actively involved in the Communist party. For a short while he was a member of the Young Communist League, and in April 1961 he was arrested in a sit-down, antinuclear demonstration at Whitehall for which he was later fined £1. In September of the same year he participated in another Campaign for Nuclear Disarmament (CND) demonstration along with author Robert Bolt (*A Man for All Seasons*) and philosopher Sir Bertrand Russell, for which Wesker and many others were sentenced to a month in jail.

He had been working to reform British theater even before he was arrested in political demonstrations on behalf of radical causes. His sudden fame as a playwright gave him a forum. In 1960, almost as soon as he had minimal name recognition, Wesker began issuing pamphlets to the trade unions calling for a socialist solution for the arts, largely in line with the nineteenth century utopian socialist William Morris.

Morris believed that machinery in the industrial age debased the function of labor, robbing workers of taking any pleasure in completing the task and destroying their creativity and pride. Furthermore, competition forced workers into meaningless, degrading jobs in unhealthy workplaces that were stripped of order and beauty crucial to the worker's health and well-being. As a curative, Morris looked to the arts for some hope of elevating the quality of their work lives and, in turn, the quality of their products. Small workshops that crafted items rather than manufacturing them on an assembly line would ultimately be more satisfying places where workers could take pride in their products and the quality of the products would in turn make their creation more pleasing. Having said this, Morris called for the elimination of cheap, trashy goods of the kind that has the highest margin of profit in a capitalist system in favor of handicrafts with integrity and workers who, understanding artistic creation, produced what they wanted. He was convinced that conversion to socialism would come about through a revolutionary form of education that would give people a greater sense of their potential as a political force and as artists. Under socialism, Morris also envisioned whole communities flourishing with plenty of leisure time and healthy living.[2]

Imagining Morris's ideals for a society that turned to its artists for a truly pleasant way to live, Wesker talked about places all over England that could serve as collecting points for artists and audiences. In 1960, two years after his initial successes at the Royal Court Theatre, Wesker issued two pamphlets to the secretary of every trade union in Britain—"The Modern Playwright, or 'O, Mother, is it worth it?'" and "Labour and the Arts: II, or 'What, then, is to be done?'"—in which he exhorted the unions to consider a more vital relationship to the arts. In the first pamphlet he argued that an increased exposure to the arts could assure a better life because "working, playing, laughing, crying, eating, singing, dancing, studying, leisure and creative art [are] not separate aspects of living for separate people, but natural manifestations of the *whole* act of living for everyone to indulge or enjoy."[3] Like Morris, Wesker argued that the enjoyment of the arts is humanizing and opens up economic opportunities to those who read books, listen to concerts, and attend the theater. Besides, the arts belong to the workers and should not be left to the care of others. He summed up by saying, "I believe Socialism—and I'm sorry about the number of times I've said this—to be not merely an economic organization of society, but a way of living based on the assumption that life is rich, rewarding and that human beings deserve it." What he meant was that he believed socialism could fan "that marvelous human spark" to "release the energy of the individual" and nurture the creative best out of every human being.[4]

Wesker was among a group of activists who then turned to trade union support to organize an artist's cooperative that would provide a greater voice for working-class writers, musicians, actors, directors, and composers. Much to everyone's surprise, four unions offered their support and two others provided small amounts of funding. Furthermore, in September 1960 the Trades Union Congress passed Resolution 42, a petition to find ways to encourage greater participation in the cultural life of the community and spawning Centre 42. Centre 42 enjoyed several short-lived successes in the early 1960s, but it was eventually destroyed by splinter groups among the various socialist factions, lack of reliable private and public subsidy, and disagreement among the board of directors about the Centre's ideological basis and future. By 1964 it was clear that Centre 42 did not have sufficient funding, and there was serious dissension in its leadership. It limped along until 1970, when it folded altogether. Since then Wesker has felt relegated to the margins of London's alternative theater and even excluded entirely by some venues.

Because Wesker's vision for labor was drawn on Morris's nineteenth-century model, it was repudiated by socialists with more radical interests. Such leftist playwrights as John McGrath, for example, considered

Wesker's approach to working-class theater romantic, paternalistic, and impractical as an instrument for social change. McGrath, a founding member of Centre 42, believed that Wesker's solution for the working classes was an adoption of those middle-class values that would eventually undermine the working-class culture. McGrath's debate with Wesker was played out in a series of letters written in 1970. Their differences lay essentially in political philosophy. Whereas Wesker and his supporters were simply seeking an opportunity for the workers to gain greater access to the middle-class arts, McGrath and others like him were pressing for significant changes—a fundamental restructuring of Britain's economic system that would put more of the nation's income in the hands of the working classes. McGrath made his point by founding the 7:84, a theater company whose name reminds us that 84 percent of Britain's wealth is owned by 7 percent of the population. Wesker has always felt that the economic system is fundamentally exploitative; nevertheless, he is loathe to call for a complete abandonment of capitalism.

McGrath attacked Wesker's old-fashioned socialist values in plays like *The Friends*. His intention was not to drive Wesker out of the movement but to engage him in debate. Demanding real commitment to revolutionist goals of his socialist friends, McGrath wrote in a *Black Dwarf* review of *The Friends*, "If Wesker had concentrated on bringing a truly socialist consciousness to bear on the mass forms of television and film, if he had tried to make the theatre he presented relate directly to the conflicts and history of the working class, or if he had at least attempted to break down the bourgeois forms and mystique of the theatre, then he would have been somewhat more convincing in his concern for the cultural well-being of the proletariat."[5]

Following the appearance of that review, Wesker and McGrath exchanged their letters fighting over the purposes and goals of socialist theater. Essentially, McGrath argued for a radical transformation of society and Wesker for gradual reform. Already feeling under siege by various factions at Centre 42, Wesker had no stomach for a give-and-take discussion, and he responded defensively. He took McGrath's attack personally to mean "If you aren't with us, you're against us." Their argument ended with a few angry words and a nagging doubt in Wesker's mind about the nature of his commitment to socialism. This was a man who had been willing in 1960 to go to jail for his pacifist convictions and yet in 1970 had been left deeply uneasy about the left's attitude toward power—lessons he had learned during the turbulent years of Centre 42 in debates with people who espoused opinions like McGrath's. The discomfort of their ideological quarrels haunted him for years, shaping his later political statements about the individual and the state, about socialism, about the role of politics in literature.

Although Wesker was at the forefront of the movement that made protest theater a box office attraction, as the 1960s progressed he found himself displaced more and more by hardline activists and performance art groups who were committed to radical social and political reform. Dedicated to a more economically egalitarian society accessible to the oppressed and dispossessed, their cause had a revolutionary fervor that was endorsed by the politics of the era. Audiences were flocking to see radical drama. In the next generation were John McGrath, David Edgar, Edward Bond, and Trevor Griffiths—all playwrights whose leftist works were suddenly very much in demand. Wesker found himself obsolete ironically at a time when government patronage to the alternative theater groups had risen substantially. Subsequently, the number of alternative theater groups—not counting the young people's theater—that originated in the 1970s jumped from a half-dozen in 1968 to more than a hundred in 1978.[6] Additionally, the number of places to stage alternative theater grew from 34 in 1968 to more than 140 in 1978, and there were at least 200 small-scale touring companies in London and the regions (Itzin, xiv). Forming theater companies under names like The General Will, CAST, Portable Theatre, Joint Stock, Gay Sweatshop, Red Ladder, Belts and Braces, and Monstrous Regiment, theater ranks in Britain soon included feminists, gays, leftists from Marxists to liberals, radical educators, and experimenters of all sorts.

Socialist theater took such a dramatic turn to the left in the late 1960s and into the 1970s that Wesker eventually began to rethink his political position. Clearly his William Morris type of politics was not confrontational enough to satisfy demands in the growing counterculture for radical theater, despite his self-avowed socialist sympathies. Just when he needed a play that would put him back into the mainstream, he wrote several box office rejects in a row. Unfortunately, several of them were weak and others disappointed audiences anticipating more productions with political themes. *Their Very Own and Golden City* (staged 1963–65) was written with insider politics in mind and therefore confused many reviewers. *The Four Seasons* (staged 1964), considered overly sentimental, was not the sort of play Wesker's fans wanted to see. *The Friends* (staged 1970) reflected Wesker's depressed mood at the close of Centre 42 and his mixed feelings about utopian experiments and radical socialism—another letdown for audiences who considered Wesker an upbeat playwright.

Some reviewers were disappointed by what seemed to be soft logic and other signs of Wesker's lack of a university education. Ironically, they were turning against his working-class background because of his lack of sophistication. Many critics felt Wesker could have corrected his problems had he stayed with his director of the trilogy and *Chips*, John Dexter. Wesker did use Dexter to mount *The Old Ones* (staged 1967), however, and it too received mixed reviews because the audiences did not understand its Jewish traditions. The oddest incident was the 1972 actors' revolt at the Royal Shakespeare Company, when they refused to perform *The Journalists*. Their objections grew largely out of a political correctness of the time that discounted Wesker's approach. They preferred the more radical play by John Arden and Margaretta D'Arcy, *Island of the Mighty*. Because Wesker's reputation was no longer on the ascendancy, the actors had the clout to refuse the play. In the end, the company ironically did not perform *Island of the Mighty* because the playwrights—even more radical than the actors were—withdrew their play when they decided the Royal Shakespeare Company's production distorted their writing. Then as now, Wesker's answer to his critics—both in the mainstream press and on his left—has been to lash out with a stream of angry letters to the newspapers. He has defended his views and his plays—whether the work in question was weak or strong. And his opinions have been routinely ignored, even though he has often been right. These letters have not improved his situation, however, because his politics is often little supported or understood; Wesker nevertheless continues to write to the *Guardian*, the *Times*, the *Independent*, the *New Statesman*, and the *Observer* when something is on his mind. His editorializing has earned him the reputation of a pesky troublemaker in an age that mistrusts emotional outbursts, idealism, and a passionate faith in human worth. Wesker has fought a lifelong battle on behalf of human rights—those of the elderly, of Jews, of Palestinians, of trade union workers, of Salman Rushdie, and even of racists—in a country where self-mockery and flippancy are commonplace and valued. He has withheld his plays from performance in South Africa, spoken out against Irish terrorists, and railed against the "lilliputian mentality" of theater critics. His outrage at injustice has struck his reviewers as rather quixotically moralistic and self-righteous, even naive. His reputation for stubbornness—earned by speaking out for sometimes unpopular causes and by insisting on taking some part in directing his plays himself—makes producers wary of financing a major production with him.

In a 1986 interview, 16 years after his exchange with John McGrath, Richard Hoggart praised Wesker for his willingness to discuss his clash with others in public, particularly with the socialists. Wesker explained his differences by saying that he no longer believed himself a socialist, at least not in the "strictly doctrinaire political sense."[7] He continues to embrace many of the socialist ideals as defined by William Morris—a belief in the goodness of honest labor, especially when the worker had direct control over the means of production, a belief in the value of education and the arts, and a belief in basic fairness in the way everyone, including the working classes, should be treated. But he has backed away from any social and economic revolution that would redistribute the wealth and power in Britain. Such a retraction should have come as little surprise to many fellow artists like McGrath, who have been long critical of his political fence-riding. Nevertheless, Wesker's admission would have been quite startling to those who were accustomed to identifying him in the early 1960s with the radicals. He himself had found the question about where he lay politically difficult to sort out at first. As soon as he made that statement to Hoggart, he asked himself, "If I'm not socialist, what am I?" (Hoggart 1986).

East End Jew

That question has remained unanswered for some time, for Wesker still embraces many of the basic tenets of socialism. He continues to bristle somewhat at McGrath's suggestion that he is not "in any way socialist" and that his work has little to say to the left. He could argue, after all, that he was raised in London's East End, a district known for its socialist radicals.

The East End, unofficially defined by the neighborhoods of Bethnal Green, Stepney, Whitechapel, Mile End Road, Spitalfields, Shoreditch, and Bow, has long been home to newly arrived immigrants, the poor and dispossessed. Ever since 1381, when peasants from Essex met with the king and his deputies to protest a poll tax in what later was called the Peasants' Revolt, it has been the place of assembly for a variety of political causes. In the nineteenth century William Booth founded the Salvation Army (1867) in Whitechapel Road, the Chartists were accused of storing arms at the Trades Hall in Bethnal Green in preparation of an alleged overthrow attempt of the government (1840), and Karl Marx's daughter, Eleanor, organized the trade unions in Whitechapel. The East End was also the origin of massive strikes organized by Jewish anarchists in 1889. Later, Sylvia Pankhurst's East London Federation of Suffragettes met in Bow, and Mohandas Ghandi stayed at Kingsley Hall in 1931.

The brand of socialism that sprang up in the late nineteenth century out of concentrations of agitators like the Jewish radicals of the East End set the pattern for socialists in Europe and America. There were, of course, the revolutionists and anarchists among the Jewish immigrants who originated in Russia and Central Europe and whose population dominated the East End at the turn of the century. In these circles were those who were recognized and supported by the Socialist League of William Morris. This group spoke out for more jobs, improved working conditions, higher wages, and greater political representation. They were strong political agitators for fair treatment of all the Jewish workers, but especially of the machinists and the garment industry, the heart of Jewish industry and probably the most powerful group of workers in the late nineteenth century. Wesker's family counted themselves among those protesters. His father, Joseph Wesker, was a tailor's machinist, and members of his family—particularly his sisters Anne and Sarah—belonged to the Garment Workers' Trade Union, one of the unions to grow out of the early Jewish socialist movement.

If anyone molded Arnold Wesker's rebellion as a child, however, it was his mother, Cecile Perlmutter Wesker, known to her friends as Leah. Wesker remembers her fondly for her ability to face failure and survive it. Whatever political, personal, or social setbacks she suffered, she bore them unflinchingly and carried on, refusing to give up. Wesker still uses her example when he feels cornered and limited by others.

Leah Wesker was born in Gyergyoszentmiklos (George St. Nicholas), Romania, one of 14 children.[8] Three died at birth, and all but one (who died a Communist in Bucharest) of the remaining 11 emigrated to England and, later, Israel. After her mother was killed in a horse-and-cart accident, Leah and her two younger brothers were sent to England in 1906 to live with her grown sister, Sarah, who was already settled there. Her *shoichet* father (a Kosher butcher) wanted to remarry, and his new wife did not want the responsibility of the three young children, so Sarah took care of her three younger siblings, even as a widow, until she married a second time in 1921. Her new spouse, a widower with four children, asked Leah, Harry (Herman), and Ignatz (Isaac, Ignatic) to fend on their own; thus they were set out on the streets for the second time. Still, they made out. Ignatz (also known as Uncle Perly) became a successful businessman making thermostats, but Uncle Harry (a dyed-in-the-wool Communist) never took to capitalist enterprise, though he tried. Leah married Joseph Wesker, a man more like Arnold's Uncle Harry than Uncle Perly.

The Weskers had landed in Swansea from Dneiperpetrovsk (known as Katerineslav), Russia, around 1910. They probably left in fear of yet another wave of pogroms. His grandfather, Mendel, was "well versed in Talmud," according to one of Wesker's aunts. His father was one of five children and had a twin sister, Aunty Rae, who's described in the story "A Time of Dying."[9] His father was "a loveable but weak personality who was more intelligent than his trade of tailor's machiner which he hated."[10] Like his brother-in-law, Uncle Harry, he was not interested in making money.

The stories of the Perlmutters and the Weskers speak for thousands of Jews who emigrated to England in those years.[11] Indeed, 1906, the year Leah arrived, was one of the peak times for Jewish immigration, especially from Central Europe and Russia because of the chaos caused by the Russo-Japanese War (1904–5) and the 1905 Russian Revolution. There was little work, and the harvest was unpredictable. The Russians blamed the Jews and persecuted them in pogroms that lasted until 1906. Thus, many Jews left their homes in search of economic opportunity and many also fled in terror of persecution and conscription.

Wesker's grandmother, Toba Bella (Teresia) Kornweiss, was born in the Hapsburg territory of Galicia, Poland, and sought refuge elsewhere after the territory became Russian and the pogroms began in 1881–82. To avoid trouble in Galicia, her family apparently migrated in the 1870s to a section of Hungary that eventually became Romania. Unfortunately, the Romanian "exodus" of 1899–1906 found several thousand Jewish families once again in a march across Europe in search of a safe haven. Many of these people settled in Great Britain, but many others moved on to Canada and the United States. By the time Leah left Romania, most of her family had already pulled up roots. Those few Weskers who stayed in Europe did so, perhaps, because they were living in a region of Russia more favorable to the Jews. Those who migrated to England became, for the most part, the fortunate members of what has been called the "most highly organized and cohesive Jewish community in the western world."[12]

The Jews brought to England a variety of skills in all trades, but they were best known for making the cheap clothing industry possible. Nearly a third of all newcomers found work in the nineteenth century in tailoring.[13] They worked in sweatshops of 12 to 18 people for so little money that they were able to undercut the going prices, making Whitechapel the center for the largest distribution of inexpensive men's clothing in the world. Jews eventually broke the barrier in other professions as well. They brought similar strategies to the making and selling of furniture and the restaurant trade. They also lent genius to the sciences and other academic disciplines, and through the shrewd managerial skills of brothers like Lew and Bernard Winogradsky, and the talents of many directors and actors, they have had an enormous influence on the entertainment industry. Not the least of these artists are two notable playwrights, Harold Pinter and Arnold Wesker, both born in Hackney of the East End and raised by Jewish tailors there.

Wesker was born in Stepney at Mother Levy's Maternity Hospital in 1932, six years after the birth of his parents' first child, Della. He was delivered by the well-known Dr. Samuel Sacks, father of neurologist/author Oliver Sacks (*The Man Who Mistook His Wife for a Hat*). For most of his childhood he lived in the heart of Spitalfield's Jewish community at 45 Fashion Street, and he had relatives on Flower and Dean Street, so these lanes are at the locus of his memories.

Socialism best served the East Enders in hard times. When the fascist movement, spearheaded by demagogue Oswald Mosley, whipped up British sentiment against the Jews in Wesker's childhood years, the East End socialists were organized to oppose it, and they attracted a following among the Jews since the socialists were the only ones to publicly confront the fascists. At this time, perhaps as much as a third of the British Communists were East Enders.[14] In October 1936, when Mosley planned an anti-Semitic protest march through Wesker's old neighborhood, East End Communists—including Wesker's parents—turned out to meet them. A force of over 2,000 of Mosley's fascists dressed in black shirts and boots gathered for the march. Ready to take them on in battle were 10,000 opponents who were jammed in Gardiner's Corner (the intersection of Whitechapel and Commercial roads) and the junction of Cable Street with Cannon Street Road. Six thousand police desperately strategized to keep them apart. Finally Mosley called off the march, but around 100 of his followers ran along Mile Road a week later smashing shop fronts and beating Jews.[15] Wesker writes about the Mosley confrontation in *Chicken Soup with Barley*.

In the ghetto the tenets of socialism encouraged a philanthropy, also a theme in *Chicken Soup with Barley*, that ran deep in the Jewish tradition of the East End. Jews all over England—but particularly those in the ghetto of the 1930s and during World War II—were known for their social responsibility that assured housing, food, clothing, education, and health care for its needy. Dozens of self-help organizations assured that Jews met their social responsibilities more completely than any other group in British society in the years around the turn of the century, despite abject poverty, overcrowded housing, and unsanitary living conditions. Even when socialism among the Anglo-Jewry declined around the 1920s, the tradition of helping one another remained alive in the East End up through World War II.

No section of London was harder hit by German bombs between 1939 and 1945 than the East End. Hitler's military goals were probably the Wapping Docks and the factories. Still, the clear line of the River Thames made the entire district an easy target. At the outbreak of the war, the young Wesker was sent to Ely with the children from his sister's school, the Spitalfields Foundation School, but he nagged his parents to return home. They brought him home just in time for the worst of the blitz that started on 7 September 1940 and continued for 57 nights. He spent most of those days in the catacombs of the Spitalfields Fruit Exchange before he was again evacuated. He came and went from London with some frequency until the last of the war, when the Germans began using the unmanned flying bombs, the doodlebugs, and V2 rockets, one of which fell on Petticoat Lane. After that, he was sent to a family in Llantrisant in South Wales, where he lived for six months.

Although nearly a third of a million people left East London in the war years, Wesker's parents courageously stayed on. Fortunately, no one in Wesker's extended family was directly injured by bombs, but they were also lucky. When the children returned home for the last time, parts of the East End were unrecognizable. Whole streets and more were destroyed. The community that had been resilient enough to withstand the sweatshops of poverty, the waves of anti-Semitic attack over several decades, the zeppelin bombing of World War I, and the blitz finally succumbed to the demolition of the neighborhoods. Whole blocks were bulldozed and replaced by modern buildings. Like many others, Wesker's family eventually left the East End.

Despite the imminent dangers during the war, much of life in London continued. Wesker attended the Upton House Technical School in Hackney until 1948, when he failed his Eleven plus exams. After that he took a brief clerical course at Upton House Central School; then he left to try his hand building furniture as a carpenter's mate and later held jobs as a bookseller's assistant and a plumber's mate. In 1950 he joined the Royal Air Force, where he put together material that became the basis for *Chips with Everything*. After his two-year stint in the National Service, he became a seed sorter and a farm laborer in Norfolk, a kitchen porter, and finally a pastry cook in London and a chef in Paris, giving him material for *The Kitchen*.

All the time Wesker was knocking about, he was looking for an entree into theater. He had been accepted for study by the Royal Academy of the Dramatic Arts (RADA) in 1948, but he left for lack of a study grant. He subsequently organized a drama group while in the Air Force and while in Paris tried to save money to attend the London School of Film Technique.

He found his niche in theater when he was encouraged by his brother-in-law to write plays in 1956, about the time that the *Observer* announced a play competition, and he submitted *The Kitchen*. The night that he saw *Look Back in Anger* and "recognized that things *could* be done in the theater," he sat down to write *Chicken Soup with Barley*. A year later when he happened to recognize Lindsay Anderson, the film and theater director, standing in line for a film, Wesker talked to him about his short story "Pools." Although nothing was ever done to film the story, Anderson sent the two plays on to George Devine for a reading at the Royal Court Theatre. His first professional production, *Chicken Soup with Barley*, was mounted at the Belgrade Theatre in Coventry on 7 July 1958 and was soon transferred to the Royal Court. As a result of its reception, Wesker was awarded an Arts Council grant of £300, which he used to marry Doreen (Dusty) Bicker the same year. *Roots* opened at the Royal Court in September 1959. Besides *Chicken Soup with Barley* and *The Old Ones*, the plays that trade heavily on Wesker's Jewish background include *The Wedding Feast*, *Shylock*, *Four Portraits—of Mothers*, and *When God Wanted a Son*. Many of his short stories also use these themes—"Pools," "Six Sundays in January," "Said the Old Man to the Young Man," and "A Time of Dying."

Wesker comes from a family with a long and deep tradition of communal and political activism with an emphasis on self-discipline, fellowship, and social responsibility—all socialist as well as Jewish values. If anything, Wesker is more proud today of his Jewish origins than ever, and he sees his work over the last 30 years as consistent with his earliest endeavors rooted in socialist causes. True to his heritage—socialist and Jewish—he vigorously subscribes to the priorities of equality and justice, the virtues of education and training, the rigid code of family responsibility and of social responsibility that requires the care of others whenever possible. He also submits to strong instincts of compassion that rise out of the golden rule of Judaism, "Love thy neighbor as thyself." He qualifies his acceptance of socialist principles, however. Although they served her in her stand against fascism, his mother's Communist values seem to Wesker rather simplistic. Barring a revolutionary crisis, the worn-out slogans have become superseded for him by a more complicated politic. So when communal responsibility or collectivism sits in conflict with his anti-authoritarian stance, another Jewish tradition—his independent spirit—takes priority.

Wesker's resistance to authority began as insubordination in his adolescent days when he abandoned both the Zionist Youth Movement and the Young Communist League. Because he objected to their "histrionic tendencies," he quit and joined an amateur acting group instead. His resistance to mob rule on the one hand and to hegemonic leadership on the other was expressed as rebellion when he was one of the Angry Young Men. The insubordination of his youth has turned into a quiet defiance in his older years. Little else has changed for Wesker. If anything, the greatest transformation has taken place in Britain's socialist theater that has rejected the old-fashioned humanist values that it espoused in the days of George Bernard Shaw—values Wesker still embraces.

Wesker has always mistrusted the herd instinct. Working with Centre 42 confirmed his fears about the way group pressures may overpower the individual. When he works these days, he prefers to take on tasks alone or to deal with people on a personal level. After watching the collapse of Centre 42, Wesker found individualism more important than ideals, causes, or articles of faith, and blindly loyal adherents who willingly subordinate their personal desires to the advancement of a belief or ideology frighten him. He addresses this fear in *Caritas*, in which Christine, the anchoress, commits herself with religious enthusiasm to a contemplative life in the mindless way Wesker dreads. Christine's devotions isolate her from any sensual pleasures of life—"[the feeling of her own] skin in the grass, sun on breasts . . . the cool winds that bring the smell of the hawthorn and the wild mint."[16] But more than that, her dedication—rather than give her spiritual strength—taxes her energy and initiative and her sense of self.

Wesker extends his mistrust of human institutions to hegemonic governing bodies. In the essay "State-right Freedom, Birth-right Freedom" he explores the conflict between the individual and the state.[17] In doing so he defines the differences between the tightly controlled rights that may or may not be conferred on the people by a government that mistrusts their ability to make choices, and the rights, which are naturally conferred at birth, that presume without question that humans are deserving of dignity and respect regardless of place or condition of birth.

Being Jewish, Wesker has cause for mistrust of totalitarian governments and group tyranny. He cannot forget, of course, the Holocaust and the hundreds of thousands of Jews killed in concentration camps. And yet many Jews who became Communists to fight fascism during World War II began to doubt their alliances after the war when Stalin revived the pogroms against Jews in the Soviet Union. Wesker not only fears the possible rise to power of another Hitler or Stalin, but he mistrusts the motives of any autocratic or charismatic leader who uses power politics to enforce group loyalty. Although Wesker is willing to defer to the practical needs of the greater good when conforming to government policy and to the suspension of rights in times of crisis, he believes that individual happiness and freedom is paramount. He therefore questions the conditions that might tip the "very delicate balance between state and individual, one that cannot be maintained by dogma and slogans" (*Distinctions*, 223–24). His point is that any governed people should be very cautious about relinquishing basic freedoms on behalf of causes, because these rights are easily lost and regained only with enormous struggle.

When it comes to making a choice between rallying behind the causes of revolutionary socialism, because it offers a more equitable distribution of wealth, and the importance of the individual, Wesker opts in favor of the individual. The question of surviving the forces that encroach upon the naturally free spirit of human beings depends on being able to recognize dangerous elements within the culture that claim moral priority. Wesker wrote in a letter to C. W. E. Bigsby that we "need to survive those who on the one hand are in power and abuse that power and those, on the other hand, who, with fanaticism try to defend us."[18] It is the "twin passions of corruption and fanaticism, of inequality and violence" that threaten us from inside society. The destructive potential of causes that commit one entirely is summed up by Raphael, a character in Wesker's story "The Visit," who says,"*All* ideology is anti-social! . . . [T]hat's why people grow away from socialism. They sense the anti-social nature of ideology. . . . Dogma is the death of spontaneous creativity, and spontaneous creativity is the life-force of existence. Ergo—political ideology is anti-social."[19]

Looking over the past 30 years of Wesker's career as a playwright, one could conclude that the East End and his Jewish upbringing probably did more to shape his plays than any other single factor. The evidence is considerable: his family's history of persecution, his experiences in the bomb shelters, his membership in the Zionist movement, his awe of the power of the intellect, and his continued support over the years by the Jewish arts network. He has repeatedly been published in the *Jewish Quarterly* and he has received encouragement over the years from the

Jewish Repertory Theatre in New York City. Added to these are his loyalty to the family and the political and religious values he has embraced. And yet to overemphasize these events might also be a misrepresentation of the facts. Wesker warns us particularly against overemphasizing his dedication to religion: "Like most writers I have been pressed to ask myself what it is that informs my work. On reflection it seems to have been a Jewish temperament. Acknowledging a Jewish temperament is not the same thing as being preoccupied with Judaism."[20] Wesker is, indeed, a secular Jew—one who lives by Jewish principles and values and remains at home in the Jewish community. Still, he cannot be read as a Jewish playwright without also considering some of the other influences on his thinking, political and philosophical.

Humanist

Because of his Jewish upbringing, Arnold Wesker now situates himself in a political niche he recognizes as unfashionable and accepts (Hoggart 1986) the labels of "radical humanism"[21] or "old-fashioned humanism"[22]—terms lent to him by sympathetic critics. With its emphasis on the William Morris vision for a democratic education, on the arts and philosophy, and on the strengths of the individual, "old-fashioned humanism" best defines the impulse behind most of Wesker's writing. By *humanist* Wesker means "that reverence for, and greater preoccupation with man and his ways" rather than with God or any ideology that might attract dedication (*Distinctions*, 255). Indeed, it was his insistence on the central importance of the individual—even in the 1960s when radicals were committed to the idea of communal power and collectivism—that finally separated him from New Left socialists.

Even though Wesker defends the rights of the individual, he continues to oppose individualism that is destructive to the point of selfishness, willfulness, ambition, and greed. He fears the dangers of the power of money in the economically competitive, capitalist system and endorses the strengths of democratic decision-making and cooperation. Moreover, he fully supports socialism's goals of general economic fairness and protection of the underdog, particularly the working classes, as long as personal liberty is not sacrificed to achieve its goals. He wrote in a 23 August 1989 letter that "to be a socialist you [have] to be able to defer to the majority. I was not good at that, and was always skeptical of the 'majority.' Too much of an individualist—which of course is what I [once] imagined socialism was about: freeing the individual spirit."[23]

For his independent thinking, Wesker has paid a certain price. As Richard Hoggart and others have pointed out, Wesker remains greatly underrated as a playwright. Partly responsible is his Jewish otherness. He told Anthony Clare, "I don't feel very English in England. I feel very alien. I'd never thought of myself as anything but an English writer until the responses to my work began to take on a special tone, and they bore no relationship to what I thought I was doing as a writer" (Clare, 52). Although he loves England's landscapes and believes in the freedoms it preserves, Wesker has never been fully at home in England and will always be an outsider as long as he fights for little understood causes. Much of this alienation is expressed in his plays and short stories, sometimes in long preachy passages; much of this irritation appears in his essays. Wesker's stubbornness about his plays and his prickly resistance to changes by directors have also made him unpopular in London, so much so that his better plays do not easily get an unbiased hearing, explaining why many of his plays (*The Mistress*, for instance) have not been staged in London, even though they are well received abroad.

Despite his present reputation as foolishly outspoken, he is less impulsive than he was as a young upstart and more reticent. Whereas he once exposed his own political vulnerabilities and those of his family in the scripts of the plays, he is much more private today about his family's history. He also avoids committee-run projects like Centre 42, where he might be forced to disagree publicly. Although he may not be an Angry Young Man, a playwright of domestic drama, a radical leftist, or whatever else the critics have wanted him to be over the years, he has remained faithful to a protest of basic injustices and continues to write about characters who defiantly maintain their dignity in the face of defeat, frustration, or misunderstanding. As ever, Wesker worries about what the world is doing to itself and has a compulsion to do something about it. Wesker continues, moreover, to be deeply committed to the necessity of a humanistic education and a belief in the benefits of the arts as a tool for education. In all of these tenets, he has held faith.

Chapter Two
Debts to the Court

One of Arnold Wesker's strengths as a writer—and one of his weaknesses—is that his writings are largely autobiographical. Believing that art is the "transformation of experience" or sometimes the "organization of experience," Wesker could not conceive of any other approach to writing.[1] He told Richard Hoggart in a 1986 interview that he had no imagination. All he had was a "ragbag of memories and metaphors." What he meant was that he reached into the experiences of his domestic and professional life for situations to write about. He told Hoggart, "If I've got any kind of talent, it's for selecting the metaphors life has offered me" (Hoggart 1986). Although this restricts the material he is willing to explore and the way in which he is willing to explore it—as he tends to reduce it to the personal level—Wesker can usually trade on his "re-creation of experience" with confidence. As Ronald Hayman has pointed out, "The more autobiographical his plays are the clearer the reflection is likely to be" (Hayman, 13). His works poignantly reveal a human being struggling to make sense of himself and the world.

That connectedness to ordinary existence appealed to film director Lindsay Anderson when he first read Wesker's *Kitchen*. Anderson wrote to Wesker, "You really are a playwright, aren't you? I mean there it is, with characters as solid as I can imagine, and a whole way of life to them, and the necessary perspective" (*Distinctions*, 4). He meant that Sarah and Harry, Ada and Ronnie Kahn seem like people we might recognize on the bus, at the supermarket, in our offices. They are as familiar as our next-door neighbors. Remarkably few writers seem able to capture commonplace people as Wesker does in his early plays. What lends Wesker's characters authenticity is his working-class perspective and sensitivity to the inner structures of family life. To examine the finer points of human behavior, he relies on naturalistic conventions, because of all the approaches to mediating contemporary reality naturalism represents for him the most faithful view of human nature, and it is the dramatic form he knows best.

Naturalism

In reaction to the artificial rhetoric and delivery of eighteenth- and early nineteenth-century theater, Emile Zola developed the concept of literary naturalism. He sought to replace with a more lifelike set of conventions the theatrical style of his time, particularly the declamatory speech and exaggerated gestures, the characterization that depended too heavily on historical figures, and adherence to other rigid rules of performance. In the preface to his theatrical version of *Thérèse Raquin* Zola outlines a new form that valorized the "return to nature and to man, direct observation, exact anatomy, acceptance and portrayal of that which exists."[2] The new style emphasized the particulars of daily life and featured everyday characters who become products of an environment by simply living in it. The props for this theater are realistic; for example, real plates and pots instead of painted backdrops set the scene, and the costume, stage design, and speech are as natural as possible to bring the performance to the highest degree of verisimilitude.[3] Zola's innovation furthermore exchanged the worn gestures and the false pitch of the "theater voice" for a more natural dramatic style, something akin to the acting we know today on the stage as well as in television and film.

Zola's interest in a more realistic style of play production grew out of his ideas about determinism, a particularly brutal view of human nature that renders the human being nearly helpless, a pawn to larger forces dictated by accidents of birth into class, national origin, race, and gender. He explored these ideas in the preface to the play version of *Thérèse Raquin* (1873) and later more fully in *Le Roman expérimental* (1880) and *Le Naturalisme au théâtre* (1881); consequently, many reference books today will define naturalism solely on the basis of determinism. Nevertheless, many of the dramatic conventions Zola launched have so outlasted the popularity of the ideas of determinism and particulars of social Darwinism that few playwrights today associate them with the outdated ideas of biological, social, or economic determinism. Indeed, many playwrights are likely to ignore its original connections because the conventional gestures, dialogue, and scenes that suggest verisimilitude have simply become the mark of traditional theater, with no social agenda attached to it.

Wesker too is more interested in naturalism for its theatrical convention than the philosophy behind it, although he has read Zola's *Le Roman expérimental* and found it interesting. He accepts the belief that physical conditions shape the individual but makes little out of that notion in his writing, and he has adopted nothing else from Zola's studies of the psychological effects of determinism. It must be remembered here that Wesker is not sophisticated as a playwright in part because he does not share Zola's interest in the psychological development of a character, and, being self-taught, he is not replying to the European theatrical tradition.

Wesker's understanding of naturalism is that "art is the re-creation of experience, not the copying of it" (*Distinctions*, 9), meaning that although his plays present action that looks and feels as "natural" as everyday life, they are somewhat stylized (not as realistic as most films, for example) in that they use many standard conventions of the contemporary theater. And to that point he adds, "I'm not a writer who illustrates ideas, or explores ideas through invented characters and situations; rather I'm a writer whose experience drives me to organize that experience into a play or story because it seems to illuminate some aspect of human behavior" (*Distinctions*, 142). Thus naturalism in Wesker's case is best defined by his desire to re-create the essence of *his* life as a working-class playwright or to capture the fundamental dynamic of human relationships as he knows them. Verisimilitude, however, is not the issue, because he recognizes that all art is an artifice to some degree.

More to the point for Wesker is his concern that an artist might re-create an experience, like life in a concentration camp, which is so compelling for the reader or viewer as a work of art that the significance of the original experience is eclipsed by the re-creation. He discusses the issue in an essay on George Steiner's review of William Styron's novel *Sophie's Choice*, in which he agrees with Steiner that "in the presence of certain realities [in this case, the Holocaust] art is trivial or impertinent" (*Distinctions*, 228). Like Steiner, Wesker is concerned that art might be more fascinating for its literary qualities than its potential for "intellectual illumination" (*Distinctions*, 231) or a straightforward account of the events that would leave nothing undetermined; nevertheless, the dramatic arts should be more than mere imitation of nature or a restructuring of the experience. Their purpose is "to illuminate . . . some aspect of human behavior" (*Distinctions*, 142), essentially to educate. He hopes that, in the case of a "horrendous reality," the work of art does not blur the lines between fact and fiction but re-creates the "most significant elements" without distortion of the facts by the form, so that a new, more thoughtful understanding of the subject matter ensues (*Distinctions*, 235).

Wesker is quite careful about certain particulars that assure a polished production, so he often includes more stage directions than most playwrights. In the prologue to *The Kitchen*, for example, he has added meticulous notes based on his four years' experience as a pastry cook that include character profiles, instructions for laying out the kitchen, for miming the cooking process, and serving. The set in this case is not entirely realistic, as real food is not used. This is how Wesker sometimes combines slice-of-life naturalism with less realistic forms. It was this mix in *The Kitchen* that gave definition to the term "kitchen sink drama" used by critics in the 1960s.

The Kitchen

Although *The Kitchen* (1956) is Wesker's first play, it followed the trilogy in production, mostly because of technical difficulties in staging the original script that was then only a one-act, particularly since it is one of Wesker's most carefully choreographed plays, calling for 33 actors, some of whom require training in food preparation, and precise timing to make it work. Despite its demands, the play opened at one of the Royal Court's Sunday afternoon performances at the Theatre Upstairs, a low-budget showcase for new writers called a "Production without Decor" in 1959. It was two years, in 1961, when the Royal Court Theatre needed to fill a six-weeks' slot in the schedule, before it was revised to two acts. *The Kitchen* has since become a favorite of the world's greatest directors. Ariadne Mnouchkine in France, Koichi Kimura in Japan, and John Dexter in England have all built their reputations on the play. Stephen Daldry's 1994 revival at the Royal Court (to rave notices) indicates its timelessness.

The setting for *The Kitchen* is the workplace in a restaurant called the Tivoli. In this kitchen are multinational workers whose ordinary interactions and passions—cultural misunderstanding, jealousy, love, humor, and anger—are heightened by the competitive system that drives the business. The pressures of profit demand so much of the workers at peak periods that their normal responses are debased.

The play's action revolves around a German cook, Peter, who turns manic-depressive when pushed by the kitchen manager's obsession to meet the schedule. On this day Peter is agitated by his own inability to convince his girlfriend, Monique, to divorce her husband for him, even though she is pregnant for the third time with Peter's child. She has aborted the others, and it appears likely that she will try to abort again, then abandon Peter for her husband, who has bought her a house. Monique's rejection of Peter, announced during the evening rush hour, sends him into a rage that ends in his attack on the gas pipes that feed the stoves and the dishes that are stacked in the dining room.

Exacerbating his personal troubles is the relentless pace of Peter's job. As Wesker directs in the introduction, "The quality of the food here is not so important as the speed with which it is served. Each person has his own particular job. We glance in upon him, highlighting as it were the individual. But though we may watch just one or a group of people, the kitchen staff does not. They work on."[4] Because time is money, the cooks are forced to meet the demands of the orders as they are shouted out, and they do whatever they can to withstand the pressure. As soon as the rush begins, each person is isolated by the task at hand while efficiency cancels out personal necessity. Workers then grow increasingly hostile to one another. To protect themselves, they fall back on demeaning and degrading defenses like racism and raw aggression. Thus normal human interaction is thwarted by the strain of the timetable, the noise of preparation, and the sound of the stoves. People must shout to communicate. Indeed, the nature of the work so readily impedes camaraderie that "people come and go and cannot stay long enough to understand each other, and friendships, loves and enmities are forgotten as quickly as they are made" (2: 9).

The pace, of course, is dictated by the profit motive that overrides all ordinary exchanges in the kitchen, shaping the workers and their products. To work long periods in these conditions, the older cooks blunt their desires with alcohol and the younger cooks live for their time off. The impersonal nature of the work has only occasionally the effect of being absurdly humorous. Peter attempts to find some way to talk to Monique through the inexorable rhythm of the food orders:

PETER *(tenderly)*:	Listen, do you want to know where I went this afternoon? To buy your birthday present.
MONIQUE:	A present?
WINNIE *(to Hans)*:	One veal cutlet.
WINNIE *(to Kevin)*:	Two plaice. (2: 62)

Shortly after this conversation and on the other side of the kitchen, Winnie doubles over in the pain of a self-induced abortion. Few, including Peter and Monique, take notice. Winnie's distress only cuts momentarily into the uncompromising pace of the schedule. Attempting to ignore the demands of the kitchen's routine, Peter tries once again to win over Monique amidst the turmoil, but his efforts are pathetically quixotic:

PETER: Listen, Monique, I love you. Please listen to me that I love you. You said you love me but you don't say to your husband this thing.
HETTIE *(to Frank)*: Two chicken. (2: 64)

During the break between meals, to offset the dehumanizing effect of the job, Peter encourages the others to relate their dreams. Many speak of the longing for more free time, more rest, more money—the dreams of employees anywhere. Peter discovers, however, that he cannot dream in a kitchen; the pressures of his job block his yearnings. Paul, the Jewish pastry cook, however, has visions of a more caring community, one in which people respect and empathize with others' needs. He tells how he once supported the cause of a striking bus driver and how he was concerned when the driver complained about a demonstration against nuclear weapons war that delayed his bus. Angry, he casually wished he could drop a bomb into the crowd of demonstrators. Paul's story suggests how the tensions of the workplace taking priority over the distress of its workers serves as a metaphor for the capitalist system as a whole. Dehumanizing work divides society, creating insensitivity and callousness to individual need.

Speed out of the necessity for profit does even more to create hostility, especially between management and staff. Out of a need to undermine the system, as much as anything, Peter donates some of the kitchen's food to a beggar at the door. Nowhere is the clash of values between economic attitudes clearer than when Marengo, his boss, flies into a rage, then walks away saying, "I give work, I pay well, yes? They eat what they want, don't they? I don't know what more to give a man. He works, he eats, I give him money. This is life, isn't it?" (2: 68). He believes his question is rhetorical, but Peter would disagree. For him life is more about relationships and human kindness than about meeting production schedules or making money.

Protest against profit motives and mass production established Wesker as a socialist playwright, especially since *The Kitchen* is a rare example in British theater of the workers' perspective, of "the daily collision of man with economic necessity."[5] The socialist themes are easily recognizable—people over profit, a cry for reasonable working conditions and worker participation in management decisions, as well as an insistence on a more cohesive and sympathetic community.

Undercutting these classic socialist issues, however, is Wesker's concern for the rights of the individual: the prerogative to speak out against inequality, a license to pursue personal inclination, and an acknowledgment that freedom is a birth right conferred by no one. These are values of humanism that converge with socialism in their opposition to hegemonic bourgeois decadence and in their outrage against the injustice of suppression. They are also values that find their roots in the Jewish tradition of compassion and justice. So what the critics of the 1960s saw in Wesker's plays as pure socialist idealism is, in fact, a mixture of socialism, humanism, and Jewish ideals. Although nominally compatible, these philosophic traditions begin to conflict over the contradiction between individual freedom and communal responsibility.

Finding himself doubting Peter's selfish morals, Wesker at that time was more inclined to think like Paul, the character who quietly and thoughtfully can understand the conflict from two points of view: labor and management. Paul makes his plea for understanding and tolerance based on socialist causes—the right to strike and the need to protest the use of massively destructive arms. But even as he speaks up for the bus drivers', the factory workers', and the cooks' rights to better working conditions, he asks about their collective responsibility to society: "I should stop making pastries? The factory worker should stop making trains and cars? The miner should leave the coal where it is?" (2: 52). In short, he wonders about where their responsibility to others ends and a concern for their individual rights begins. The workers are, after all, in a service profession, and others depend on them. Should transportation come to a standstill because a handful of demonstrators want action? Should diners go hungry because Peter is angry with Monique?

The dispute is represented in the tension between Peter, who despises the abuses of the marketplace, and Paul, who recognizes a larger set of needs that should probably take priority over individual necessity. Despite Peter's antisocial behavior, we sympathize with his cause. And yet Paul makes us question Peter's argument by appealing to our sense of common decency. This unresolved opposition lies at the heart of Wesker's plays and creates problematic ambiguities in the early ones. Because he has not sharpened his own position, Wesker leaves these questions open at the end of *The Kitchen*. He has not yet understood the disparity between the socialist values instilled in him by his mother and the alarm he feels about the loss of individual freedoms in Germany and the Soviet Union in the 1940s and 1950s. Because Wesker is unsure of the answer, the conflict between social need and individual rights will continue to haunt him and his writings. In *Chicken Soup with Barley* we see the rebellion of an individual against the oppression of an institution, in this case the Socialist party.

Chicken Soup with Barley

The first of Wesker's plays to be produced, *Chicken Soup with Barley*, was presented at the Belgrade Theatre, Coventry, on 7 July 1958 and was transferred a week later to the Royal Court Theatre in London. It maps the decline of the Kahn family and, by implication, other Jewish-socialist families like the Kahns, over three different decades of British history. Disintegration is marked through the failing health of Harry Kahn and its effect on his wife, Sarah, who tries to nag him into being more of a fighter. Their constant bickering, which eventually divides the family, serves as a metaphor for the decline of the Socialist party in Britain of the 1930s, 1940s, and 1950s, a political institution that has practically gone defunct in the 1980s and 1990s because of insider fighting. The Kahns' struggle for democratic rights and middle-class security marks as well other significant historical moments for Jews and Britons during that time. The play is deeply autobiographical.

Act 1 opens with the Kahn family in an uproar. The mother, Sarah Kahn, wants to mobilize the family to participate in the human barricade against Oswald Mosley's blackshirts, who have planned an anti-Semitic march through the Jewish East End of London in October 1936. This scene is based on an actual incident, when the conservative Jewish Board of Deputies ordered Jews to boycott the march to reduce tension and lessen the attention the press might give Mosley, but the East Enders were too anxious to fight to obey the board's directives. They turned out by the thousands with banners that read "They Shall Not Pass." The city tried its best to keep the warring groups apart by calling 6,000 constables into service. Finally late in the afternoon, Mosley's men were dispersed by the police, but not before some minor outbreaks, looting, and damage occurred. Some of the defense tore out pavement stones to use as projectiles, and they overturned carts to set up barricades. While breaking up the mobs, the police seemed to be more sympathetic to the fascists than the Jews since, in the end, many more Jews than fascists were arrested.

Despite chagrin at their own capacities for violence, socialist Jews won a moral victory from this confrontation. As Wesker shows us in *Chicken Soup*, families were brought together, neighborhoods became more cohesive, and eventually the nation turned against Mosley when England entered the war against Germany. Not long after this incident, in a show of sympathy and fair-mindedness, Parliament passed a bill outlawing the civilian use of the sort of uniforms that had given Mosley's men the psychological advantage. With the intensity of World War II, the fad of fascism in England soon waned, and with it diminished the popularity of the Socialist party and the Jewish lobby in the East End.

Mosley's attack on the East End helps to explain why Sarah Kahn and her Jewish family and friends dedicate their energies to socialism. For Sarah, the socialist affiliation is a vehicle for her rage against injustice and an outlet for her maternal instincts. For the Kahns' friends Monty and Prince, socialism provides the mechanism for fighting fascists in Spain, and, like so many of their mates who have volunteered, they thrill at the prospect. For Dave Simmonds, a belief in socialism becomes a way of resolving some conflict he feels between his pacifist and his Jewish convictions by giving him permission to oppose Mosley's blackshirts. Sarah's factory-working sister-in-law, Cissie, finds strength and vitality in the East End trade unions that include in their ranks a number of socialist leaders. The only family member who does little to resist Mosley's threat is Sarah's husband, Harry, a man with a penchant for doing as little as possible, whatever the situation, and depending too heavily on his wife for survival.

Act 2, set in 1946, tangibly illustrates the immediate aftereffects of World War II on British families: the Kahns have moved to London County Council flats (low-rent apartments) because their neighborhood was destroyed in the German air raids. Furthermore, the state of Israel is being shaped out of the Palestinian homelands, and a Labour government has won the elections. The Socialists are excited about their two newly won seats in Parliament and about the prospect of nationalization and the National Health system. But the party also shows signs of taking its newfound political power for granted by demanding more of the Socialist party than it can deliver and by working less among the rank and file.

Ronnie's anticipated homecoming from his job as a pastry cook in Paris also raises hopes. Nevertheless, family life is not as healthy as it may seem. Ronnie, Sarah and Harry's son, is returning because he has quit his job, and Harry, who has had a stroke, has become even more passive. Ronnie's sister, Ada, is fed up with waiting for her husband, Dave, who has fought in the Spanish Civil War and World War II, to come home permanently. Furthermore, she has become impatient with the bureaucracy of the Socialist party. She and Dave want to go to an isolated farm and live close to the land, using their labor as a weapon against the "jungle" of industrialization, the complex of business and politics that squelches individuality. She berates her father for refusing to attend party meetings and for doing little to take charge of his own affairs. She believes he would secretly rather be an owner in the means of production than share in the making of it.

Her anger at her father who, as Sarah says "sits and sits and all his life goes away from him" (1: 53), becomes an analog for the party that seems to be failing the needs of its younger generation as it gets mired in layers of administration and compromise politics. Because he has not found a viable profession, Ronnie sees himself in his father and is frightened that he too may someday become passive and ineffective. Perhaps referring to himself, he says to Harry, "You're not tired, Harry—you're just drowning with heritage, mate!" (1: 54).

November 1955 and act 3 find the family even more isolated than they were nine years earlier. Harry has had his second stroke and is near paralysis. Their Jewish friends and family now live in the regions among the *goyim*. Monty and his wife, having reaped the benefits of postwar affluence as green-grocers in Manchester, speak nostalgically about socialist activism as a thing of the past. Auntie Cissie has become a charity case for the family.

Like Harry, the Socialist party has grown old and is almost paralyzed, in this case by the violent excesses of Stalinist Russia, where members of the Jewish Anti-Fascist League have been shot. This is shocking news because the anti-fascist socialists had long been allied with the Communist party, and the shift in policy signals a less tolerant Soviet Union, one that would once again be persecuting the Jews. Even more alarming, the Soviets violently suppressed the people's revolution in Hungary in 1956. Stalin's acts of brutality have alienated British socialists who at one time had sympathized with Russia's cause. Britain's leftists, disillusioned by the failures of the National Health system and too burdened by red tape to get adequate treatment for their sick and aged, are unable to respond to yet another disappointment.

Once optimistic about the Socialist party and nationalization, Ronnie has become disgusted with "political institutions, society—they don't really affect people that much" (1: 72). He and his mother quarrel bitterly about the direction their lot has taken. He cannot understand why she supports the party when it has become nothing more than a totalitarian form of government in the Soviet Union. Ronnie asks, "What's happened to us? Were we cheated or did we cheat ourselves? I just don't know, God in heaven, I just do not know! Can you understand what it is suddenly not to know? And the terrifying thing is—I don't care either" (1: 72).

His mother is appalled and defensive. She cannot understand why he is attacking the core of her beliefs in the strength of the family and in the basically humane values of the party. The two are inextricably intertwined in Sarah's mind: "All my life I worked with a party that meant glory and freedom and brotherhood. You want me to give it up now?"(1: 73). She then tells a story about a Jewish neighbor whose chicken soup with barley saved Ada from dying of diphtheria. For Sarah, the party is the only institution that could replace the communal generosity of her own family and her old Jewish neighborhood. So for all its faults, the party is better than nothing: even an ineffective health system is better than none at all. If it betrays its principles, then it is no worse than the weakest of its members who are, after all, human beings. But that is no reason to give up on basic socialist tenets: "There will always be human beings and as long as there are there will always be the idea of brotherhood" (1: 75). Sarah has faith that the party will survive its mistakes.

Ronnie does not share her sense of loyalty. He takes a more cynical stance. "It doesn't mean a thing," he tells her defiantly. Ronnie does not have the energy to embrace the suffering that her form of loyalty would require of him: "I—I can't, not now, it's too big, not yet—it's too big to care for it, I—I . . ." (1: 75). His resignation infuriates Sarah, who shouts at him, "You'll die, you'll die—if you don't care you'll die" (1: 76). She is angry with him for his rejection of her values, for his desertion of the party, and for his apparent lack of ambition. Like his father, he would rather do nothing. We are reminded of a story she tells earlier about three men in the hospital with strokes. One eventually goes back to work, one dies, and one neither lives nor dies. The one who recovers completely is for Sarah the one who has cared enough to recover and the only one with a meaningful future.

Chicken Soup with Barley echoes many themes of *The Kitchen*—the need for community and compassion, the power of activism against repression, and a search for a clearly defined role for the individual. Wesker seems to want to embrace his mother's unquestioned acceptance of socialist values, but ultimately he finds himself doubting the party's usefulness for him. In the absence of a strong identification with the political institutions that were at one time a source of family strength, Wesker discovers instead a solace in traditional Jewish practices—the celebration of the extended family, the healing force of food, and confidence in the virtues of reason and argument. Superficial reminders of the Jewish heritage are also here—the passing reference to the formation of Israel in 1947 and to chicken soups, as well as the use of Jewish dialect. Most important, however, is Wesker's discovery of that place where Jewish and socialist values converged in the fascist resistance, how the British Jews experienced another diaspora after the war, and why they eventually abandoned the party. This play about political disillusionment explains much about the playwright's own turn against the more militant strains of socialism today.

Wesker often describes *Chicken Soup with Barley* as pessimistic (as he has in an interview with me).[6] Indeed, he regards the trilogy as a statement about Ronnie's political disillusionment and failure. Nevertheless, readers and audiences still respond to the plays for what is perceived as Sarah's uplifting message. Audiences still identify strongest with the can-do spirit of indomitable women like Sarah Kahn and Beatie Bryant (in *Roots*) and their determination to be resolute and committed even in the face of loss. The feistiness of these women especially struck a responsive chord in audiences of the 1950s who, anxious about Britain's uncertain economic future, wanted something to believe in. After watching *Chicken Soup with Barley* or *Roots*, middle-class audiences sense some hope for themselves and even recognize in these plays inspiration for courage and resistance.

Roots

By Wesker's own personal account, the character of Sarah Kahn is based on his mother, and the story of Beatie Bryant is based on his wife, Doreen (Dusty) Bicker.[7] His own story had a different ending from that in *Roots*. Arnold Wesker met Dusty in 1952 while he was working as a kitchen porter and she as a waitress. Two years later he trained as a pastry cook and eventually went to Paris to work as a cook. Unlike Ronnie, however, Wesker did not abandon his fiancée. After Wesker entered the London School of Film Technique and wrote two plays, they married on the money that he received from an Arts Council award for young playwrights. They have three children—Lindsay Joe, Tanya, and Daniel—and two grandchildren, the daughters of Lindsay Joe Wesker and Jacqueline Rudet. Like Beatie, Dusty Wesker is warm, enthusiastic, resilient, and determined.

Of the plays in the trilogy, *Roots* tells us more about the Bickers than the Weskers, and so it says little about the Jewish traditions that he celebrated in the other plays of the trilogy. It tells us a great deal, however, about those characteristics that Wesker most admires and about those he mistrusts in the working classes. The Bryants, a rural family rooted in Norfolk, speak with a distinct East Anglian dialect indicative of their simple education and way of life. Mistrust of the working classes surfaces again as a theme in *The Wedding Feast* (1974).

Beatie Bryant has been living in London under the influence of a young Jewish intellectual, Ronnie Kahn, and has returned home full of the ideas he has planted in her. She berates her sister Jennie Beales for the family's lack of culture—not enough books, too much time spent on rock music and football pools. Their laziness gives them exposure only to what Beatie identifies as the most inferior and dissatisfying forms of art—"the slop singers and the pop writers and the film makers and women's magazines and the Sunday papers and the picture strip love stories" (1: 147). She wants her family to be like Ronnie's—interested in politics, the fine arts, and socialism. She has been persuaded by him that the working classes can improve their quality of life through education, not so much in the way of better jobs and opportunity for employment but through a richer daily routine.

Much of Ronnie's (and Wesker's) concept of a "richer" life is based on William Morris's ideals for a "new birth of art" that would improve the quality of life for every worker and his or her products (Morton, ed., 153). As I have discussed earlier, Morris proposed that by educating people to a sense of their capacities, particularly their ability to produce their own art, they could work under less anxiety and can improve their leisure through a rediscovery of the solace and fulfillment they once had in the arts. As Beatie tells her mother, "Socialism isn't talking all the time, it's living, it's singing, it's dancing, it's being interested in what go on around you, it's being concerned about people and the world" (1: 129). Although shaped largely by Morris's vision, Wesker has the fine arts in mind more than the folk arts that Morris admired. Neither he nor Morris, however, is validating popular culture—a trend that they both believe has robbed the arts of aesthetic values. Wesker's admiration of the fine arts and crafts is articulated by Beatie: "I ask him exactly the same questions—third-rate. And he answer and I don't know what he talk about. Something about registers, something about commercial world blunting our responses" (1: 115).[8]

As soon as she returns home, Beatie becomes a disruption in her family's relatively comfortable routine by denouncing their way of life that she believes keeps them divided against themselves. She wants family members to straighten up their rooms, patch up their differences, and open up their minds to each other—all before Ronnie Kahn comes to visit. Even the threat of Mr. Bryant's layoff is overshadowed by Beatie's railing. On Ronnie's recommendation, she prevails upon them for a more substantial and honest exchange in their discussions. Language is "bridges," Ronnie has told her, "so that you can get safely from one place to another. And the more bridges you know about the more places you can see!" (1: 90). She tries to explain to them that conversation draws people together by giving them the tools for helping each other. Language may be consoling in times of crisis.

Beatie wants her family to entrust honest feelings to each other, listen to one another, and ask after the others' needs. She decries their lack of curiosity and genuine interest in each other, "There are millions of us, all over the country, and no one, not one of us, is asking questions, we're all taking the easiest way out. Everyone I ever worked with took the easiest way out. We don't fight for anything, we're so mentally lazy we might as well be dead" (1: 147). She realizes that asking questions can establish common values, can build community through understanding and lessen fear. Somehow she knows that the process of posing questions is an important tool because, beginning with dialogue, it nurtures the educational process. Questioning engages the listener, forcing responsible analysis and reducing indifference and ignorance. Since this argument is obviously more complex than we would expect of Beatie and her family, we have to recognize that Ronnie (i.e., Wesker) is speaking through her. Wesker's point is that education is essential as a prerequisite to the compassionate treatment of others. His concern, of course, is not only for all humanity but especially for the protection of ethnic minorities like the Jews who have historically suffered torment. According to Wesker, the Jews dread ignorance above all else; it is the evil force that has led to pogroms and persecution.[9]

Beatie believes that through language and art the family will find its roots—its connection to others in a larger cultural sense. Wesker expanded on this point in an interview with Richard Hoggart: "Beatie Bryant is not talking about recognizing the strength of family ties . . . but about 2,000 years of history that make us" (Hoggart 1986). She is talking about "the roots of civilization," an image that represents the foundations of the Judeo-Christian and Muslim cultures that inform our history, shape our imagination, and create common bonds in the Western world, the law and literature, social customs and scientific attitudes. Elsewhere Wesker has said those roots are important because "with roots it's possible to grow tall and branch out anywhere."[10] Beatie tries to explain that we know too little about those roots, those links: "Listen to me! I'm tellin' you that the world's bin growing for two thousand years and we hevn't noticed it. I'm telling you that we don't know what we are or where we come from. I'm telling you something's cut us off from the beginning. I'm telling you we've got no roots. . . . We don't know where we push up from and we don't bother neither" (1: 146).

Indeed, Wesker demonstrates in *Roots* that language and the empowerment of self-education are so potent that they provide Beatie with the means to carry on without Ronnie, even though he is supposed to be the committed intellectual. In the end, Ronnie backs out of his promises to her and never appears at her mother's house. Instead, he sends a note in which he tries to apologize by saying he is one of the "sick and neurotic" intellectuals who "couldn't build a better world even if we were given the reins of government" (1: 142). Beatie is understandably shaken and self-castigating. She blames everyone but Ronnie. And then she begins talking freely. As she tries without Ronnie to explain the concept of roots to her mother, Jimmy, and Pearl, she realizes that these ideas are her own. She no longer needs him to think for her. Beatie's own words become a bridge to her independence.

When *Roots* opened at Coventry's Belgrade Theatre in May 1959, Joan Plowright starred as Beatie Bryant, and she played the role again at London's Royal Court Theatre in July, when the play was transferred. Plowright's memorable performance, most critics agree, made the role famous, so much so that every serious actor to play Beatie since then has been compared with Plowright. The normally sardonic Kenneth Tynan wrote, "She grips one's attention throughout, and rises glowing to the challenge of the final scene. . . . Her astonished cry of self-discovery brings down the curtain on the most affecting last act in contemporary English drama."[11] Plowright's identification with Beatie might have been the key to her success in the role. She must also have recognized in Beatie a grit and indomitable spirit that transcends Wesker's paternalistic treatment of the character because she played Beatie as an irrepressible force bottled up all too long.

Wesker's treatment of Beatie has provoked a variety of responses—pro and con—over the years. While reproving her family in the first act, she seems to comprehend little of what Ronnie has taught her, nor does she seem to care. Being in love with Ronnie, she mouths most of his words without thinking much about them. In act 2 she strains to win over her family since her own explanation of his arguments is too superficial to be persuasive. By the end of act 3, however, she has found her own voice and begins to articulate her clear understanding of Ronnie's arguments. Through talking them out, she has grasped their nuances and breathes life into them. Nevertheless, that she does not know her own opinion until her man teaches her and abuses her has come under sharp criticism from feminists. Today Wesker himself seems somewhat discomfited by the naive implications of his play. When *Roots* played at the National in 1989 he remarked that Beatie's character is "perhaps a little stylized."[12] Certainly evidence that he has become more sensitive to women's issues is the large number of women's roles he has developed in recent years.

Less controversial, oddly enough, has been his curiously uncomplimentary depiction of the working classes in this play. The rough Norfolk dialect, their humorous ignorance of medicine, their lack of common sense and social graces leaves Wesker open to the charge that he exaggerated these idiosyncrasies to dehumanize the very people who became his in-laws. Wesker defends his images of these bumpkins in his introductory notes to the play: "My people are not caricatures. They are real (though fiction), and if they are portrayed as caricatures the point of all these plays will be lost. The picture I have drawn is a harsh one, yet my tone is not one of disgust—nor should it be in the presentation of the plays. I am at one with these people: it is only that I am annoyed with them and myself" (1: 80). Hardly a defense. It is ironic that one of the century's best-known working-class playwrights employs embarrassing stereotypes to depict the farmer and family as the disfunctioning proletariat who bring on their own misery. Here is Jennie, the working-class housewife who has lost control over the order in her home and lives in happy-go-lucky squalor. Like her mechanic husband, she is isolated and politically unsophisticated. When he spouts off, he spits out narrow-minded rural sentiments about patriotism and the Labour party. The rest of the family seems similarly unreflective and careless. The Bryant's marriage, too, is unsurprisingly hostile. The stingy Mr. Bryant controls every small amount of money Mrs. Bryant needs for the household, and, seemingly as an extension of that paucity, he has very little to say to anyone.

When asked about this play in the early 1960s Wesker was quick to declare his affection for these people and deny any intended insult. Nevertheless, his early characterizations of his family are something of an embarrassment to them. He could have explored the admirable simplicity of their lives, their easy-going resilience in the face of hardship, and their tightly knit neighborhood, even if he wanted to pursue these themes without sentimentalizing or romanticizing them. Certainly one of the most interesting characters in *Roots* is Stan Mann, who epitomizes the ability of these people to endure suffering with quiet stoicism. Even in Stan's dour greetings we get a glimpse of the stubbornness and stoicism that others of his community share. And finance schemes—like Pearl's "buying club" as an alternative to buying appliances on "the H.P." (hire purchase, comparable to lay-away)—indicate a cooperative spirit of the type that Richard Hoggart describes in *The Uses of Literacy*.

One can only speculate that Wesker's treatment of the Norfolk people stemmed from some misgivings about some of the working classes and his ambivalent feelings about the communal, rural values that at once suppress individualism and discourage self-improvement and personal ambition.

The Working Classes and the Arts

Beatie's self-righteous condemnation of the working classes at the end of this play—so vigorous that it silences a rebuttal from her family—is one of the moments that provoked leftist playwright John McGrath to question Wesker's allegiance to socialist values. In a 1970 exchange of letters, McGrath challenged what he perceived as Wesker's limited comprehension of the working classes and the arts: like Morris, Wesker defined bourgeois values too narrowly by the standards and practices of the urban, moneyed, dominant classes. For McGrath, the lack of appreciation by the working classes of the so-called fine arts is less a matter of being able to understand writers or composers than of taste. He believes that the fine arts that are commonly rejected by the working classes are arbitrarily given value by a middle-class concept of culture that arrogantly excludes the contribution made by popular art forms, especially from television drama, popular music, and film. He raises the example of excellence in some television series that have "the same potential as the Victorian weekly magazines held for Dickens. Similarly, the pop song today has, if anything, rather more potential than the Tudor lyric as Wyatt found it. In the cinema, the comedy, the adventure-story, the drama, the epic are all forms which may not yet have revealed their full powers" (6 July 1970 letter). McGrath's solution is to expand aesthetics to include the best of the popular forms to reach the working classes. (He has consequently explored the Scottish folk celebration Céilidh, film, and a television police series as ways of reaching the working classes.) He advised Wesker that "it is no way to improve matters by thrusting alien art forms—the product of the class enemy—at a backward proletariat and expecting them to like it" (McGrath, 15). For McGrath, our roots must include more than a few worn-out, culturally received art forms.

Wesker's answer to McGrath is that too many artists have underestimated the ability of the working classes to appreciate the fine arts, which he considers a form of self-education. Remembering his own childhood when he was lifted out of the desultory conditions of the working-class environment by his family's interest in classical music, books, and the cinema, he laments those who are cheated of similar experiences. Indeed, throughout the 1960s Wesker worked tirelessly for the success of Centre 42 with the hope that an arts center for the working classes might open up an exposure in music, theater, and literature that they too might also use to escape the tedium of their daily lives.

Convinced that the fine arts are superior to any of the popular forms, Wesker was bound to clash with McGrath and other founders of Centre 42, who wanted to use the forms of popular culture to reach their audiences.

Although Wesker strongly believes in education in the fine arts for the working classes, the character that represents his interests in *Roots*, Ronnie, backs away from the opportunity to educate Beatie and her family when he deserts her. This is Wesker's way of illustrating Ronnie's weaknesses: his lack of vision, his self-centeredness, and his lack of resolve. *Roots* ends, instead, with Beatie's rescue of herself, setting up a self-help theme that underscores the importance Wesker places on working-class self-discipline—an inherently Conservative approach to class difference. It becomes one of the earliest signs that Wesker was not the socialist playwright he seemed to be. Beatie's willingness to assume responsibility for her own education becomes Wesker's message about the work ethic intended not only for the working classes but also for the middle classes, and it played very well at the box office.

What we get from Ronnie's desertion is yet another example, in addition to *The Kitchen* and *Chicken Soup with Barley*, of a young socialist who fails the very people he is supposedly committed to help. We see in these early plays an emerging pattern of doubt about the effectiveness of socialism and a yearning for a more socially responsible model, possibly in the determination of individual spirit, that could actually fulfill promises.

With this Conservative critique of the working classes, the trilogy demonstrates the limitations that Wesker sees in the socialist movement. Ironically it was these very plays that earned Wesker his reputation as an outspoken socialist playwright. The confusion is not simply the result of a critical misreading. He had taken his platform as the son of a Communist and a family in London's East End and a self-avowed socialist. Everyone, including Wesker, believed that the disillusionment his trilogy expressed was idiosyncratic, particular to the Kahn family or at the most a sign of the postwar dissatisfaction that most Britons shared at that time. Very few could see that Ronnie's doubts about socialism were revealing Wesker's own unconscious mistrust of socialism for the Jewish working class. Few could have predicted that his hopes for change in Britain were bound to be so frustrated that he would eventually withdraw from its ranks. Nevertheless, bitterness about the shortfalls of socialist values comes through quite clearly in Wesker's next play, *I'm Talking about Jerusalem*.

I'm Talking about Jerusalem

Continuing the story of the Kahn (and Wesker's own) family in *I'm Talking about Jerusalem*, he writes about the abortive attempt of his sister Della and her husband, Ralph Saltiel, to live in the country simply and by their own values. Harold Ribalow, author of Twayne's first volume on Wesker, knew Saltiel as a radio operator in Ceylon and describes him as a person very much like the character Dave Simmonds: "Ralph was a brilliant, dynamic, exciting human being who swore that, should he survive the war, he would live as a simple working man, using his hands as a carpenter. He was a socialist, a Jew, and a man with a strong sense of justice and idealism."[13]

Ribalow further explains that Wesker's sister and brother-in-law lived for 10 years (a slightly shorter length of time than the Simmondses) in a "humble shack in Norfolk" where they tried to build a new Jerusalem, a utopia somewhat like the one William Morris describes in his *News from Nowhere*. In Morris's book the economic revolution has already taken place, and workers, having rejected modern technology, have discovered the pleasures of handicrafts and the enjoyment of industry for its own sake.

Dave and Ada expand on the life they envision as they move into their "house in the middle of the fields" in September 1946 to the sounds of Beethoven's *Ninth Symphony*. They want to rekindle Morris's nostalgic dream of living away from cities, where technology and mercantilism dominate, by settling in little communities among gardens and green fields where no one feels any want because possessions are shared communally without monetary exchange. With their dream of a new Jerusalem, fairly common for a young couple in the 1960s, they seek a place for themselves away from the "dark Satanic mills" of William Blake's hymn, so well known that most Britons readily recognize these lines from *Milton: A Poem in Two Books: To Justify the Ways of God to Men*:

> I will not cease from Mental Fight
> Nor shall my Sword sleep in my hand,
> Till we have built Jerusalem,
> In England's green and pleasant land.

Dave yearns to recapture some of the pride a worker feels for his tools, his products, the sort of pleasure in the work's process that Ralph Saltiel witnessed in Ceylon. He believes "that a man is made to work and that when he works he's giving away something of himself, something very precious" (1: 163).

It is not long, however, before Dave and Ada's dream is destroyed when Dave's boss fires him for stealing linoleum. Dave is so angry that the linoleum is not considered communal property that he lies about taking it. His ambitions are further dashed by his own lack of business sense. He does not know how to draw up sound contracts and short-changes his assistant, who eventually moves on to the factory for more money and the excitement of working around big machinery in lieu of some abstract reward of pride in one's creations and a romantic dream. Dave's business eventually collapses.

On the day Dave and Ada move out, Ada's bother Ronnie returns to help. It is 1953. Ada's father, Harry Kahn, has died, and the Conservative party has won the election by a wide margin. Ronnie is deeply angered that his family, as part of yet another socialist experiment, has failed to succeed. He tries to persuade them to carry on. But Dave will not listen. He and Ada plan to set up shop in a London basement apartment where he will turn out furniture. He has lost faith in his ability as a craftsman; moreover, he refuses to talk about any socialist victories like the Spanish Civil War because it has not changed matters either.

Dave's loss of idealism makes Ronnie desperate. Ronnie too has lost his confidence in the future of socialism, but he wants someone, anyone really, to reassure him that visions "*do* work! And even if they don't work then for God's sake let's try and behave as though they do—or else nothing will work!" (1: 216). Only the women in the Kahn family—Sarah and Ada—remain steadfast to their old ideals. Sarah, particularly, is philosophical: "Did you expect the world to suddenly focus on them and say 'Ah, socialism is beautiful,' did you silly boy? Since when did we preach this sort of poverty?" (1: 215). And Ada stoutly maintains that a life in the country is only a part of the experiment. "In the end," she maintains, "they're going to have to turn to us" (1: 215). What she means is that this is only one small setback in a socialist revolution. Ronnie does not believe her. He "cups his hands to his mouth and yells in protest to the sky with bitterness and sarcasm, 'We—must—be—bloody—mad—to cry!'" (1: 218).

I'm Talking about Jerusalem ends on much the same note as *Chicken Soup with Barley*: the men, being pragmatic and brutally realistic, hold little hope for the future of their ideals. They stand in marked contrast to the women, who refuse to abandon their optimism in the face of defeat. In *Jerusalem*, however, there are some differences. Ronnie, though discouraged, clings weakly to a fragment of his mother's old political dreams. The ending, however bleak, has no real sense of finality or absolute defeat. There is some suggestion that their plans might be realized at another time.

I'm Talking about Jerusalem once again raises the question about the role of the individual in society. Like Peter in *The Kitchen*, Dave argues that his move to the country is strictly an isolated act of personal preference—one with no social implications—but his old friend Dobson, like Paul in *The Kitchen*, challenges that deluded notion. Endorsing the importance of social responsibility, Dobson remonstrates that someone has to work in the factories to produce screws and other modern necessities; without this farms and the rest of the industrial world would not prosper. Wesker's stand in this debate remains unclear in *I'm Talking about Jerusalem*. Even so, the mood he leaves at the end of the play expresses a glimmer of hope, however tenuous, and a reaffirmation of the individual's right to make choices regardless of social need.

Still, the argument set forth by Dave—that he should drop out and "do his own thing"—was not widely recognized by early audiences of *I'm Talking about Jerusalem* as particularly selfish or irresponsible, so they overlooked the conflict between Dobson and Dave. Instead, audiences responded to Dave's frustration at trying to live the simple William Morris life of a craftsman. Biased by romantic desires to leave the city and live off the land and by their expectations that Wesker was endorsing socialist causes, audiences glanced past the argument between Dave and Dobson that would have signaled Wesker's interest in individual identity, a distinctly antisocialist impulse. To be sure, both thrusts—the desire for a socialist solution and the critique of it—are there, but because Wesker does not completely let go of socialism until after the 1960s, and does not make his views public until the 1980s, his ambivalence led Kenneth Tynan to charge Wesker with "intellectual flabbiness" (Tynan, 299) and John Russell Taylor to call his plays "oddly muddled and out of focus" in their effect.[14] Similar comments by a number of critics indicate that they did not understand Wesker's waffling, even in those years, about his ideological convictions. Although Wesker did not understand his own political convictions at the time, most of his attitudes about the primacy of the individual are surprisingly consistent from that period to the present.

Despite the mixed messages of his plays, Wesker's early works, especially *Chicken Soup with Barley* and *The Kitchen*, have remained remarkably popular among community and university audiences. Only *Roots* has not held up well, partly because of its grating paternalism and naive treatment of both women and the working classes, partly because few actors have been able to repeat Joan Plowright's premiere performance.

Much of the credit for the success of these plays should also go to John Dexter, Wesker's director during those years. As Wesker acknowledges, Dexter's ability to catch what Wesker was after and insist on certain cuts and additions while the plays were in rehearsal lent the early drafts of the first five plays much needed shape and clarity.

Indeed, Wesker credits much of the success of his early plays to Dexter. He points in particular to the middle section of *The Kitchen* and the coal scene in *Chips with Everything*.[15] The last play Dexter directed for Wesker was *The Old Ones*, which he took to the Royal Court Theatre, and by then the strain of working intensively with one director had begun to wear on both of them. Following that, Dexter decided to take on other contracts to show that he could direct someone else's work; furthermore, being less than enthusiastic about Wesker's later plays because he thought that Wesker had not sufficiently "digested" the material, Dexter did not want to direct Wesker's plays simply out of a sense of duty or friendship.[16]

Wesker, too, was ready to break away from Dexter, although they parted friends, because he wanted to try directing his own productions. He defended his decision in a 1974 article for *Plays and Players*. Essentially, he wanted to eliminate the middle man "to ensure that his own voice emerges through all those filters,"[17] meaning the producer, the director, the actor, and the critic. Although he had the impression that he had taken charge of his own productions, Wesker's decision probably accomplished the reverse. As long as he has insisted on full authorial control, fewer and fewer theaters have taken the financial risk of signing on his untested plays because directors have less freedom to make changes. The risk of failure became the issue, particularly after Wesker experienced a couple of failures in the mid-1960s. As long as Dexter was directing his plays, however, Wesker experienced one gratifying success after another, even if production results did not always match his original expectations.

Chapter Three
Theatre, Why?

If British theater of the 1950s had not become largely a repository of hackneyed and tired works revisited again and again by an almost closed circle of middle-class playwrights and audiences, Arnold Wesker and others might never have found a voice in the 1960s. But the theater industry needed a new idiom that could only come out of the formerly excluded working-class writers and others who likewise had alternative points of view.

Periodically, mainstream theater in Britain has opened itself up to "fringe" (counterculture) elements. Most often, however, their influence has been minimal in the form of working-class perspectives couched in satire, folk song, folk theater, locally inspired historical reenactments, and biting melancholia that momentarily resuscitate the slow-paced, predictable portrayal of middle-class life. The previous window for alternative theater had been in the 1930s, when the oppositional and socialist Unity theater pressured the West End to recognize a fresh form of thinking and new attitudes. One full-scale play in particular, Walter Greenwood's *Love on the Dole* (1935), had been a run-away hit; Clifford Odets's *Waiting for Lefty* (1935) and Richard Llewellyn's *How Green Was My Valley* (1939) also had good seasons, but once World War II came along London's theater fell back into the old rut.

By 1960 the political climate had again changed. With a new wave of revolutionary thinking, the time was ripe for a fresh assault on mainstream theater. Around Christmas of that year several artists (mostly playwrights and directors)—John McGrath, Shelagh Delaney, Ted Kotcheff, Bernard Kops, Clive Barker, Sean Kenny, Doris Lessing, Alun Owen, Tom Maschler, Clive Exton, and Jeremy Sandford among them—met informally to toss around ideas for establishing their own means for producing artistic works, particularly a venue that would select its works more for their ability to speak for the people than by their potential at the box office. The artists wanted a multimedia cultural center that would feature all sorts of working-class arts, including music, night club entertainment and films, as well as theater, dance, and the visual arts. They also wanted a means for bringing together neighborhoods that had been cut off from one another by shifting economic trends at the end of World War II, and they aspired to reach out to the regions outside London, to communities that had been overshadowed by big-city needs.

The group continued talking into the spring about what they hoped to create, and they readily agreed that the purpose of this center would be, as Clive Barker put it, to "wrest artist activity from commercial domination and, in combination with the trade unions, to establish a new social role for the arts."[1] They aimed, most of all, to bypass the stranglehold that high rent, fashion-minded producers, croneyism among the directors, and bourgeois tastes had placed on theater in London.

Quite independently of the others, Wesker had already thrown his opinions into the arena with two pamphlets[2] aimed at trade-union audiences. In a lecture delivered first at Oxford in April 1960 and later published as "The Modern Playwright, or 'O, Mother, is it worth it?'" he challenged the unions to make the fine arts accessible to the working classes. Basically his argument was twofold: the working classes could realize a higher quality of life through the arts; moreover, the unions could promote the arts for workers by launching an inquiry into how this could be done. The assumptions behind Wesker's arguments probably did more to win over the leadership than the rank and file, since in the lecture he complained pointedly about the millions of workers who sit night after night mindlessly watching their television sets instead of attending the theater. Comparing his own childhood to that of his working-class friends, Wesker suggested that their development had been stunted, or "stultified," by empty forms of entertainment. Because of cultural starvation, workers were only "enjoying half of life" and they deserved more (*FF*, 16–17).

In his second pamphlet, "Labour and the Arts: II, or 'What, then, is to be done?,'" issued in May 1960, Wesker spelled out the details of what he wanted the trade unions to do, why it would benefit them to sponsor the arts, and what the results would be if they failed to do so. Wesker and his co-author, Bill Holdsworth, chairman of the Mayfair branch of the Association of Engineering and Shipbuilding Draughtsmen, called for the Trades Union Congress (TUC) to underwrite a new theater, a film movement, and an orchestra. They also suggested a sponsorship of writers, folk music, contemporary artists, and children with talent. Their argument was that this was the most effective means for the TUC to promote quality of life in a "culturally bankrupt community" and that doing so would humanize the lives of workers who are otherwise exploited as mere tools of a mechanized industry.

Wesker and Holdsworth persuasively claimed that without giving the workers "a rich voice of their own" the role of the Labour movement would diminish along with the quality of workers' lives. Indeed, much about what they had to say seems somewhat prophetic today because, in fact, the TUC never was fully generous with substantial sums of money for the arts and eventually the Labour movement did lose a great deal of its hold over the lives of most Britons. Had the movement been making more significant contributions to workers' lives—educating them through theater to the basics of economics and power struggle—workers might not have voted the Labour party out of power in 1979. What Wesker, Holdsworth, and others were witnessing in the 1960s without realizing it was the peak of labor power in England before the union busting of the Thatcher era. Had the TUC taken more of a leadership role in the arts—one that led to contributions by workers—the Labour movement might well have bargained from a different position 20 years later.

Whether Wesker's and Holdsworth's pamphlets, which were distributed to the secretary of every trade union in the country, had an immediate effect or not, the TUC, meeting on the Isle of Man in September 1960, did pass Resolution 42, calling for a greater participation in the arts by Labour. It read, "Congress considers that much more could be done and accordingly requests the General Council to conduct a special examination and to make proposals to a future Congress to ensure a greater participation by the trade union movement in all cultural activities."[3] For many, Resolution 42 signaled the possibilities of significant financial support, but when the report of the inquiry was handed down a year later, it became clear that the TUC had decided not to become involved in any substantial (i.e., monetary) way. But the TUC did endorse union participation in local festivals and that alone opened the door for Centre 42, named after the TUC resolution.

Union encouragement was enough, in any case, to push the Steering Committee for Centre 42 to move ahead. By this time Arnold Wesker had joined them. But organizers shaping Centre 42 had divided along two lines—those who wanted an organization that would simply act as a clearinghouse for talent that would play in the regions and those who wanted an actual physical plant for showcasing talent in London. Before they could resolve that issue, Centre 42 was incorporated in September 1961 and invited almost immediately to participate in the Wellingborough Arts Festival, 1–4 November 1961. Not surprisingly, the festival was hastily thrown together, and its publicity was belated; nevertheless, it was by all accounts a success. Because the festival drew unexpectedly large and enthusiastic crowds, Centre 42 was invited to mount festivals in five other locations in 1962—Nottingham, Leicester, Birmingham, Bristol, and Hayes and Southall. Then Centre 42's Council of Management announced in the Annual Report that the six festivals had gone in the red £33,400, even though its directors had raised £15,450 in addition to a £10,000 grant from the Gulbenkian Foundation to cover two years' work.

To keep the enterprise afloat, Centre 42 attracted a collection of business types and artists in 1962–63 to put the enterprise on sound financial footing. The roster read like the who's who of British arts and letters—Peggy Ashcroft, Robert Bolt, Graham Greene, Vanessa Redgrave, Laurence Olivier, Joan Plowright, J. B. Priestly, Terence Rattigan, Herbert Read, Peter Sellers, Alan Sillitoe, C. P. Snow, Kenneth Tynan, and Raymond Williams, among others. But many of the original Steering Committee had dropped out—Doris Lessing, John McGrath, Alun Owen, and Clive Exton left for a variety of reasons, but mostly in disagreement about the direction that "42" was headed. Doris Lessing, for example, thought Wesker lacked "the education, the judgement, the administrative expertise to be Centre 42's Director."[4] And John McGrath, among others, disagreed fundamentally with Wesker's understanding of the project.

Once Centre 42 was under way, its founders began losing sight of their original goals because there was no consensus of purpose: some simply wanted to entertain; others wanted to provide a voice strictly for the worker. Wesker had said all along that he wanted to "teach" his audiences and to that end he would even "undermine people's existing values and impose our own upon them."[5] Hoping to subvert the football-betting habits of the working classes, he exhorted his writing colleagues, "We must pick up our poems, our plays and films, tuck them under our arms and go out to the public and do battle with them." It had not occurred to him that his remarks were condescending or that he was speaking from the contradictory perspectives of both the working class and the cultural elite. He was later accused from many quarters of "taking culture to the masses." He was surprised when readers of all sorts took such offense at his remarks.

Nevertheless, Wesker plowed on. His mission was to redress injustices played on uneducated workers shut out by the snobberies of Britain's class system. He believed that a self-constructed education in the arts would not only improve daily life but could minimize class differences and open doors for the excluded. Acculturation might boost many workers into a middle-class life; more than that, however, it could help a worker differentiate between the frustration of low pay, which is merely low-level exploitation, and "soul-destroying" work, the most pernicious form of exploitation.[6] For this reason he repeatedly insisted that "art is the right and need of every civilised community. As such, it should be subsidised and not forced into paying for itself."[7] Wesker's detractors, however, accused him of "cramming culture down the throats of unwilling workers," and he has subsequently spent years trying to live down journalist's questions about paternalistic snobbery and "taking culture to the masses." From Wesker's point of view, the arts—especially painting, classical music, and theater—are universal (indeed, a common heritage) and therefore know no class boundaries. So he categorically refuses to discuss the matter of foisting unpopular forms on the workers.

The issue of "Whose Arts?" manifested itself in Centre 42 as a debate among its co-directors—Clive Barker and Arnold Wesker—about whether to use popular music and other popular forms in the festivals. Wesker stood against the others in Centre 42 in his opposition to the use of rock music, which he deemed paralyzing to its listeners and trivial.[8] Although he has claimed to enjoy some popular music, he was always rather uneasy about the defiant tone of rock concerts and fans. In the 1960s bands such as the Beatles and Rolling Stones played to huge audiences and were enormously popular, and so the question about using rock stars in local concerts was particularly acute. What frightened Wesker, perhaps irrationally, were concert gatherings of young people seemed hypnotized by numbingly loud music and swept away by mob hysteria. He was also concerned about the attitude of political indifference expressed by both pop singers and their audiences (*FF*, 68).

To their credit, Centre 42 planners tried to solve their differences by selecting a variety of entertainment with a broad appeal. At the festivals there were time slots for poetry readings, a hairdressing demonstration, documentary films, and a wide assortment of music. Organizers also attempted to reach out to the needs of young audiences heard to remark that "only snobs and sissies go to the theater" or "I don't like going to the theater because the older people turn round when I laugh." To their discredit, the planners never really surmounted the problems of the generation gap that had crept into the debate about popular forms; nor did they ever resolve the question about the rock music or the value of popular culture.

Centre 42 died a slow death, but not before purchasing the expansive Round House in Camden Town, a Victorian engine shed or car barn on Chalk Farm Road in London. It had been Wesker's grand dream to build a center for artists and showcase for the arts where all sorts from the working classes to the leaders of Britain might gather to talk about and enjoy the arts. He said in a letter to the Round House's architect, Ron Allio, "We are not looking for a working-class art—we do not know what this is. There is only good and bad art and there should never be any other criterion" (*FF*, 61). No longer did he speak of arts specifically done by or for the working classes. He envisioned, instead, a center that had a broad educational and social potential with rooms for meetings for the trade unions, the churches, and schools, with an auditorium, technical area, and exhibition areas for the arts. He also wanted places for restaurants and projection rooms for films, classrooms and book stalls. In short, he wanted a building that could begin to integrate the arts with daily activity in a working-class district of London where neighborhood people could wander in and out, yet one that could still function as a center for the national and international leaders as well as artists.

After receiving £50,000 for the Round House—£40,000 raised by Prime Minister Harold Wilson at a Downing Street tea party and £10,000 donated by the British Arts Council—Arnold Wesker convinced Louis Mintz and Alec Coleman to donate the remaining 16-year lease on the building to Centre 42. In exchange, however, Wesker promised Mintz the successful completion of a £650,000 campaign drive, but that goal was never realized. In the meantime, the original founders watched their original goals for Centre 42 slip through their grasp as they turned the reins over to the Round House Trust, numbers men like Robert Maxwell, who was their treasurer from 1965 and who understood little about "wresting artist activity from commercial dominion." Purchasing this building was not the only factor in the termination of Centre 42. Enthusiasm for the project had already begun to wane even in the earliest days of incorporation during disputes about the Centre's goals. The 1960 Steering Committee could agree on a need for artistic freedom, arts on a local level, and opposition to mainstream theater, but in the throes of operation its members could not agree on how to achieve those ends. Then, too, the chaos of the early festivals had taken its toll in energy expended for shows but not for planning.

It must be underscored that the biggest single obstacle to a flourishing Centre 42 was always a lack of money—a problem that could easily have been solved with government support. With adequate subsidy, all the competing factions in the Steering Committee could have been satisfied. They had, after all, managed to mount six festivals at much less than the cost of producing one major West End production, even in 1962 terms. And the pending debt was equally manageable: the £50,000 needed to retrofit the Round House could have been meted out over several years by the British Arts Council, which easily gave £302,000 to the Royal Opera House in 1957–58.[9] Centre 42 closed its doors permanently in December 1970, shortly after Wesker decided to resign. Ironically and sadly for Wesker, the Round House became in the 1980s the site of occasional rock concerts, and it largely remains unused.

The Nottingham Captain

The campaign to promote Centre 42 and its subsequent failure exacted a large price of Arnold Wesker personally and professionally. In 1962, once Centre 42 was under way, Wesker deliberately chose to curtail his playwriting to devote his energies full time to the project, and this decision proved a big mistake because it cut deeply into the momentum he had established as a writer. During the early 1960s Wesker completed very few plays for production. One of them, *The Nottingham Captain* (written and performed in 1962), leans too heavily on original speeches by historical characters like Lords Byron and Castlereagh and Jeremy Bentham.[10] Compiled hastily in a weekend after the originally scheduled playwright pulled out at the last minute, it was written to serve as part of the entertainment at the Wellingborough Festival and to commemorate 1812 events at Nottingham, one of the festival sites, when weavers destroyed machines that would replace them as workers. It opens with a well-known speech by Lord Byron, who ridicules the proposal of a death sentence for the rioters, called Luddites. The narration set to music is mostly a rehearsal of events leading up to the trial of three key rebels— Jeremy Brandreth, William Turner, and Isaac Ludlam—and, as Glenda Leeming has pointed out, much of the documentary is taken verbatim from an 1817 issue of *Gentleman's Quarterly*. She speculates that Wesker also borrowed very heavily from Ernst Toller's *The Machine-Wreckers* (1922).[11]

Although the speeches are stiff and bookish and the chain of events rather disjointed, the play is still noteworthy for its format, which Wesker draws on for such later historically based productions as *Beorhtel's Hill*. It is also interesting for its combined use of Brechtian song and signboards that act as a choruslike commentary on the speeches. This was the only concession to Bertolt Brecht's method of "alienation," or *Verfremdungseffekt*—considered de rigueur for the socialist theater of the 1960s and 1970s—that Wesker made in his entire career. Because of the Brechtian elements, *Nottingham Captain* outweighed two other plays written at this time—*Menace* and *The Four Seasons*—partly because the latter contained few of the social themes that had made Wesker famous and because they had no hint of Brecht's influence.

Chips with Everything

For many, Wesker's last great play was *Chips with Everything*, written in 1960–61 as the tide for Centre 42 was on the rise. He based it on letters he wrote and a journal he kept during the first eight weeks he was serving in the Royal Air Force in 1950. At first the material went into a "very bad novel," but it was reworked in 1960 as a play. It opened simultaneously in Glasgow and Sheffield, was quickly transferred to the West End, and premiered on Broadway in 1963. Although the initial reviews of *Chips* were mixed, everything else seemed to be going so well that Wesker decided to invest the £10,000 that he received from the film rights into the future of Centre 42. That decision proved to be a mistake, given the financial hardships he has suffered since that time, but his friends would say that Wesker is often generous to a fault and not very wise about the way he spends his money.

When it first appeared, *Chips with Everything* was reviewed by critics as another socialist play about the destructive consequences of class conflict—a misunderstanding generated by audience expectations about Wesker's works. The problem is that the critics' undue emphasis on class tensions slights *Chips*'s more central theme, which examines the forces that destroy the individual and spread the poison of suppression.

Pip Thompson is one of several fresh recruits newly conscripted into the Royal Air Force. Although he is born to wealth, attends British public school (private school), and is university trained, he has chosen to be drafted as a noncommissioned airman. His presence in the wing as one of the regulars antagonizes everyone from the most groveling working-class conscript frustrated in his fawning desire to please Pip to the wing commander who suggests that Pip should stop slumming and become an officer. Essentially no one likes Pip because there is not much to like. He is not only cold, detached, and selfish, but he also refuses to fit anyone's expectations of a young man from a wealthy family. Because he fails to find a niche for himself in either the upper or lower ranks, Pip's reasons for rejecting officer status is unclear, but his background suggests that he is rebelling against his family, which has many members with distinguished military careers, and his father's expectations of him. Whatever Pip's reasons, he has a certain untested and romantic yearning to be what he calls "one of the toilers" (3: 42), so he apparently fancies that he gets along with the others better than he actually does.

In fact, Pip cannot place himself among ordinary men and spurns their friendly gestures at every turn. Early on he reveals his distaste for the masses by describing a working-class tea room in the East End, which he happened to visit when his car broke down. While Pip is eating a piece of "tasteless currant cake" and drinking tea from "a thick, white, cracked cup," an old man with rheumy eyes sits down next to him. The man is neat, but his face is lined with grains of dirt and something about him must have reminded Pip of everything he did not want to become. Pip says disdainfully, "And then I saw the menu, stained with tea and beautifully written by a foreign hand, and on top it said—God I hated that old man—it said 'Chips with everything.' Chips with every damn thing. You breed babies and you eat chips with everything" (3: 17).

At another point, when his working-class mate Charlie tries to connect with Pip, Pip insults his nickname and makes it clear they cannot communicate on any meaningful level. Part of Pip's aversion to Charlie may have been the lad's blind awe of wealth, which Pip symbolizes. Like Pip, Charlie is unable to transcend class stereotypes to become a real friend. The difference between them is that Pip, not knowing what it means to be a man like Charlie, does not particularly want to taste that experience.

Still, middle-class mates have no more success than Charlie assimilating Pip into their group. When Pip finds he lacks the killer instinct even to bayonet a dummy, Andrew tries to comfort him. But Pip recoils from that sort of intimacy, and Andrew attacks Pip's arrogance. As soon as Andrew assures the haughty young man that he is only trying to help, Pip dismisses him. Pip simply cannot be comfortable around middle-class friendliness. He surrenders to an *esprit de corps* only when he can lead the others in a nighttime raid on the coal yard, and he warms to the game only because it becomes a way to subvert authority.

If ordinary conscripts irritate Pip, the officers infuriate him. He flares up when the pilot officer sidles up to him and addresses him with alternately familiar and intimidating language. The officer indicates that he considers Pip one of them, the officers: "Your mates are morons, Thompson, morons. At the slightest hint from us they will disown you. ...You, we shall make an officer, as we promised" (3: 59). Threatening Pip with court martial, he tries to pressure him to join his peers. Pip rejects the man out of hand: "I WILL NOT BE AN OFFICER" (3: 59). Nevertheless, something the pilot officer says haunts him: "We listen but we do not hear, we befriend but do not touch you, we applaud but do not act—to tolerate is to ignore" (3: 59). Wesker later glossed these lines in the article "Art Is Not Enough": "We listen to you [rebels], we let other people listen to you, and we show no offence; we even applaud you, we even flatter you for your courage and idealism, but little else. It goes right through us. We listen, but we do not hear. We befriend, but we do not touch you [who oppose us]. We applaud, but we do not act. We have, in other words, tolerated and thereby ignored you. All our rebels have been defeated like this."[12]

Although Pip might believe that he hates this arrogance of power, he obviously registers the officer's words because he later repeats them to Charlie as a way of showing his contempt for the officer. When Charlie asks about their meaning, Pip's explanation is, "We'll do anything they want just because they know how to smile at us" (3: 63). Pip indicates at that moment that despite his own protestations to the contrary, he knows he will eventually be forced to yield to the pressures from the top.

In the end the officers break Pip's will just as they destroy the spirit of another misfit, Smiler, a harmless, young recruit who naturally wears a silly grin on his face. The corporals so hate the odd grin that they brutalize Smiler until he runs away from camp. When he returns with bleeding feet, he is arrested and ordered to submit to more of the same treatment. Although his mates make every effort to protect Smiler from the reprisals, they are ineffective. They are about to be thrown into the brig for refusing orders when Pip steps forth, smiles at the pilot officer, and begins changing into an officer's uniform.

Pip's motivation for capitulation to the officers' corps is unclear. He might have feared his own merciless harassment to the point of a complete breakdown like Smiler. Or he might have wanted to avert the possibility of mass court martials for the entire company. Or he might have decided to take his place among the officers because he would never fit with the others, but he could deliver them by undermining the military from the top. Whatever his reason, the results are tragic because the evidence is clear: hating physical violence and holding little more than contempt for groups, Pip does not have the disposition for leadership in the military and will likely become a vindictive officer. Being forced to conform to a role he despises, he has, however, sacrificed his integrity and jeopardized the future of the enlisted men. Just as tragically, Smiler is bullied until he too is crushed by the system. Both have become victims of institutional necessity.

Because the protagonist is an aristocratic misfit and not the working-class hero that audiences expect from a "socialist" playwright, many find themselves at the end of the play with misplaced antipathy for Pip, looking past his rights as an individual to his character flaws. But that is not Wesker's intention. He asks that we question the way we allocate freedoms on the basis of social acceptance and class: "The important thing is that justice belongs to even personalities who are unattractive, and so right should be right no matter what cap you wear, and the fact that he wears an upper-class cap should not make his rightness less right" (Bigsby 1977).

Similarly, some misguided critics, such as Irving Wardle of the *Observer*, interpreted the play as an indictment of class differences or, as Wardle put it, "a bitterly personal expression of loathing for the class tyranny of service life."[13] But the purpose of *Chips* is less about class struggle than the invidious strategies of those in charge to retain their power. Wesker described *Chips* as "a warning. It says—though again one is theorizing after the event—to the ruling class: you can no longer kid us. We know the way it happens. And to those who are ruled: look, boys, this is the way it happens, and this is the way it will end if you continue not to recognize that you are very sweetly but very definitely being put in your place."[14] The object of his remarks is not only the ruling classes (in this case corporate types and officers) but anyone like Pip who has the right-minded impulse to liberate the others from oppression, especially from those whose means of controlling may be much more terrifying than snobbery. The distinction that Wesker makes here between the lesser threat of class dominance and the greater menace of destruction of the human spirit is significant because it demonstrates all too well Wesker's dread of persecution—regardless of its source or justification—a theme that runs through all of Wesker's work.

A milestone in the development of a serious playwright, *Chips with Everything* is one of Wesker's first attempts to move away from the straight naturalistic forms of drama to a more stylized or poetic form. In it Wesker experiments with the effects of mime, folk song, and minimal scenery to see if he could develop a cleaner, simpler style without the trappings of naturalism. He also tried a more charged but spare language, with strict attention paid to rhythms and sharp give-and-take dialogues like this one in which Andrew plays the pilot officer for a fool:

ANDREW:	*(saluting)* Good morning, sir.
PILOT OFFICER:	Haven't you been told the proper way to address an officer?
ANDREW:	Sorry sir, no sir, not yet sir.
PILOT OFFICER:	There's dust under that bed.
ANDREW:	Is there, sir?
PILOT OFFICER:	I said so.
ANDREW:	Yes, you did, sir.
PILOT OFFICER:	Then why ask me again?
ANDREW:	Again, sir?
PILOT OFFICER:	Didn't you?
ANDREW:	Didn't I what, sir?
PILOT OFFICER:	Ask me to repeat what I'd already said. Are you playing me up, Airman? Are you taking the mickey out of me? I can charge you, man. I can see your game and I can charge you.
ANDREW:	Yes, you can, sir.
PILOT OFFICER:	Don't tell me what I already know.
ANDREW:	Oh, I wouldn't, sir—you know what you already know. I know that, sir. (3: 24)

Rather than try for naturalistic detail, Wesker chose a few key scenes with drills, bunkhouse inspection, and bayonet practice to represent life in the military. It should have been clear from the coal scene alone, in which the men steal coal in a beautifully orchestrated mime scene, that Wesker was not attempting a faithful reconstruction of life in the National Service. Nevertheless, he was repeatedly taken to task for the play's retreat from realism. Many reviewers complained that the military was never like that, as though Wesker did not know (after serving for two years in the National Service) that he was taking some literary license. Undaunted by the mixed reviews, he tried many of the same artistic strategies—minimal scenery, rhythmical dialogue, and lyrical language—in *Menace* and *The Four Seasons*. With these plays, however, he had even less critical success, perhaps because the language was more self-consciously "poetic" and the plots fell short of that of *Chips*.

Menace and *The Four Seasons*

Menace, screened as a television play in 1963, was another experiment for several reasons. Wesker wanted not only to concentrate more on poetic language but also to see how he liked creating for television. Looking back at *Menace* and *The Four Seasons* through the plays about extramarital affairs, which Wesker wrote in the 1980s, these plays do not seem so out of the ordinary. At the time of the great fanfare over Centre 42 and the stir over "socialist theatre for the masses," however, these plays were entirely unexpected, partly because *The Four Seasons* appeared after Wesker's 18-month hiatus during peak activity at Centre 42. Both plays are love stories in which the characters talk their relationships into disintegration. Written in 1961, three years before *The Four Seasons*, and published in *Six Sundays in January*, *Menace* served as a dry run for the later play and could well have drawn on *Look Back in Anger* for the idea of a class conflict between a wealthy woman, Harriet, and her lover, Garry, who has no appreciable means of income.

What menace lurks in this play is entirely unclear. The most obvious threat is that of the three boys who harass Garry, Harriet, and their three misfit housemates. Leaning on Garry for moral support are a half-blind accountant; Sophie, a woman on pension; and a tailor's machinist who plays the football pools. When young gang members shadow the near-sighted Sophie, the others rescue her by inviting the boys to tea. The boys, disturbed by their unexpected hospitality and the neuroses of these motley hosts, find every excuse to escape. Their threat has suddenly diffused.

Another possible menace is the pending loneliness that hangs over all their lives, each clinging to the others in a fragile alliance. "It is a play," wrote Wesker in a memo, "about insecurity, about a threatened world that menaces our security so that we never have a chance to develop fully, to finish things" (Ribalow, 94). The menace, therefore, that seems most disturbing is Harriet and Garry's tense relationship in which she nags him about his lack of work and he nags her about managing their dinner party. Here are two people who need each other, and yet he ridicules her about "looking for life . . . amidst the despair," and she taunts him with insinuations of impotence (*SS*, 94–95). The play ends with the threat of her walking out and of his throwing her out. The inevitable is deferred, if only temporarily, when they impulsively decide to whitewash a wall together and dance in a slow, expressive dance—a strange ending to a barely coherent play.

Because the play is hardly more than a potpourri of images, it has no real center or plot, but many of its disjunctive parts are pregnant with suggestion and provide material for Wesker's later works. His concern for the forgotten aged is further developed in *The Old Ones*, and the quarreling between mismatched lovers is a theme Wesker uses again and again in the plays of the 1980s, especially those that feature intense women. The difference, however, is that Wesker is more generous and balanced in assigning faults than he is with later reincarnations of bickering couples. Garry and Harriet are equally culpable; she is willful, but his attacks on her are petty and mean-spirited.

The seeds of the relationship in *Menace* germinate into the love affair of *The Four Seasons*. The couple in *The Four Seasons* is middle aged and on the rebound from earlier, hurtful relationships from which they are trying to recover and start anew. The trouble is that they bring to a deserted farmhouse their old defenses and self-protective strategies, which prove destructive to the new relationship. The cycle of their love affair parallels the change of seasons beginning with winter. Beatrice, thoroughly wounded by a failed marriage and love affair, can do little more than sit nearly inert, while Adam tries to help her heal. By spring she has emerged from her paralysis and has begun speaking. Their love grows, but sarcasms borrowed from earlier relationships creep into their exchanges:

BEATRICE: Why should you imagine I can't cook, or run a household? You mistake my silence for inability.

ADAM: You're cheating. Obedience and false modesties—there is no time.

BEATRICE: Come now, if I have false modesties you have false innocence.

ADAM: Aaaaaah!

BEATRICE: Did that hurt?

ADAM: Didn't you mean it to hurt?

BEATRICE: I'm sorry. Old reflexes.

ADAM: But it came so easily, so quickly. (2: 2)

By summer their love has fully blossomed, but we still hear defensiveness and latent acrimony in every exchange. They seem to talk past each other: she cannot forgive herself, yet she belittles him; he cannot be satisfied, since he has only one ideal in the perfect woman: "There are two kinds of love and two kinds of women. The woman whose love is around you, keeping its distance lest the heat of it burns you; and out of that warmth you emerge, slowly, confidently, as sure as the seed in her womb. And the woman whose love is an oppressive sun burning the air around you till you can't breathe and drying every drop of moisture from your lips till you can't speak; and she has a passion no part of which relates to any living man or any living man could share" (2: 93).

Apparently "oppressive woman" describes Adam's ex-wife, a woman he finds mad because she would "rave and regret, applaud and destroy, love and devour" (2: 94). He seems doomed to repeat his mistakes, since Beatrice too is this sort of woman.

Insulted by his confessions, Beatrice explodes, then takes the blame of their failing relationship, but they both realize that they have been used and abused and bring those crippling memories to their relationship. Beatrice says, "But if we'd met each other before we'd met anyone else then the right hour would have sung clear and ringing at the right time, every time" (2: 98). Still, she is bitter that she has never found "peace, majesty and great courage" in a lover, and he wants a woman who has "passion without deceit, wisdom without cruelty, pity without abuse" (2: 106). He also wants someone to depend on him without complaint and respond to his needs but demand little of her own. He wants to be able to teach her and provide her with a sensitive, but strong companionship that cradles her. The trouble is that Adam's partners, like Beatrice, reject co-optation by this paternalistic exuberance—what Adam calls his "laughter." Beatrice fights him for control and escapes through self-absorption and demands of her own.

In the autumn they abuse each other again and reconcile by baking apple strudel together, but their declaration of forgiveness is clearly tentative as they drift toward a deadening indifference. By autumn's end Beatrice openly resents Adam's laughter. They reminisce sentimentally about their past lovers while Adam tries to re-ignite a fire among the damp, cold leaves and Beatrice packs her clothes with a "chilling" calmness. We know that the cycle will repeat itself either with these two people or with a new set of partners.

Although *The Four Seasons* suffers from a weak, predictable plot and embarrassingly sentimental lines, it is a seminal play for what it suggests about themes of male-female strife in other Wesker plays. A reader of *The Mistress, Lady Othello,* or *One More Ride on the Merry-Go-Round,* in particular, would do well to study *The Four Seasons,* because many later works dealing with dissatisfied couples become extensions of the arguments begun here. It not only offers some explanation for what drives Wesker's "devouring woman," but it also lays out the familiar trail of an affair from the exhilaration of those first days of discovering each other to bitter cruelty after disappointment. Moreover, *The Four Seasons* connects some of the disappointment to earlier memories, some of them out of Wesker's childhood. It is difficult to know if the failing affair between Beatrice and Adam is autobiographical, but the reminiscences at the end of *The Four Seasons* record some of Wesker's memories about his parents.

The play is also interesting for its albeit less than successful experimentation with "heightened dialogue" (Wesker's description) and controlled speech rhythms. Its impressionistic movement of time, stylized set, and emblematic costume changes are marks of a playwright growing into new forms. The patently naturalistic preparation of the apple strudel, although inventive and playful, seems a jolt amidst less referential images.

The Four Seasons drew a great deal of criticism from those who found it too bourgeois for socialist theater. Wesker's disclaimer at the end of the play attempts to answer those who question why a socialist playwright would isolate Beatrice and Adam in a deserted farmhouse away from any viable community. Well aware of the accepted practice in socialist theater of situating human interaction in its ideological and historical context, Wesker speaks out for a less "cold-hearted and chastising" theater—one that recognizes the primary importance of love (2: 113). Against the "puritanical attitudes towards art and the artist which are shared by a perplexed, narrow-minded bourgeoisie," he defends his departure in theme and focus: "There is no abandoning in this play of concern for socialist principles nor a turning away from a preoccupation with real human problems" (2: 114).

To some extent Wesker's defense begs the point because socialist theater is not necessarily defined by such rigid moralistic and economic judgments as he would suggest, nor does it abandon the primacy of human relationships. Still, there is a revealing subtext to his remarks. He is determined not to submit to what he perceives as a sacrifice of his artistic integrity or a subordination of individual expression to political, especially socialist, allegiances. His message surprised many, since it was timed to address the pressures by socialist peers and critics, especially those at Centre 42, for more radical theater. It also defined a stance that distinctly set Wesker apart from the others. Coupled with his new play, *Their Very Own and Golden City,* written in the same years as *The Four Seasons*, the works of this period mark a turning point for Wesker: he is publicly declaring his own brand of socialist drama, one that is only tangentially interested in ideological themes.

Their Very Own and Golden City

Their Very Own and Golden City was written in 1963–64 by a disillusioned and dispirited Arnold Wesker. Mounted in 1966 after the devastating reviews of *Four Seasons*, its reception was lukewarm and it was followed by a prolonged dry spell before Wesker wrote *The Friends* in 1967, which also received crippling reviews.

Although Centre 42 would not officially close its doors until 1970 when Wesker resigned his directorship, the project as Wesker had envisioned it with a large cultural center for the working-class districts of London was already being threatened by 1963. *Their Very Own and Golden City* marked the beginning of a dark period in Wesker's life when he tried to understand the failure of a movement to which he had been fully committed.

Essentially the two-act play is his version of what happened at Centre 42, and it is the only record we have of Wesker's story of that period. The first act begins in 1926, when a group of young dreamers conceive of a better life, and ends with the beginning of World War II—a period that interrupts the progress of their hopes to build six model cities that will act as seeds for a new way to live. The second act chronicles the frustrations that the Trades Union Congress (TUC), the city planner, the industrialist, and the chairman of the movement offer to impede the realization of this dream. Now and again scenes with the young dreamers return as an ironic reminder of how easy and exciting these ideas seemed to be in the discussion stage and how difficult they were to execute because of institutional resistance. Because the play is set in 1926, all the later events become flash-forwards that narrate what eventually happens to the group's plans for the "Golden Cities." Act 2 in particular slides quickly through a period that spans "1948–1985 or thereabouts" (2: 126), a head-spinning turn of events that leads up to the finale that is a postmortem on the plan's failures.

Their Very Own and Golden City begins with the dreams of a young man, Andrew Cobham, and his friends Stoney and Paul, who want "the chance to change the pattern of living for all time" for the inhabitants of six New Towns or New Cities—fully self-contained settlements with carefully designed systems that anticipate social and economic need. Andy's youthful vision is vague and idealistic but appealing. He describes "cities of light and shade . . . with secret corners" and "cities for lovers . . . and crowds and lone wolves." He wants "cosy cities . . . family cities . . . with wide streets and twisting lanes . . . full of sound for the blind and colour for the deaf . . . that frighten no one . . . that sing the praises of men" (2: 160). The question is how to achieve his dream—with a grand project that builds all the cities at once or with a piecemeal approach that risks the danger of incompletion. At first Andy admits only to a modest goal, to know "that change is possible" (2: 131), but from the start he wants six "Golden Cities," however this is to be achieved.

Also in the project is Andy's sweetheart, Jessie. Much of what we learn about the Golden Cities we learn through Andy's instruction of Jessie—conversations reminiscent of Ronnie's instruction of Beatie, Adam's instruction of Beatrice. Andy later meets Kate, to whom he is initially attracted although he is married to Jessie, but his admiration for Kate sours over the years. She is a curious figure. As the "coldhearted, unsympathetic" socialist whose drive to serve the cause and the program takes precedence over personal and family need, she is the sort of individual whose single-minded ideology concerns Wesker. (Trussler and Marowitz, 86). Kate tells Andy, "Your family is your family and your work is your work, and you have not the right, no right at all, to neglect a project involving so many for the sake of your own good life" (2: 176). And yet she is someone Wesker can approach, as she too advocates the fine arts for the "common man." She says sardonically to the working-class person who wants to learn about and produce in the arts, "Haven't you noticed the patronizing way we say, 'He's artistic, how touching—give him pottery classes and amateur theatricals'—but the masters continue to hang on our walls and the big theatres are our habitat, not yours" (2: 168–69). Like Wesker, Kate also claims to be classless, a term that probably refers, in Wesker's case, to one who is born of working-class parents and educated to middle-class tastes and profession.

After earning his credentials in architecture, Andrew Cobham (whose name in earlier drafts was Martin Wadham and Andrew Wadham, echoes of Arnold Wesker's name) sets out to garner trade union support. His TUC mentor is a crusty but principled old cynic, Jake Latham, who tries to convince Andy that he should never submit to compromise: "Defeat doesn't matter; in the long run all defeat is temporary. It doesn't matter about present generations but future ones always want to look back and know that someone was around acting on principle" (2: 141). Latham is the old-line party member who acts as a conscience to the rest about their standards and values. He is the one to preserve the integrity of their program. As a good old socialist Latham looks forward to the revolution and he wants nothing short of a complete reform of the economic system in Britain. As a test he asks Andy, "Is it better to risk defeat in defence of a principle or hang on with a compromise?," and Andy answers much too quickly, "Compromise." It is an answer he eventually lives by as he tries to build his Golden Cities, but it is a solution he lives to regret because he finds himself bargaining away so much that he ends up with "patchwork," a small piece of what he hoped to build.

The problem with "patchwork," as the chairman of the local town planning notes, is that "one day the chaos will overwhelm the tiny bit of order, won't it?" (2: 163). His observation is rather prophetic, however, since he will support other, equally untenable projects that he admits are also "bits of an oasis in the desert that the sun dries up" (2: 163). Andy is frustrated by these responses from petty bureaucrats, who typically refuse to design projects that are comprehensive enough to be effective. He mumbles in reply, "A cheapskate dreariness, a dull caution that kills the spirit of all movements and betrays us all—from plumber to poet. Not even the gods forgive that" (2: 163).

Eventually it is the small-minded officials and factional fighting in the TUC that block progress on the six Golden Cities. Even Cobham's boyhood friends, being diverted by personal problems, fall away from the project. By 1936, with a world war in view, Andy has only accomplished two small projects. Out of frustration he decides to put his friendship with Jake Latham on the line to break up the in-fighting among the unions. He opposes Jake publicly in an open debate before the annual TUC. Again, he later rues his actions because in the end—after allowing the erosion of his plans by the demands of an industrialist, TUC members with petty grudges, and a minister of town and country planning—he has gained little but aggravation and alienation for his dedication. Not only that, he has lost the trust of a close friend and mentor. Similarly, the group of friends who once dreamed of the Golden Cities together break apart and go their separate ways.

Between 1948 and 1985 Andy Cobham doggedly pursues the Golden Cities until he receives the funding to build one of the six. But his is a Pyrrhic victory because he has to abandon the other five to achieve that much. Furthermore, he has jeopardized his marriage with Jessie, who grows tired of being treated like a housekeeper. Walking around the city site with Jessie and Kate, Andy realizes that his efforts are only "patchwork" and in some way mere scraps thrown to him by the political and economic powers to appease and quiet him. He caustically notes, "I don't suppose there's such a thing as a democracy, really, only a democratic way of manipulating power. And equality? None of that either, only a gracious way of accepting inequality" (2: 197).

The final scene returns once again to the young dreamers—Jessie, Andy, Paul, and Stoney—who speculate about possibilities for the Golden Cities. There are two ways their dreams could have taken them—toward a realization of their vision, or to failure. As they walk around the cathedral that inspires their vision, Jessie suddenly notices, "They've locked us in" (2: 198). Her words are ironically insightful, predicting the time when institutional forces around them curtail their plans and thereby determine the less than satisfactory outcome. When Paul finds an open door, Andy says with naive trust, "We knew the door was open"—again, a wry reminder that they were more bound by invisible constraints than they could recognize at that moment. "How did you know, my ragged-arsed brothers?" asks Jessie. Full of confidence and unbridled enthusiasm, Andy answers, "Because we're on the side of the angels, lass . . . and people are good" (2: 198–99). As the curtain falls, Andy's words ring with ambiguity—either sounding a hollow pride and offering hope for success, if people only care, or articulating a sardonic commentary on an inevitably disappointing conclusion.

Critics immediately noted the parallels between the dismantled plans for the Golden Cities and Centre 42. Both projects, consisting of six parts, end up as "patchwork." Their original conceptions are killed for a lack of money and by the foot dragging of small-minded government and TUC officials, who could have made a difference. The Golden Cities' uncultured industrialist, the unimaginative minister of town and country planning, and the querulous union members surely had their counterparts in the history of Centre 42. Arnold Wesker clearly imagined his counterpart in Andrew Cobham.

Like Cobham, Wesker walked away from his project nearly empty-handed and convinced that no political movement was worth the personal cost of family, friends, and professional satisfaction. He had begun to learn that lesson with the shock of the Soviet invasion of Hungary in 1956, the year he became most disillusioned with what he thought was the humaneness of socialism, and he learned it again after a few years in the Centre 42 movement. Like Cobham, Wesker believed that he could have made real changes in the system but achieved far less than he planned, because systems have a way of appropriating the individual and even hegemonically crushing individual integrity by forcing a compromise of principles. After losing so much on behalf of a questionable goal, Wesker would never again throw himself into support of another cause like this.

Still, both Cobham and Wesker had weaknesses of their own. They too often acted stubbornly without consensus of their natural constituents and political allies, and they did not know when to compromise and when to accede. Their quest was frequently too personal—a barrier to connecting with others. Realizing, at least, that Cobham had a problem with collaboration, Wesker focused his theme in *Golden City* largely on the breakdown in the spirit of cooperation. He said, "I spend more time lamenting that than having them pat themselves on the back because they've built a beautiful city" (Hayman, 90). Wesker's fatal error, however, was his inability to recognize that failure in a project of that magnitude was as much the fault of the leader who tends to work alone as that of his followers, who lack real dedication and loyalty and are unable to realize that the leader must work toward agreement to broaden the base of support and bring others along.

As a result, both the character and the author express similar frustrations. Cobham wanted six cities and got one. Centre 42 mounted six festivals, but at the expense of its own future. There was no energy or financial support for continuing. Wesker had wanted a permanent home for Centre 42 that would "embrace all the arts" and "act as a reservoir for talent which outside communities could invite" (Trussler and Marowitz, 95). Centre 42 got the building but lost all managerial control to commercial interests that lacked political commitment. Once the Round House activities were appropriated by the Round House Trust, Ltd., many hard feelings shattered friendships that had been based on a common resistance to the "incestuous elite." Wesker eventually experienced strained friendships among people he admired—like Tom Maschler, to whom the *Golden City* is dedicated, and Clive Barker who wrote Wesker on 6 May 1969 to say, "I don't need to remind you of the sacrifices that I made in the three operative years of Centre 42 or of the total involvement I had with the dream, I don't want to labour the point, but don't forget Arnold, it wasn't your dream, it was our dream and I would like to know what happened to my dream."[15] Like Andy Cobham, Arnold Wesker got only "patchwork"—and that at the expense of old friends.

Although the Round House became the flashpoint between Wesker and several others, the underlying debate had already begun with a difference about whether the time was right for a full-scale social upheaval and whether Centre 42 should become the vehicle for such a revolution. Although Wesker fundamentally agreed on the need for changes, he was no longer clear about what sort of revolution he wanted, and he did not believe it was time for a complete social reform that would replace capitalism with an entirely new system. As Andy Cobham says to his friend Paul, "The alternative [to accepting a compromise] is that complete revolution we all used to talk about, but today? Here? Now?—there's no situation that's revolutionary, is there? face it, all of you. There—is—no—revolutionary—situation" (2: 170). Wesker said something similar in a 4 October 1970 letter to John McGrath:

> There's no dire circumstance to force us into the excitement of taking to arms, secret plottings or threats of violence. We might wish we were such people and that the situation was so straightforward. It is not and we are not and there is in the dishonesty of pretending otherwise an inbuilt bomb to explode our hopes, frustrate our energy, disappoint our friends and consign us pathetically to the growing heap of left-wing factions while those controlling power more subtly than we have cared to analyse it, look on and thank God for our callow fervour.[16]

As the 1960s drew to a close, Wesker's analysis of the nation's political situation proved accurate. Although remarkable events rattled institutions in the United Kingdom, a cataclysmic upheaval did not occur, and British theater was forced to think realistically about the changes it could effect. The final scene of *Golden City*, written in 1963–65, suggests two potential outcomes, neither revolutionary. Looking ahead, we know that these young optimists will either experience the kind of failure that comes with a half-finished project, in which case Andy's lines resound with bitter irony, or the faint possibility that the vision of the Golden Cities would be seen to its conclusion, in which case his lines seem bravely naive. As Wesker wrote the play the future of Centre 42 was also hanging in the balance—it might have received a massive infusion of money that would have enabled the directors to renovate the Round House and continue with the festivals, or it might have collapsed, becoming a blip on the timeline of theater history. Knowing the actual outcome for Centre 42, however, makes it difficult to read any hope into the final lines of *Golden City*. The comments of young Jessie and Andy become bitter reminders of what could have been. Whatever we construe after the fact, Wesker had realized even by 1964–65 that Centre 42 at best would achieve no more than "patchwork," if that. It alone would never have made a significant difference in Britain's political structure, no matter how fully its plans were realized, and that realization reflects on the general hopes of leftist politics in Britain (Trussler and Marowitz, 92).

The Friends

Wesker continued to chew on the problems inherent in the anticipation of a revolution in his time as he wrote *The Friends*, the last of his works anticipating the demise of Centre 42 and expressing deep reservations about the social and political chaos of the 1960s. He wrote *The Friends* between 1967 and 1970, the years that registered the assassination of Martin Luther King, the burning of barricades in Paris, the Soviet invasion of Czechoslovakia, and anti-Vietnam demonstrations worldwide, including Britain. When it opened at the Round House in 1970, *The Friends* met with many negative responses from the critics (although some prominent critics like Martin Esslin were fairly complimentary), who were often confused about its lack of political solutions and put off by its maudlin tone. Still pained by scathing reviews of *Four Seasons* and *Golden City*, Wesker recoiled at these comments, mainly because, as director of *The Friends* and artistic director of Centre 42, he had taken an intense personal interest in the play's success.

In *The Friends* are working-class colleagues who have banded together for more than a decade in the employ of a cooperative that produces designer goods for the interiors of workers' homes. The concept recalls the ideals of William Morris's company founded in 1861. One among them, Esther, is dying of a terminal disease. Her impending death becomes the occasion for a reevaluation of the friends' work, their relationships, and their beliefs. As they talk they argue, and the unspoken question of whether they will remain together hovers over their exchanges like a dark cloud. After Esther dies at the end of act 1, everything that has held them together—the workshop, shared political commitments, feelings for one another—seems to be in doubt as they cast around for a focus to their lives, for something certain to believe in once again. At the end of act 2 they lift Esther's body and dance with it in an erotic burial ritual that Wesker borrowed from a Romanian village custom.

Sitting the entire time in Esther's room, the friends attempt to recapture the cohesion they once felt. Although their discussion is often rambling and shapeless, they return to several key themes—the significance of death and loss, their disappointment with the cooperative and what it should have accomplished artistically, and what they must do at this point to reshape the revolution. Since Wesker anticipated the imminent dissolution of Centre 42 and harbored many reservations about the turmoil of the 1960s, he is setting forth his final stand on a number of central issues.

Like many debates between Clive Barker, technical director of Centre 42, and Arnold Wesker, artistic director, the friends discuss the quality of their workshop's products. The crucial difference is that all the voices in *The Friends* are largely Wesker's, as he makes little effort to represent the views of leftists. Crispin, a friend and partner in the cooperative, believes they could have created better designs, but Roland, Esther's aesthete lover, reminds him sarcastically that they chose to give the people what they wanted "in the name of 'democracy'!" (3: 80). Crispin and Roland share a certain amount of doubt about the quality of their products and agree that they might have accomplished much more had they followed their own artistic instincts instead of allowing the working-class market to dictate their choices:

ROLAND: Couldn't say our tastes were superior to theirs—

CRISPIN: —that would place us in a class we were asking them to overthrow! What long discussions we had.

ROLAND: I always remember a character in an Eliot novel asking: "Don't you think men overrate the necessity for humouring everybody's nonsense, till they get despised by the very fools they humour?" (3: 80–81)

Brutally aware of contradictions in trying to establish an honest vehicle for working-class expression, they also cringe at the fact that, despite their efforts to the contrary, their consumers were mostly middle class.

Another friend, Macey, is so disgusted by the futility of their work that he wonders what good it would have done, anyway, for the working classes to buy these products. He feels that the ideological reasons for their actions are overblown and opposes donating one-third of their profits to support revolution in the Third World. As the more fiscally responsible member of the group, he questions his friends about opening *five* more shops after the first one was a success (again, an obvious reference by Wesker to the six festivals sponsored by Centre 42). And as the most cynical and politically conservative member of the group, he confesses that he simply does not like the proletariat, "The working class, my class, offend me. Their cowardly acquiescence, their rotten ordinariness—everything about them—hate them! there!" (3: 107). Later he asks why the friends choose some sort of reverse-snobbery, working-class tastes to guide their designs: "So tell me this, you idiots, you: if bourgeois values were only decadent and working-class values were only beautiful, then what were you complaining about in the first place? One minute you claim the need for revolution because inequality has left the people ignorant and the next minute you claim you want to do nothing but what the people want. But why should you want to do that which an ignorant people want? What kind of logic is that?" (3: 123).

This argument echoes, of course, the debate that raged at Centre 42 between Wesker and Barker among others about the value of popular culture. Here, however, Wesker has omitted in *The Friends* any mention of Centre 42's original purpose that was to provide a working-class vehicle by establishing a new popular culture in Britain and by breaking down "all barriers, social, economic and psychological that stand between the people of this country and full participation of the arts."[17]

John McGrath had attacked Wesker for paying lip service to socialism but ignoring the Marxist/Leninist expectations of a worker uprising. Dreading such a possibility, Wesker began in *The Friends* some exploration of what *revolution* had to mean in the 1960s, during which a shakeup, rather than upheaval, seemed inevitable. The only middle-class member of the workshop, Simone, articulates desire of most Britons (and Wesker) to attain change gradually through a lawful system: "There's a difference between the order that cripples and the order that liberates" (3: 121). Her companions largely agree. Their discussion is prompted in part by Esther's fear of a revolution that would unleash violence, erase history, increase human suffering, and leave an uncertain future. Believing in bettering life for the worker by reforming the system from the inside, Esther says, "Rabble-rousers frighten me, they're only rebels, not revolutionaries. . . . My brother is a rebel because he hates the past, I'm a revolutionary because I see the past as too rich with human suffering and achievement to be dismissed" (3: 106).

Simone believes that science, having produced principles out of barely discernible patterns in the chaos, has brought about true revolutions—revolutions in thought. Almost imagining herself standing against the guns of the Soviet militia in Hungary, Simone defiantly concludes her defense of Esther: "*I* will neither wear cloth caps nor walk in rags nor dress in battledress to prove I share [the working man's] cause; nor will I share his tastes and claim the values of his class to prove I stand for liberty and love and the sharing between all men of the good things this earth and man's ingenuity can give. Now shoot me for that!" (3: 125).

Esther's brother, Manfred, agrees with Simone. Hardly the dangerous anarchist that Esther described, even though he does support books for Cuba, medical supplies for North Vietnam and arms for South African blacks, Manfred's idea of revolution commits him to less visible social revolutions like those discoveries made by Albert Einstein,

Robert Millikan, Ernest Rutherford, and Niels Bohr. Their collective works caused a paradigm shift in the sciences of the twentieth century.

Exploration of revolution in contrast to rebellion as a theme in *The Friends* becomes Wesker's message to his colleagues at Centre 42 and to other leftists. He wants to say that preparation for a revolt by the workers is destructive at best and something of a waste of time. There were other, more immediate aims that should occupy the attentions of Centre 42. Wesker questioned whether his colleagues had truthfully examined the implications of Marxist/Leninist thought or whether they swallowed its tenets whole without a real examination of its arguments. Like Macey, Wesker was telling his friends that there were no radical changes in the offing, no dawning of the Age of Aquarius. He and his friends would eventually grow old and die and so would their aspirations, because no real reform could come of stale political rhetoric that no longer applied. Tacitly he was calling on socialists to recognize the full value of nonviolent revolution, the only agency to respond effectively to the pernicious forces of their time.

Even as Macey was speaking on the Round House stage, however, the Council of Management at Centre 42 was making plans to close its doors once and for all. Fully aware of the lack of funds at Centre 42, Wesker pitched a note of despair over the death of Esther and the collapse of the working-class cooperative in *The Friends* based on his own sense of futility. He had resigned almost seven months to the day after *The Friends* opened at the Round House under his direction without achieving the dialogue he sought. By that time socialist theater had shifted even further to the left, and Wesker found himself standing nearly alone.

Although some sensitivity about the Centre 42 debates still remains in 1990, the idea of bringing together participants in alternative theater, oddly enough, continues to have its appeal. At a 1988 conference, "British Theatre in Crisis," chaired by Clive Barker, attended by John McGrath, and supported by Arnold Wesker, many of the questions that had begun the debate about nonmainstream theater 28 years earlier were reopened. Participants called for more pluralism in theater, although concerns now included gender, ethnicity, age, sexual preference, and educational level as well as class. Echoing the complaints of their predecessors, the conferees fumed at the emphasis that government funding placed on "building-based, professional, middle-class-oriented theatre" and pleaded for more cooperation among artists to build alliances, exchange information, and seek innovative methods for finding new sources of funding.[18]

The pulse of the Centre 42 movement still registers an occasional but faint beat. And the failure of Centre 42 in the 1960s did, ironically, open up hitherto unimagined possibilities in the 1970s for funding alternative theater. Demand for Centre 42's program made the British Arts Council recognize the danger and unfairness of pumping disproportionately large sums of money into a national opera, ballet, theater, and symphony orchestra that would be enjoyed only by elite audiences largely from the London area and, concomitantly, the value of small theater venues, localized production companies, and touring companies that could make the arts accessible all across Britain. Shortly following the termination of Centre 42 there was an explosion of possibilities in the lively arts, mainly following the infusion of Arts Council money into these projects. Even though a people's theater never was established at Centre 42, its founders could claim with some satisfaction that they had paved the way for others. An assessment of the legacy of Centre 42, even 30 years hence, would, however, be premature.

Whatever else may be said about Centre 42, the project was unfortunate for Wesker since it interrupted the momentum he had established in his writing, sapped his vitality, and undermined his sense of direction. The contacts he had established at the Royal Court Theatre had dried up following the death of George Devine in 1965, and Wesker made political enemies along the way as he discovered his ideological position. Moreover, following the disappointments with Centre 42 in 1962–63, Wesker spent the next 10 years coming to terms with what he perceived as a crushing defeat. And never again will he take up the banner for people's theater.

Chapter Four
Distinctions, Intimidations, and Hysteria

Arnold Wesker's writing changed direction in the late 1960s after he found himself thwarted by events at Centre 42. Conscious of a manifest difference between his beliefs and the widely shared political views among his contemporaries in alternative theater, he began in the 1970s to explore what it meant to be an outsider in England. Two factors have made him feel the outsider—his politics and his religion—each inextricably bound up with the other. Over time Wesker has turned his back on socialism because, given the swelling numbers of leftists in the 1970s and their growing political control, their voices seemed to him to have grown ever more strident and demanding. Their rising anger at the political system and his own sense of failure had driven Wesker into isolation. His stories and plays of the 1970s—painful to read because they wrestle with themes of disappointment and estrangement—eventually evolved into considerations of what it means to be Jewish. Wesker found in Judaism both a refuge as a place where he belonged, as well as a rationale for his aversion to radical ideology. In the 1980s his despondency found its expression in several one-woman plays. Both series of plays—those of the 1970s and the 1980s—raise the voices of characters—Jews and women—who feel powerless, marginalized, vulnerable, and yet centered with a sense of purpose.

Six months after the closing of Centre 42 Wesker delivered a speech at a conference in Finland on the Writer in the World of Increasing Conflicts, "Distinctions, Intimidations, and Hysteria." He summarizes, "In a world of increasing conflicts the writer needs to distinguish and protect himself from the intimidations of false messiahs, shallow prophets, the jargon of politics, the hysteria of impotence and the misplaced anger of friends" (*Distinctions*, 179). No other statement could have better represented his fears at this time, and so it became his writer's protection against external pressures of any sort. In it he seems to make a silent vow to shield himself from the hysteria of others and fight publicly for the rights of the tyrannized everywhere, particularly writers.

Wesker perceives his enemies as largely of two types: colleagues with whom he sometimes has professional difference, and narrow-minded ideologues out of religious fundamentalism and the political right with whom he has deep philosophical differences. He has fought most vigorously in his writing against the ideologues. These are the "Lilliputians" who threaten the artist out of small-mindedness. They are the bigots who would silence unconventional ideas if they knew how and had the means. He sees them particularly among politicians and religious leaders like Iran's Ayatollah Khomeini, who ordered the death of writer Salman Rushdie because he believed him to be a blasphemer. About Khomeini, Wesker wrote to the *Independent* on 17 February 1989, that here was a man "whose petulant and tortured heart, so obviously engraved in his eyes, was about to wreak destructive and revengeful havoc for something someone seemed to have done to him long ago. The idea that such a man can dare to pass sentence of death, on anyone, let alone someone so far beyond his jurisdiction, is monstrous, barely believable."

Wesker's first line of defense against such excesses in human nature has always been education through the arts. Rather than suppress the voices of the racist, the bigot, the gainsayer, Wesker believes in the power of the artist to awaken "a generosity of the spirit and the senses" and enlarge understanding. Instead of censorship, he turns to the artist to reform cruelty by introducing new ideas and questioning authority. He believes, almost naively, that the very nature of art, being subversive and transforming, keeps dramatic thought alive. He wrote in an unpublished essay, "Art fans the conflict and celebrates the chaos.... Art animates doubts. Doubt, chaos and conflict are absolutely unacceptable in a well-run, orderly society."[1] But he has also fought back when squelched by directors and actors.

Wesker first felt an assault on his work in the days of the fight for the survival of Centre 42, but his anxiety increased after 1970 with a string of events that undermined his confidence significantly. Still stinging from bad reviews of *Four Seasons* and disputes with director William Gaskill about *Their Very Own and Golden City*, he mistakenly decided to take full direction of *The Friends* himself for the May 1970 production at the Round House. The results were, by his admission, unfortunate. The cast so rejected his leadership that for 12 weeks of rehearsal he was barely able to maintain control and civility.[2]

For the first run-through readings he invited the cast to his cottage in Wales where he fed and entertained them for a week. His intention was to build some cohesion and camaraderie among the participants, but his hospitality had the opposite effect. Suspicious of Wesker's sincerity and callous to the idea of prearranged gregariousness, the cast, led by Victor Henry, were privately disdainful, to say the least, and sometimes even openly rude. Why Henry was belligerent is unclear, but he became the leader among the actors who did not respect the process. Wesker then tried through rehearsals to pull the actors together and win their affections, including the offer of many rehearsal meals cooked by Dusty Wesker, but he never was successful. They obviously did not like his style of directing and refused to communicate or cooperate with him. This experience was devastating to Wesker, both because it irreparably damaged his reputation as a director and because it destroyed their production of *The Friends* just at a time when Wesker desperately needed a success.

In May 1972, barely a year after the debacle with the cast of *The Friends*, Wesker's new production, *The Old Ones*, was withdrawn from the schedule at the National Theatre. Kenneth Tynan, who was then literary manager of the National, cited casting problems as his reason, even though that determination was not within his purview.[3] Incensed, director John Dexter eventually took *The Old Ones* to full production at the Royal Court Theatre on 8 August 1972, but the incident was unnerving.

Since that time Wesker has successfully directed a number of his own productions, including *The Old Ones* in Munich in 1973, *Their Very Own and Golden City* in 1974, *Love Letters on Blue Paper* at the National Theatre in 1978 and in Oslo in 1980, *Annie Wobbler* in Birmingham and in London in 1984, *Yardsale* and *Whatever Happened to Betty Lemon?* in London in 1987, and *The Kitchen* at the University of Wisconsin, Madison, in 1990. Having ripened as a director, Wesker now works quite effectively with actors, especially young actors, and occasionally even takes on plays by other writers, such as John Osborne's *The Entertainer*, staged 1983 at Theatre Clwyd, and Shakespeare's *Merry Wives of Windsor*, staged in 1989–90 in Oslo. He also has successfully collaborated with directors like Russell Vandenbroucke at the Northlight Theatre in Chicago (1988, 1992), but major theaters in London have still not found a place for him, in part because he insists on strong directorial powers.

He was struck by yet another actors' revolt in October 1972. In this case the actors at the Royal Shakespeare Company rejected the text of his play *The Journalists*, possibly because it was not sufficiently leftist. They somehow had decided they would rather perform a play by John

Arden. Ironically, they ended up fighting as well with Arden, who left the theater never to work with them again. Taken together, these incidents diminished Wesker's trust in the goodness of human nature and served to teach him about the terror of group hysteria. Within two years of these actors' revolts he had written a short story and a play that may reveal something about his feelings at the time—"The Man Who Became Afraid" and *The Wedding Feast*.

"The Man Who Became Afraid"

Written originally for a 1974 publication where it appeared with the short story version of "Love Letters on Blue Paper," "The Man Who Became Afraid" is about Sheridan Brewster, who laughingly claims to be afraid of things and begins eventually to believe his joke. Then he suffers three anxiety attacks—one that grows out of a fear of anti-Jewish terrorism while he is working in Israel, a second in Munich triggered by the *foehn* (unsettling, even clinically depressing weather conditions in southern Germany) winds, and a third aboard a plane when an inconsequential malfunction occurs.

In a delayed response to the increasing distress, Brewster begins to purchase protections of all sorts—fire appliances, safety belts, vitamins to ward off the flu, house insurance. And his neuroses manifest themselves even further by compulsions to collect—art, books, stamps. Finally he breaks down entirely by entering a midlife crisis and becoming deeply melancholy about aging:

> Pleasure *had* gone, irretrievably, from his work. Fervour *had* evaporated from his political beliefs, and curiosity no longer drove him into relationships with people. It seemed to him he understood the state in which men take their lives: not for hatred of life itself but for the incontrovertible fact of their own scant calibre for which *they can see* no remedy; of their own self-doubting for which *they* know no answer; of that awareness which each man possesses of and for himself and cannot articulate, and which no one, no one, no one else can explain away. (*LL*, 100)

Brewster buys a sports car, ostensibly for his wife, becomes so inflexible that he can no longer carry on a decent discussion with a friend, and discovers he is sexually impotent. The steady decline in his marital relations ceases when he admits to himself that he has broken faith with socialism and admits to his wife that he is "frightened of everything." From that point on, she feels no more than maternal pity for him.

The emasculated Sheridan Brewster, once a match for guerrillas in Africa and gun runners, now "catastrophe-dazed," alarms Wesker because he represents the person he might have become had he surrendered to his own apprehensions. Brewster's surrender to his fears is also reminiscent of his father's capitulation to life when he too felt defeated.

The Wedding Feast

In 1974, the year *The Wedding Feast* was written, Wesker acknowledged in an interview that he had shouldered much of the blame for his directing disaster and had not been able to forget those three miserable months: "I don't think I've quite recovered from that disastrous production of *The Friends* in London. It was the director's fault—my fault. I allowed the actors to be terrorised by one other actor."[4] The lesson, of course, that has haunted him is that kindness can be misunderstood and sometimes even misplaced.

The Wedding Feast (which premiered in 1974 in Stockholm and opened in Leeds in 1977 only after it had been performed in Czechoslovakia, East and West Germany, and Belgium) demonstrates the effects of group tyranny on an indefensible victim and how raw emotion rather than rational analysis often determines the outcome. The mob in this case is a Norfolk working-class family (distinctly similar to Beatie Beale's family in *Roots*) that turns against Litvanov, a Jewish shoe manufacturer who fancies himself a generous and liberal employer. The plot is based on Dostoyevski's short story "An Unpleasant Predicament," and it bears some Pinteresque marks with the chilling invisible violence that lurks behind every domestic scene. The industrialist may be based on Wesker's Uncle Perly, who was the only successful businessman in the family and known for his exceptional generosity and kindness. The play is divided into two acts, with a prologue that employs a narrator who is also one of the characters, Stephen Bullock.

In the Prologue Louis Litvanov is described by Bullock as the sort of businessman who believes that he has done all he can for his employees. Litvanov has been generous to a fault. He has given his workers bonuses tied to profits in prosperous times and a fixed bonus in hard times. Furthermore, he has voluntarily offered sick pay, even though it has obviously been abused by his workers, and he tolerates feather bedding (requiring two of three people to do the job of one) and sponsors a football team that costs the company money for equipment and lost production. Although Bullock is a Marxist, he distrusts these generous impulses by Litvanov toward the workers. He believes Litvanov is dishonest about trying to buy his workers' goodwill, about assuming that the benefits are sufficient to assure worker cooperation and confidence.

One evening Louis Litvanov learns this lesson firsthand when he stumbles onto the wedding party of one of his employees after one of his tires has blown out (echoes of Pip's story in *Chips with Everything*). Deluding himself about his standing among the workers, he invites himself in. From the start it is clear that he has no place of honor here. These are Christian, working-class rural English whose culture is totally alien to Litvanov's, the son and grandson of poor, Jewish, Eastern European cobblers. He knows the Slavic peasant life from his parents' stories, but he does not begin to understand the local British working-class culture. These people tell jokes he does not get. He falls flat when he makes a "Jewish toast" to them. They call him Liftoff, their Anglicized version of his name, and he fails to appreciate the in-group significance of their nicknames. Moreover, he can only relate to them as their employer, as their superior. Although he hates their tastes in things like amateur art, he can be magnanimous about them as long as their interactions are in his office where he can pretend to be fair-minded while maintaining control, but at the wedding party, where his CEO status carries little strength, he must be honestly democratic. What he discovers is that the cultural gap between them could not be greater.

Latent hostility toward Litvanov is brought to the surface during the shoe game once everyone, including Louis Litvanov, is drunk and out of control. The person who is "it" is blindfolded, stands in the center of a circle, and tries to catch the one on the edge of the circle with the shoe. The shoe, of course, is moved around the circle, and the person in the center follows its movement by gentle taps from those holding it. At first the game proceeds in well-meant fun, but when Litvanov takes his turn, the game becomes violent. Eventually he is beaten to unconsciousness. Rather than recognize their own culpability and take responsibility for the outcome, the players rationalize their behavior. They consider the incident just a stroke of bad luck and turn to more immediate concerns.

Kate, the one educated member of the White family, blames Litvanov for trying to ingratiate himself with ordinary folk. Like Bullock, she is a Marxist who hates the boss's generosity, since it is offered paternalistically; she chides him with sarcasm, "Just give them the rate for their work and the sweet, sweet *illusion* that they're equal to any man. Stop pretending it's a reality. And don't be kind or ashamed or apologetic for your money. You go around behaving like that, how shall we be able to hit you when the time comes, bor?" (4: 168).

Because Kate is a Marxist, someone ostensibly fighting for the well-being of workers, one has to wonder why she would not welcome worker benefits and the boss's goodwill. One could make the case two ways when construing a remark like this coming from a Marxist. To her credit, she calls attention to Litvanov's condescension and the illusion that he has tried to create of an egalitarianism that he has not been prepared to honor. Although he is willing to improve working conditions, Litvanov is not willing to open a constructive and cooperative dialogue with his workers; nor is he willing to hand them real authority.

One has to wonder why Kate does not seize the moment to educate Litvanov about how to achieve a genuinely egalitarian and cooperative relationship without paternalism. And she does not seem to like the new egalitarianism any better than he does. Kate struggles with her own motives because she hates having Litvanov at her table. Tacitly she yearns for a return to the old hierarchical structure where everyone knew how to behave: it was easier to deal with the unambiguous villainy of an employer who exploited everyone. The boss's old abusive ways defined a clear role for leftists who could regard him as their enemy.

Like Pip in *Chips with Everything*, Litvanov deserves humane treatment by his employees, regardless of his well-intentioned but offensive behavior. Wesker said in an interview, "The point I was trying to make—and the critics have missed—is that anybody who comes from a working-class background, but who through fame or accident or whatever is brought into contact with industrialists or politicians or the aristocracy, will obviously discover that many of these people are not evil monsters" (*Distinctions*, 128). Indeed, Litvanov, for all his paternalism and boorish manners, is represented more sympathetically than the Norfolk bumpkins whose crude manners and stupidity are used as comic relief and cheap laughs. The question that surely must haunt Wesker today is how many of his disappointments in London's theatrical world should be attributed to a veiled anti-Semitism. The answer is probably that he does not know, nor would he want to calculate it. He does, however, sympathize with the Jewish Litvanov: "He's not me, but I do identify with him. He's warm, attractive, and he not only wants to behave justly but actually does do so. Yet he's caught up in a situation that will inevitably humiliate him" (*Distinctions*, 127). In many ways Wesker *is* the big-hearted, warm father figure who understands Jewish jokes more readily than pub humor and is more at home with Yiddish than with

London's street language. Referring to Wesker's Old World sense of responsibility as a host and father, Margaret Drabble once asked, "How [has] the word 'paternalism' acquired quite such derogatory overtones—there is nothing wrong, surely, about being fatherly, though there may be good or bad fathers?"[5] Recognizing his kinship with Litvanov, Wesker indirectly acknowledges the animosity he too has endured—animosity that has some basis in religious and therefore cultural differences. He also recognizes that he lives in a country that rejects old-fashioned paternalism, but he might have been happier in a more traditional culture.

Although Wesker has been consistent while espousing his own mix of religious and political views, it has taken some years for him to sharpen his positions and assume full responsibility for them. While working on the trilogy Wesker relied on the vexed Ronnie Kahn, the young Jewish man who could not wholly swallow his mother's leftist teachings, to try to sort out his reservations about socialism. In *The Kitchen* he balanced Peter's anarchic outburst with Paul's quiet questioning, and by the time he had written *Chips* and *The Friends* his ideas about the sanctity of the individual were coming clearer to him. But it was not until "The Visit" (written in 1978) that he was able to articulate with full clarity what he had been thinking all along about dogma and authoritarianism.

"The Visit"

Wesker's arguments may be easily identified in this short story, as he is only thinly disguised as Raphael and Dusty, his wife, as Maddeau ("Miniautobiography," 253). Raphael and Maddeau are visiting Danish friends over the Whitsun holidays. Their vacation is planned around the luxuries of gourmet foods, lying in the sun, bicycling, classical music, and intellectual political conversation. The agenda suits Raphael because he is deeply concerned about the disintegrating political conditions that threaten this comfortable, upper middle-class way of life and social order.

Fed periodically by "circles of veal neatly tucked up with dressings and juices," pommes de terre lyonnaise, farmhouse butter, fresh chola, rounds of pickled cucumber, gefilte fish, chopped liver and matzos, soft cheese, and small sweets and chocolates, the friends catch up on the latest news about each other and relax.

Karl-Olaf has received a terrifying letter probably meant for the former occupant, who was a writer: "Dear Sir, the envelope in which this letter arrived could have contained a lethal explosive device" (*SOM*, 102). They briefly discuss their concerns about the possibility of PLO terrorism and its implications. Later, while cycling through lush country landscapes, Raphael suddenly reminds them of the ever-present nuclear threat: "If the big mistake were made now they'd have no place to hide. They'd have to stand, in the blinding flash, watch each other wither, melt away" (*SOM*, 112). Janika confesses that she often contemplates the threat and does what she can—hoarding food and keeping supplies on hand—to meet the possibility of "some kind of anarchy with all the accepted and expected patterns of behaviour between people breaking down" (*SOM*, 113).

At dinner in a haute-cuisine restaurant they are bullied by a manager who once showed his true colors in a supermarket-sponsored contest that allowed him and his wife to scoop up as many groceries as they could in three minutes. His story confirms Janika's fears about the unpredictability of human beings who can suddenly push aside their good naturedness. After truite à la Marguery and a bottle of Chateau La Tour Ballet '67, they discuss Libya's dictator and whether he would possibly offer some leadership to his people.

And so their weekend together progresses with sumptuous meals and lazy activity in generous surroundings, always tempered by serious talk about what Janika calls "a temporary lapse in human kindness, a cracking of mutual confidence, a time of—awful aberration" (*SOM*, 113). They share a mutual concern about human cruelty: a woman who had been beaten by her husband, American soldiers who act like gangsters in Vietnam, the sexual revolution, and pornography. Because Karl-Olaf and Janika have reached a troubled point in their marriage, their quiet sniping adds to the underlying political tensions and serves to illustrate the difficulty of reconciling human aggression.

On their last night together, while listening to a radio lecture by Isaac Deutscher taped at the London School of Economics on the pending collapse of capitalism, Raphael begins to see the center of the problem. Deutscher explains that conflict arises from a contradiction in socialism "between the social character of production and the anti-social character of state control" (*SOM*, 174). The humanitarian good in a socialist state is canceled by the very nature of its collectivist function when the individual spirit is by necessity suppressed for the greater good. He concludes that the most effective management of resources on behalf of the people is antisocial at its core because individuals become subordinated to causes. Making matters worse for the ordinary person is the inevitable turmoil caused by any transition from capitalism to socialism, when the privileged few resist changes and terrorists use the rich as an excuse to justify more violence.

Raphael regards the ills of socialism with his own Jewish horror of human violence: "harm man and you insult God" (*SOM*, 171). Human beings, in the Jewish view, are unique in nature because, having been created, he believes, in God's image, humans possess some part of the divine and may therefore serve as God's partner in building and completing His creation. In this respect, human life requires spiritual as well as physical nurturing. If violence were not a threat to human life and if individual or group oppression could confidently be ruled out, Raphael would have little trouble embracing an unqualified form of socialism. But in a trade-off of individual against group rights, he has to defend the sanctity of the solitary human being: "the Jew [shows] no respect for historical imperatives, only human ones: man [is] a sacred thing, to be cherished" (*SOM*, 177).

Talking this out with the others, Raphael begins to understand that dogma is not only the death of the life force but also of spontaneous creativity, "ergo—political ideology is anti-social" (*SOM*, 178). Finally, Raphael arrives at the linchpin of his new realization—"values should *measure* our actions, not *determine* them" (*SOM*, 179). Individual conscience, not ideology, must therefore set the course of right action.

In "The Visit" Wesker has worked out for the first time his credo of individual rights and "the conflict between the social nature of co-operation in a socialist society, and the anti-social nature of state control" (*Distinctions*, 128). Although he has taken this position more or less all along, it is from this point that he knows precisely where he stands politically, and every other political position he has taken becomes clearer as well. What Wesker never comes to grips with, however, is what happens when individuals become isolated, fragmented, and suddenly vulnerable. Everyone needs someone else at one time or another. The loner has made no provisions for that. Wesker fails to ask when the group is beneficial and even necessary to counter malicious forces. What happens when the unprotected loner must throw up a defense against antisocial behavior, and yet no communal support is in place to provide a shield? These unanswered questions hang over his plays of the 1980s, in which lonely and isolated women find themselves vulnerable to external forces that they cannot control alone. Although he has expressed some apprehension for the unprotected individual, he fears groupthink more.

As these privileged friends—Karl-Olaf and Raphael, Janika and Maddeau—converse in their Cambridge surroundings with the music of Corelli playing in the background, they seem oddly unconscious of the economic pressures that make socialism an issue. Here for the first time

Wesker is deliberately showing a conservative preference for social stability over the benefits that might be gained through socialism's protests, primarily because he has become suspicious of causes and ideological values that determine our actions. He regards social disruption as a more persistent human failing and a more lasting and potent threat to social order than poverty, at least in industrialized countries. As he said in 1966, "I believe that a new economic order, when men are not competing for survival, is going to solve problems but because I believe there is such a problem to being a human being at all that to complicate it even more with economic problems is to confront people with the wrong battle. So this being my view of socialism it follows that once the economic battle is over there is still the battle of being alive, of being a human being."[6] Once socialism solves the grievous question of economic disparity, then problems of power struggles, discrimination, fanaticism, corruption, and hatred will still need solutions because they are more fundamental to the human dilemma and more difficult to solve.

A couple of years after writing "The Visit" Wesker mapped out his stand on the conflict between the individual and the state in a succinct radio talk, "State-right Freedom, Birth-right Freedom." The difference between these terms lies in how much power is allocated to the people: "Where 'birth-right freedom' operates we feel it is rulers of states who can overstep their authority; with 'state-right freedom' there exists a sense that it is only the citizen who can over-reach the freedom *he's been permitted*" (*Distinctions*, 223). Wesker warns BBC listeners not to relinquish their birth-right freedoms too quickly. There will always be national emergencies and crises, but very few will justify the forfeiture of individual rights. Unscrupulous leaders, tyrants, and dictators will try to persuade the public that the state could run more effectively with stricter regulations on aberrant behavior, but the public should be educated to recognize this rationale.

Leftist colleagues have never been able to grasp the reasons behind Wesker's mistrust of his working-class neighbors, nor could they see why he denigrated pub life and football pools, why he promoted the fine arts, why he insisted on the fine arts at Centre 42. They never fully realized that it was not so much the imposition of cultural forms on the masses that interested Wesker as his fear of valorizing forms of entertainment that keep workers from being able to step back and achieve some critical distance on themselves. As long as they are enjoying their own preferred forms of entertainment—the pubs, rock music, the football pools, television sitcoms—they are rarely challenged to see themselves with some self-reflection. Without that outsider's perspective they cannot be trusted to stand up for the rights of the minority, particularly the Jews. He later confessed that British Jews harbor from their parents' stories "that slight distaste for the *lumpenproletariat* simply because they bring [a dread of persecution] with them from central Europe where they experienced it in the form of pogroms. The *lumpenproletariat* got drunk, were ignorant, and were easily stirred into violence."[7] Three plays based on historical events—*Badenheim 1939, Beorhtel's Hill*, and *Blood Libel*—illustrate Wesker's anxiety about the political conditions that threaten the Jews—conditions created by the uneducated lumpenproletariat and resulting in an historical memory of their ongoing struggle against the evil of prejudice. In all three plays, however, the Jews are unable to act against dangers that they seem to face generation after generation.

Beorhtel's Hill: A Play for Basildon

In *Beorhtel's Hill* Wesker is largely interested in the ways intolerance affects working-class communities that must absorb Third World people from far-flung parts of the old British empire. These are towns that now look less and less like the homogeneous villages that used to characterize Britain. Wesker wrote the play for Basildon, a New Town in Essex, to commemorate its fortieth birthday in 1989.[8] The play closely resembles *Nottingham Captain*—a large-scale production (more than 130 Basildon citizens were included in the cast) with narrator and set pieces. Here, the narrator supplies short vignettes about life in Basildon, and a large Greek chorus, hooded and mysterious, comments on the positive and negative aspects of living in Basildon.

Beorhtel's Hill, the Anglo-Saxon name for Basildon, has been home to the newcomer for many centuries, so much so that it could serve as a symbol for the multicultural revolution in Britain. In the 1870s Jews branching out from the ghettos were among the first to discover acreage for planting and an escape from the bricked walls of London to fresh air and earthy gardens (they were called "Plotlanders"). Although they lived in substandard housing, these families became the freeholders (settlers with unlimited rights to the use of the land) displaced by a new wave of Jews rehoused there in 1951 alongside their old Cockney neighbors from the East End. From the town's inception as a planned community set up by the New Towns Act in 1949, families of all races and nationalities have chosen to settle there. With fresh generations of newcomers, old-timers have had to find a way to accommodate them. By 1983 the town had 160,000 inhabitants, three times the planned number of residents, and racial conflicts have not always been easily resolved. Among the most recent arrivals have been Asians expelled from Uganda, who have found the welcome less than warm.[9]

Great Britain created New Towns after World War II to ease the overcrowding caused by bombing and to increase housing after the building industry had come to a near standstill during the war. After many Jews lost their apartments in the East End, they became among the first to move to one of the newly built urban areas like Basildon, which were supposedly planned with the people's needs in mind.

It is the ongoing struggle to absorb strangers into this community that interests Wesker. Act 1 contains a series of fragments—nostalgic vignettes that recall Basildon's past. Beginning with the 1870s, they evoke daily life before technology—old irons, butter churns, hoop rolling, bungalows built out of discarded fish crates, and paraffin used for heating and cooking. They also recall blueberry and blackberry picking, a wooded countryside with bluebells, and generous gardens. These pastoral scenes are shattered by memories of World War II—of pitch that is loaded onto boats to build Germany's autobahns before war is declared, and later of the Holocaust and death camps.

The bittersweet vignettes—a montage of the energetic communal life—contrast with scenes of the postwar era taken from the diary of a woman who moves to the New Town in 1964. With deep apprehension and a need for a place to belong, she writes about lots cleared of their trees, ugly blocks of cement, neighborhoods bereft of social interaction, and painful isolation. Governmental committees have ruptured Basildon's history to convert housing for the poor into boring and sterile modules; people in that self-contained community are buried in their boxed homes like living dead. Worse yet, "life is a conflict of interests between the vain and the vain, the greedy and the greedy, the fanatic and the fanatic, and it's all sanctioned by the unthinking, the ill-informed, the pious, the lazy, the illiterate, the easily-incited-led-by-nose-flattered-and-fooled majority." In this wasteland stripped of natural and artistic beauty and pleasure, the meanest human impulse thrives: gangs of children bring war on one another, alcoholism destroys hope, people remain strangers to one another. And yet, as the Chorus repeatedly reminds us, "All things tire of themselves." And so the quiet revolution occurs in which "unhappiness wearies also. . . . Contempt withers. . . . The sneer dissolves," and that period of turbulence is replaced by "The city of its dreams," even though it too does not last.

Act 2 opens at the end of World War II, with conflicts among the working classes competing for land at Basildon. Angry shouts from Plotlanders resisting the onslaught of strangers who will rob them of their freeholds are offset by the calm arguments of the minister who welcomes the strangers and warns the Plotlanders that the outcome of their resistance could be chaotic development and shoddily built houses. His threats are prophetic.

The Plotlanders, like Andy Cobham in *Their Very Own and Golden City*, begin to dream of a utopian city, "a Phoenix. . . . From the shadows into sunlight / From the night's fears into morning / From the dark myths and the squalor." They dream of diversity with black and white, art and industry, doctor and dustman. Unfortunately, the New Town is so poorly planned that developers take their high profits, but everyone else is the loser. Ten thousand buildings are destroyed and auctioned off to make room for modern structures, and the Plotlanders are forced to sell out at below market value. As the old community disappears and unimaginative architecture consumes the landscape, new resentments arise among various ethnic groups.

Tensions come to a head with the arrival of five Ugandan families, who, having survived Idi Amin's tortures, have fled to England as British dual-citizens seeking refuge. Following a bitter fight in Basildon, in which ignorant demagoguery plays on human fear, the city council votes to defer the families' request for emergency housing, effectively turning them away mostly for reasons of skin color. Many in Basildon are ashamed. The hope of the future lies in the children, however, who leave, according to the play, to look for a rainbow. They are headed toward Stanstead, Gatwick, and Heathrow airports to take gifts to the arriving Ugandan refugees. With this announcement the stage fills with hundreds of roses representing hope in a bleak landscape and a natural ebb and flow of things in which "all things tire of themselves." At the end of act 1 we hear echoes of the Chorus, who explain the dynamic of these cycles in which good replaces evil and evil eventually overcomes good, which overtakes evil, and on and on:

> . . . if madness follows
> Will that too not tire of itself
> As all things do?
> Though no joy lasts
> No pain lingers.
> Though the sower flags
> The flower blooms. What tires of itself—revives.
> Be glad. Be comforted.

Thus *Beorhtel's Hill* ends with grave disappointment and only a faint suggestion of hope—all vintage Wesker. The tone is reminiscent of the dialogue between Sarah and Ronnie Kahn in *Chicken Soup with Barley*, in which he tells her, "It's too big—it's too big to care for it," and she counters fiercely, "Ronnie, if you don't care, you'll die." Although Wesker fears the worst in human behavior, he leaves room always to hope for something more. As Heiner O. Zimmermann put it, "On the one hand, it is the contrast of historical social criticism and utopia; on the other hand, it is the contradiction between imperturbably believing in the ideal and failing to actualize it."[10]

Blood Libel

Blood Libel is another unpublished play, written between 1987 and 1992, that draws almost verbatim on the original historical account by the monk Thomas of Monmouth for its story.[11] It holds deep foreboding about the sort of group hysteria that ultimately destroys outsiders in the community. Commissioned by the city of Norwich for a production in 1993, *Blood Libel* (originally entitled *William of Norwich*) faithfully chronicles the fateful history of Jews living in a small East Anglia town in the twelfth century.

According to Thomas, who tells this story in 1172 from his monastic cell, William of Norwich was a young boy, born in 1132 or 1133 on Candlemas Day to Elviva and Wenstan. Before her son was born, Elviva had a dream about a fish that is splashed with red, like blood, and has 12 fins on each side. The fish asks to be laid upon her breast. As soon as she picks it up and puts it to her bosom, however, it grows larger, sprouts wings and flies away. The dream instantly becomes an omen that tells her something special will happen to her child when he turns 12.

As a boy William works for a skinner who sells pelts to the Jews, who have great affection for William. On the Monday after Palm Sunday a stranger comes to William's mother and asks to take William to the Archdeacon of Norwich, who wants the boy as kitchen help. At first Elviva is reluctant, but she relents after the stranger offers her 30 pieces of silver, the amount of money offered to Judas to betray Christ. He leads William away, and the lad is later found in Thorpe Wood, raped and murdered.

Who the murderer was has been open to speculation for centuries. Thomas of Monmouth set this version of the story down in Latin 28 years later on the basis of little more than hearsay and supposition.

Wesker uses the story almost exactly as Thomas told it, but he uses it to draw attention to its anti-Semitic content. The child, so the historical account goes, spent the night with the Jews on Tuesday night and is treated kindly. On Wednesday, the day of Passover, he is bound and gagged, nailed to a makeshift cross, stabbed on his left side, and splashed with boiling water to cleanse him and stop the bleeding. The body is found on Good Friday by a nun who had had a vision, according to Thomas, which points her to that spot in the woods where he was buried. The boy's body is fully clothed, but his head has been shaved and there are scars on the scalp marking a crown of thorns. He is buried, then later dug up by others who want to see the body. When they open the shallow grave, they swear they see the body move, even though William is dead. Because Thomas of Monmouth seemed to have William's martyrdom in mind when he told his story, conscious parallels to Christ's passion are predictable.

Thomas's historical account continues at great length with full retellings of testimonies from the trial. William's mother, Elviva, is certain that the Jews murdered her son for cult reasons. Although she has no hard evidence, she believes that the stranger must have been a Jew because "he were evil-lookin' an' ugly." Her suspicions are confirmed by a dream that her sister has about Jews in which they tear off her right leg as she is trying to flee from them. Elviva testifies that she sent her niece to follow William and the stranger. The niece supposedly tracks them undetected through the maze of alleys and streets of the Jewish ghetto, even though the stranger is unlikely to have allowed her to go along with him had his intentions been nefarious.

In *Blood Libel* the niece's fabrication is called into question by Elias, the prior of the Church of Norwich, a level-headed man who, according to historian M. D. Anderson, rejected facile explanations for the child's death and blocked any emotional campaigns by the church to establish the child as a martyr or a saint.[12] Anderson further explains that Elias's attempt at trying to discover the truth was opposed by Aimar, the prior at St. Pancras who reminded the brother of his duty to the church. The historical Aimar apparently asked for the boy's body to be moved to his own church to serve as a relic. Another witness, whose testimony Wesker uses ironically in *Blood Libel*, is Maudie the maidservant, who cleaned for the Jews. She tells the court that she saw them put a teazle, a gag made of rope and wood, around the boy's throat and into his mouth and she is able to produce the instrument of torture in the courtroom. She also claims that she had observed the religious ritual that killed the boy. A third witness, whose spurious story Wesker also uses, testifies that he once came across two Jews in the woods who had a human body in a sack. Although belated and unsubstantiated, the information is accepted as additional evidence that the Jews are the murderers. Still another witness, Theobald the Jew, comes forth to say that Jewish teachings require Jews to shed blood each year to win back a place for themselves in the Holy Lands from which they are exiled. The year that William was slain the lot had fallen to the Norwich Jews in England to perform the ritualistic rite.

As Wesker demonstrates in *Blood Libel*, the English were quick to believe these stories since Jews were held in great suspicion in the twelfth century and anti-Semitic sentiment was continually kept alive through the pulpit. Although they were forced to live apart from Christians, the Jews prospered because they had the only cash reserves, since the lending profession was canonically forbidden to Christians. Consequently, the king of England protected Jews, drawing on them for emergency revenue in times of war, fire, disease, and crop failure. But their social and religious insularity made them easy targets for scapegoating and superstition. Secondhand stories about Jews and witchcraft abounded. Especially popular were those about Jews who used freshly drawn human blood medicinally and human flesh ritually (Anderson, 56–66). The source of these blood libel stories, repeated throughout history, originates in part with distortions about the traditions of Passover in which it is said that an angel marked Jews' homes with blood. The myth may also be a perverse twist that ignorant peasants gave to their misunderstanding of the food laws of Kashrut, which require Jews to kill animals with a minimum of suffering.

Another story about the Jews that Wesker draws on was told by the founder of the Priory at Norwich in the pulpit in 1110. Bishop Herbert de Losinga incited righteous indignation among his congregation with a tale probably borrowed from a sixth-century legend in Constantinople about a Jewish father who threw his child into a furnace for receiving the Eucharist. The hysterical mother called out to Christians for help. When they opened the furnace, the child emerged unharmed. Because it was told largely for its anti-Semitic value, Wesker opens *Blood Libel* with this story.

As the trial proceeds in *Blood Libel* Brother Elias refuses to be gulled by sensational stories. He cross-examines the witnesses closely and debates Thomas of Monmouth about the suitability of William for martyrdom. The plays ends in a clash between Thomas and Elias. In fact, history indicates that Elias probably did ridicule Thomas, so much so that Thomas's suit might never have been successful had Elias not been succeeded at his death by Prior Richard de Ferrariis, who believed in the religious significance of the story. Thomas of Monmouth then had several mystical visions about the boy that encouraged the monastery to move William's body from the Chapter House to the cathedral. Thomas's delusions were validated by the bishop and petitioners who began to report their own visions almost weekly (Jessapp and James, xii). From that point on the church and those connected with the story began to capitalize on the boy's death by selling relics and promoting miracle cures for all those who came into contact with William's grave.

Wesker's play ends wryly as he allows the bitter irony of praises for the boy and Thomas's religious ecstasy to speak for themselves. It is clear that the villains are those who would stir up bigotry and hatred for personal advantage, especially among those who claim to be Christians. Accessories to the crime are the ignorant peasants who too willingly turn against the Jews because that explanation easily suits their anti-Semitic bias. Both the church and the community saw a way to profit from William's death by conferring sainthood on him; never mind the hatred for the Jews that persisted for generations after dozens of copycat stories were told about other boys being tortured. William's death eventually led to the expulsion of all Jews from England. In 1290 a writ was handed down to the sheriffs of England banishing Jews on the penalty of death, but this fact is not a part of the play.

Badenheim 1939

The tragedy of the stories Wesker tells in these plays—about the anti-Semitism of East Anglia in the twelfth century and the Plotlanders and Ugandans of *Beorhtel's Hill*—is that the stories lay out a pattern, which Wesker uses as a reminder not only of superstitious ignorance and religious persecution, of intimidation and terror, but also of the most regressive forms of human behavior that do not seem to meliorate with time. Wesker writes plays about discrimination in different eras and different cultures to make it clear how each successive generation has to learn about these horrors anew as both the persecutor and the persecuted experience the real potential of human degradation. *Badenheim 1939* shows us Gentiles and Jews who have either forgotten the lessons of the past or have chosen to deny them out of a fear that an acknowledgment would somehow prove prophetic.

Badenheim is a quaint little Austrian spa town where Jews of all nationalities have congregated every year to attend its renowned music festival. Some Jewish families have been going to Badenheim for generations to hear the music, lie in the sun, and eat wonderful food. It is spring or early summer when many arrive in good spirits, but something in the air tells us that this year is not like the rest. Although preparations are being made for the festivities, everyone is fearful, and yet very few are willing to talk about what is really on their minds, so their underlying fears are displaced by complaints about day-to-day vexations.

The impresario Dr. Pappenheim arrives and announces the musical groups he hopes to book but still has not fully secured. Frau Zauberblit and Samitzky arrive; she is deeply in love with him, and he is homesick for his country, Poland. No one talks about the Germans. Karl is happy to have come, but his newfound friend, Lotte, is apprehensive for reasons she does not articulate. The shapely Mitzi has come to sunbathe and make love, but her academic husband only wants to check the proofs of his latest book. Trude, the wife of the local pharmacist, is deeply anxious about her married daughter whose husband probably beats her, and at the end of part 1 Trude wakes up screaming with night terrors.

Throughout part 2 the sanitation inspectors seem more and more ubiquitous. They have been sent to ready the town for the festival, but instead of asking about health conditions they are listing the inhabitants. With each registration they inquire about the registrant's marital status and religious affiliation. Everyone seems to have Jewish connections in one way or another. Because people seem to be mysteriously disappearing, we guess that behind the scenes people are dying, but in the public places they are enjoying the rich food and cultured conversation. Though most of the visitors seek out the entertainment, Karl is obsessed with the fish in the hotel aquarium. An earlier tank of blue cambium had eaten all the others. There are red ones and green ones now; the green ones are "very modest and retiring." His unspoken suggestion is that the Jews might similarly disappear without a trace.

In part 3 the long-awaited musician, Mandelbaum, arrives. He was delayed in Reizenbach, where all Jews have been quarantined, but he is unexplainably permitted to leave for Badenheim without any objections by the officials. The child prodigy has also arrived, so it appears that the music will start at any time. The sanitation inspectors have put up concrete pillars and barbed wire to build what could become a festival site or a concentration camp, but no one will openly speculate about it. In an attempt to save her daughter's life, Frau Zauberblit has signed forms to renounce her daughter and the titles her daughter was given when Frau Zauberblit married her first husband. As though they were planning their next holiday, the musicians rush to the bookstore to buy maps of Poland that are on sale.[13] The visitors discover that they have lost contact with the outside world since the post office has shut off services. At the end of the act there are sounds of gunfire and singing.

In part 4 a stranger arrives who rejects every explanation offered for his being in Badenheim. He denies he is Jewish. In an unspecified interim, the tennis courts and swimming pool have closed, and the town has grown dilapidated. A former prostitute, Sally, assures everyone, "Nothing is ever as bad as it looks." They all seem to be leaving soon on the train. Pappenheim wants to make certain that his pension will be recognized in Poland, or wherever it is they are going. Trude and Martin's daughter has escaped her brutal husband. They are relieved to have her with them in Badenheim. Frau Zauberblit leaves with two sanitorium men. Anticipating her death by tuberculosis, she has written her will, leaving her jewelry to the child prodigy for his education and instructions that Dr. Pappenheim is to say Kaddish. The rest dance and laugh, eat chocolates, pecans, peach preserves, caviar. The head waiter shoots the Doberman pinschers, which the sanitation inspectors have brought to Badenheim, because the dogs have tried to run away.

In the end the guests pack up to leave, possibly for Poland. Summer has come and gone, and the air is frosty. As they approach the station, everyone chats about far-away places they would like to see again—Majorca, Vienna, Poland. They appear to be in high spirits about their impending trip. Just before the train arrives, "a strange, glorious light breaks over them. It is a light which tells of the earth's beauty and abundance." Everyone sees it as a positive sign. But when the train arrives, there are no passenger cars. There is only a freight train with cattle cars. "Well!" says the proud and important Pappenheim, "If the coaches are so dirty it must mean that we have not far to go."

Wesker adapted *Badenheim 1939* in 1987. The unpublished, four-part script is at the time of this writing being considered for a film or possibly an opera. It is closely based on a 1980 novel[14] by Aharon Appelfeld, whose own story about repeated escapes from the Nazis during World War II (his story is the subject of the film *Europa, Europa*) supplies a profoundly chilling message about those who would maintain the appearances of normalcy, especially when things look the gravest. What makes these people most vulnerable to tragedy is their lack of willingness to act on their own behalf, possibly because they never question their faith in basic human decency. Wesker offers no real remedy outside of the salutary effects of a universal education that may create change eventually.

Regarding the tragic consequences of poverty, racism, and other instances of inhumane treatment, Wesker had to concede in a 4 October 1970 letter to John McGrath that education cannot match a revolution for its sheer ability to transform culture quickly and restructure the system overnight. Even though the impact of art and education—in contrast to that of revolution—is gradual, Wesker pointed out in the letter that "their effects accumulate over a period of time"; they can therefore hope to transform conditions without suffering, in the way that "revolutions in art . . . changed ways of seeing, revolutions in thought . . . changed notions of liberty, revolutions in science . . . took cameras to Saturn" (*Beorhtel's Hill*).

Chapter Five
Two Roots of Judaism

Although Arnold Wesker has not been active in the Jewish religious life since his days spent briefly in youth organizations like the Habonim and in the Zionist movement, he credits his style and outlook as an author to his identification as a cultural Jew. His family's linguistic patterns, their "reverence for the power of the intellect," the close bonds they have with the Jewish community, and the traditions of his Jewish origins have shaped his thinking and his works profoundly.[1]

About theological matters, however, he seems deeply conflicted and therefore vague. Even though many of his plays, essays, and short stories are marked by an identification with the Jewish community, he hastens to explain that he is not particularly religious. In his essay "The Two Roots of Judaism," for example, he argues for humanitarian principles on the strength of the Abrahamic covenant with God, and at the same time he says that, for all the Jewish cultural values that drive his thinking at the unconscious level, he is agnostic: "I do not believe in the God of the Jews—or any other God, though I quite enjoy the thought of him, and certainly I am left full of awe and respect and profound admiration at the way he speaks through his Bible's prophets" (*Distinctions*, 252–53). This apparent contradiction between saying he does not believe in God and yet acting on a faith in God may be clarified by a statement he wrote as a 17-year-old, distinguishing between wanting to believe and actually committing to a belief:

> Faith, the need to submit to something we imagine is bigger than ourselves, is an effort to supplement our inadequacy. It is a faith because it does not explain but comforts . . . all the great theological and philosophical works [are] an attempt to explain the mystery of life. . . . But because I do not believe the inadequacy can ever be supplemented or the mystery explained, I am concerned neither with religion as a faith nor science as an explanation. It is sufficient that the inadequacy never leaves me rest and that the mystery fills me with awe and keeps me sufferably humble enough to enjoy its beauties. With what, then, am I concerned? Let me say it is with THE CONDUCT OF LIFE. (*Dare* MS; Wesker's ellipses)

Whether he believes in God or not, whether he is a member of a synagogue or not, one point remains: his strongest spiritual identification is with Jewish thought, and he has become more conscious of these roots with age: "I feel a Jew, I am a Jew and because I'm a Jew I feel and write in a particular way" (Bigsby 1977). Even as a secular Jew he is compelled by the responsibility accepted by the Jewish people to address injustices. He must be a "fixer," one who gathers the sparks of God's light in the world and does *"tikun olam,"* repairs the world. As a fixer, the Jew is God's partner in completing creation, in showing concern for those in need, bringing dignity to all people, and arguing on behalf of others. It means acting in an ethical way to repair the world—to welcome strangers, free captives, settle disagreements on behalf of others, give generously of one's self. Judaism in this sense becomes code of conduct that Wesker lives by. It sets a standard not only for helping those in need, but also for resolving questions with an ethical dimension.

Furthermore, Wesker's identification with the Jewish community shows in what way his family feels different from the others. He has remarked on several occasions that he is always aware of the tradition outside the Anglican culture shaping his thoughts, "Though I was born in Britain, I know no other language and feel the rhythms of my dialogue and prose to be unmistakably English, yet I feel myself an alien writer in this country" (Bigsby 1977). Wesker says he is not exactly sure what makes his voice alien—whether it is a "Middle Eastern-European tone of voice, an old-fashioned Victorian voice, or a Jewish sensibility"—but he knows he is somehow different from his contemporaries. Because he "feels Jewish," he also has never felt fully at home in England. Being a Jew in a predominantly Christian culture like Britain creates daily reminders of what it means to be a stranger in his own land. He captures these experiences in his short story, "Six Sundays in January."

"Six Sundays in January"

Written between January 1966 and July 1967 and originally published as a special supplement by the *Jewish Quarterly* in the summer of 1969, this story features Marcia Needham, a young Jewish woman in her thirties, who finds herself restless and even depressed on Sundays in a Christian country like England. For her they are "dead" and "aimless" days—a time that fits into the ebb and flow of others' lives, but not her own.

On the first Sunday Marcia impulsively bolts from the house and takes the children for a walk on Hampstead Heath. Because her Gentile husband, Bud, does not understand her need to get away, she ends the day chiding herself for a lack of gratitude for her marriage. On the second Sunday she again feels confined and needs to walk. Twice on that day she indulges herself in sensual pleasures—waking up to Bach on her clock radio and tearing loose in a madcap run, like a woman in full flight. On the third Sunday she wakes in foul humor, "a woman's-own-and-ageing madness" Wesker calls it, and the family stays clear of her all day.

On the fourth Sunday while ice skating with the family at Whitestone Pond in Hampstead Heath she spots an acquaintance, Crispin Peterson. Impetuously she begs to show him the places of her childhood in the East End. Marcia takes him to Wesker's old neighborhood at Flower and Dean Street and No. 43 Fashion Street where Wesker grew up. Intoxicated with pleasure, she rehearses her history—a tradition she can now talk about without shame or fear of recrimination: "I'm not being sentimental and I know it's not unique, but suddenly I just feel enormously happy to have a past to show someone" (SS, 124). They walk through the Liverpool Street Station and up to a small shop on Brick Lane where she recommends the borscht, chopped egg and onion with chopped liver, and salt beef with latkes. For the time being she is elated with anticipation for her newfound friendship and for the newly defined pride of her identity.

As they are eating, a childhood acquaintance, Katerina Levinson, stops to speak with them. After a few polite exchanges Crispin finally notices the women have shared a message of recognition about their husbands in their coded silence. "You're beginning to make me feel like a foreigner," he tells them, "if returning to the East End on Sunday mornings disturbs you so much then stay away, don't indulge in sentimental journeys you've no stomach for" (SS, 128). The women recognize instantly that he does not understand the full extent of their alienation. "It's Sundays—we hate Sundays, don't we, Kate?" Kate replies, "The whole bloody family weekend, all of it." Still without any real sensitivity to their dilemma, Crispin asks, "Is the tale of Jewish family bonds also a myth? What about those proud fathers?" Kate can hardly tell him, "Our fathers were not Sunday fathers" (SS, 128). Crispin's answer is glib and sanctimonious: they should take comfort in their families and the heartwarming Christmas cards they receive. They have, after all, plenty of friends.

Kate is clearly suffering from the bruises of being boxed in by Anglocentrism, a form of exclusion weighted heavily with normative attitudes and perspectives that neither woman is able to label as anti-Semitism exactly. Nevertheless, Kate mumbles something about the stupidity of political leaders, friends accepting "facile images of themselves," racist slurs on buses and trains, Auschwitz trials, atrocities, accidents, children dying, and suddenly she is gone. When Marcia leaves Crispin to go home, she replays the tragic implications of that meeting. Convinced that Crispin never could comprehend why she too wanted to weep, Marcia aches for meaningful connections. She takes her anger out on her children.

On the fifth Sunday Katerina's husband calls Marcia to say she has committed suicide. On the sixth Sunday Marcia sits at home in despair. She has grown paralyzed, crippled with the awareness of her "double otherness"—that of being a Jew in England and being married to a Gentile.

"Said the Old Man to the Young Man"

Wesker set out once again to depict the "otherness" of being Jewish, this time with a more positive emphasis, in a 1978 short story. In "Said the Old Man to the Young Man," traditional Jewish values of an old Jew remedy the jaded values of a young man whose sole desire is success in a Gentile-dominated business world.

Martin, the old man in the story, is "a heavy, determined, club-fingered Jew who, when thirty years earlier his sweet and beloved 23-year-old daughter was knocked down and killed by a bus in Balls Pond Road, Dalston, had given up smoking his forty cigarettes a day and returned to the religious rituals of ghetto Jerusalem" (*SOM*, 29). The old man represents everything that is lovable and annoying about the older generation, anyone's older generation. His character is incurably fixed by both good-natured and irritating traits. Martin refuses to eat anything but kosher food, flirts with Jewish women in search of a second wife, cannot hear very well, cackles to cover his insecurities, and becomes openly aggressive when his sense of justice is violated. He finds himself almost immediately in conflict during a visit with his great-nephew, Amos, who—doubtful about the sincerity of his own religious commitments—considers the old man a liability and an embarrassment.

Amos, "the stern product of an age of computers, complex business corporations, think-tanks and a time of 'hard facts, man,'" knows little about the history that shaped his great uncle, and cares less (*SOM*, 29). He is ignorant of the old man's socialist activities with the Bund, a select group of devout and ideologically pure Jews who based their activities in the 1930s on a workers' union established by the General Jewish Workmen's Union of Russia and Poland. Moreover, Amos is impatient, self-centered, and impressed by experts, "efficient men with square-rimmed glasses, and the ethics of profit" (*SOM*, 30). He has a loud American accent as well as a Yankee desire to work in a fast-track position in the United States. Amos's girlfriend, however, has breast cancer and may need an operation that would tie him to Britain and take him out of the American fast track. Therein lies the conflict. Amos cannot decide whether to leave her to take the job he wants in America or to remain by her side in Britain.

Since Uncle Martin has come to London for the high holidays (*yom tovim*) of Yom Kippur and Rosh Hashanah, Amos has been relegated to accompany him to the synagogue. Being too wrapped up in his own problems to stand by the old man's side at the synagogue while he cheerfully buttonholes strangers, Amos agitates to leave before the services begin. Martin understands and asks his nephew to return at half-past seven, but Amos, not trusting this information, searches out the synagogue's expert, the *shames* (custodian), who tells him incorrectly to return at nine o'clock.

During the service Amos wanders around in London's drizzle searching his conscience for a clue as to what he should do about his girlfriend. He knows his family places a high value on humanistic compassion and just action. Their values belie that commonly accepted definition that describes Jews as "grasping" or someone who "cheats." As Jewish humanists, Amos's family abhor "production at the expense of man's leisure, property profiteering at the expense of the homeless . . . censorship to avoid unrest, unemployment to reduce inflation, random assassination to promote political aims, the revolution's 'unavoidable' slaughter of innocents in the name of nationalism, independence, equality" (*SOM*, 49). Amos struggles with the values he's been taught from a young age: "Confronted with a choice between the well-being of an institution, as which a fully elaborated ideology can be described, or the needs of human beings, then a humanist would choose the happiness of the human being" (*SOM*, 49). He weighs out these humanist values against his offer from the American firm. Attracted to the prospect of making a comfortable income, he wants to buy into their firm loyalty, and yet he recalls the gentle morals of Fabianism and balances these against the American work ethic.

He is not sure what he thinks, but he does know that the mere act of struggling with these questions makes him a moral man, and he is surprised by that potential: "I'd taken amorality to be an intellectual stand, a state of mind arrived at through reason. Perhaps amorality is simply like a physical defect, some people are dyslexic, some tone deaf, others amoral"

(*SOM*, 72–73), he muses. In his delight with himself, he goes to take a hot bath and tell his girlfriend that he is staying with her. He is proud of his ability to make a responsible decision. Ironically, he has forgotten the old man who has been left standing in the rain at the synagogue.

"Said the Old Man to the Young Man" is loosely based on characters in Wesker's family. Martin is based on his maternal Uncle Perly (Bernard Perlmutter), who lost his daughter when she was hit by a bus during a blackout in World War II. Sarah is probably based on his mother, Leah Wesker, and Millie may be based on his Aunty Ray; the young man who discovers his family's values in himself could be Arnold Wesker in a more callow moment.

The Old Ones

Another play inspired by wonderful characters right out of Wesker's own Jewish family is *The Old Ones* (1972). Like "Said the Old Man to the Young Man," the generation gap is a central topic, but the play's primary focus is on the pain of growing old and survival in a life of "chaos and contradictions" (3: 149). It is shaped by an ongoing debate between two elderly brothers who raise large questions about the nature of suffering in old age. Ultimately they are asking what makes life worth living. In an introductory note Wesker describes the play as not about being Jewish, although almost all its characters are Jewish, but about "defiant old age." Even so, the influence of Judaism as a spiritual anchor for Wesker is apparent throughout the play, especially in the verbal battle between two brothers who reflect many of Wesker's inner conflicts about spiritual values.

These two brothers (twins in an earlier draft), Emanuel (Manny) and Boomy, have led roughly similar lives, but each brother registers his particular circumstances differently and attempts to convert his sibling. Manny suffers from wracking nightmares that rob his sleep and harass his daytime hours; nevertheless, he is continually searching out life-affirming forces that push back the dark. He takes exuberant delight in nattering at his wife, singing socialist and Yiddish songs, and hurling quotations at his brother. Manny believes that life is ultimately just: there is reward for hard work with one's own hands, a natural law based on Torah rationality, progress for mankind, and God's essential goodness. He thrills at the decline in religious wars and subscribes to a naive but reassuring confidence that destructive human behavior like anger and fanaticism can be reformed. Even after Gerda, Manny's wife, is attacked by angry youths, Manny continues to hope that human cruelty may be reduced by lessening fear.

Boomy, on the other hand, finds little comfort in religious pieties or principles; instead he dwells on what might have been in a better world. After Gerda's assault he becomes infuriated that his brother would make excuses for the attackers and concludes from that experience that "men of principle" in particular are endangered when confronted with irrational behavior (3: 168). Even so, Boomy's "quarrel is with God not men" for the numerous injustices of life and its trials (3: 152). Boomy's son, for example, has been arrested for student protests and needs £100 to pay his fines. Out of a lack of will to fight the law, Boomy lets him go to jail. Another ongoing source of aggravation is their financial loss when Manny throws the family's diamonds into the Thames. Furthermore, he is annoyed by the improvidence of his "dabbler" artist nephew and his niece who struggles as a mere teacher. For every one of Manny's hopeful arguments, Boomy responds with his own selection of gloomy quotations. He finds life a burden.

Carefully preserving the balance of voices between the nay- and the yea-sayers are Sarah, their sister, and Teressa, a neighbor in the Greater London Council flats. Both characters were seen briefly in "Said the Old Man to the Young Man." Sarah and her daughter Rosa are building a Succah, a tent decorated with branches and leaves that serves as a temporary shelter during the meals of Succoth, a harvest festival and time of thanksgiving. The holiday is important because it attempts to assure those who are suffering that God provides. The wealthy are reminded of the temporariness of good fortune, bringing "man face to face with the realization of the frailty of human life and the transience of human existence" (3: 137). Sarah, a much less politically committed version of the mother in the trilogy, is not ordinarily so religious, but she wants to celebrate in the memory of her joyful father. Once a person like Manny, he might have taken pleasure in the fact that "Judaism recognizes the natural instinct of joy and makes no attempt to repress it, but rather to encourage natural self-expression" (3: 137). Her sensible and easy-going outlook is carried over into the next generation by her daughter Rosa.

In contrast to Sarah, who is sociable and maternal, is her friend Teressa who is an isolated and driven scholar living in a "dishevelled attic living-room." Maniacally absorbed in the job of translating the poetry of a little-known Polish woman whose tragic life led to one fatal mishap after another, Teressa bitterly laments that "one cared then and no one cares now" (3: 141). There is also the old cockney neighbor who tells slightly risqué jokes and goes around repeating, "Jack is a-dying, the young folk is living, Jack is a-going, the young folk is coming," hardly words of comfort to the old ones because the next generation seems largely made up of ruffians and ne'er-do-wells.

The debate between the optimists and pessimists comes to a climax when Manny tells the holiday celebrants that he has had a revelation. Without resorting to one more quotation, someone else's words, he announces that it does not matter if life's struggles bear little or no reward, because satisfaction is in the labor: "to cry 'vanity of vanities' at foolish or evil men and then to abandon your true work is to abandon not them but yourself; it is to be guilty of an even greater vanity: for you knew what they did not" (3: 193). While Manny jumps up and down in self-congratulatory delight at his own wisdom and Sarah and Rosa dance, Boomy has the last word, in which he gleefully quotes from Ecclesiastes: "Because to every purpose there is a time and judgment, therefore the misery of man is great upon him. For he knoweth not that which shall be; for who can tell him when it shall be? There is no man that hath power over the spirit to retain the spirit, neither hath he power in the day of day . . . neither hath he power in the day of death . . . neither hath he power in the day of death" (3: 194).

The play's ending has that perfect Weskerian balance of recognizing both the utopian ideal and its defeat—a viewpoint that he has called his "melancholy optimism" (British Council 1988). Nevertheless, the suggestion is there, just as it persists in many of Wesker's plays, that mere commitment to an ideal may be sufficient for survival.

Written in 1972, a time he was trying to recover from the disappointments of poor reviews and a failed Centre 42, *The Old Ones* is a reflection of Wesker's refusal to concede defeat to anyone—and at the same time to admit that he has very little enthusiasm for life. It is a statement about his stubbornness and his bruised spirit. Many readers, including Margaret Drabble, find the works of this period bleak because "They take the reader into the familiar territory of doubt, the homely land of self-doubt and disillusion. . . . [Wesker's] defiance, his largely unrewarded faith and perseverance, have made us uneasy: perhaps something in us would like to see him forced to accept the grim, dull realities of life more quietly" (Drabble, 20). And yet plays like *The Old Ones* also show how a defiant refusal to yield to the forces of darkness protects the spirit. The play seems to be the best example of Wesker's struggle to summon some resilience in the face of visible failure and loss of faith. Calling himself a "happy pessimist," he told Drabble, "I do have this capacity for retaining, for squeezing out some pleasures, some joys. I won't let Them get me" (Drabble, 28).

His comments here and elsewhere also remind us about the process of aging—they are sobering reminders of what he anticipates for all of us. In "From a Writer's Notebook," a journal Wesker kept about the time he wrote *The Old Ones*, he expresses portions of both Manny's grasping at hope and Boomy's anguish: "Growing old involves being able to cope less and less with those human faults whose inevitability one had always suspected while still young but had ignored. The sadness of it. . . . [Nevertheless] growing old is not a losing of faith—no point in losing that, there's too much goodness. No aging involves being less cheered by goodness than one is tormented by evil. And it's without control—we cannot order or pace it out comfortably. It takes us up in its own way and its own time, this feeling" ("Notebook," 8). Not even Judaism helped him shake the depression of this period. In the 1971 essay "Distinctions, Intimidations, and Hysteria" he said that aging for a writer was "to grow in understanding of his limitation as an artist" (*Distinctions*, 173). He also spoke sadly of being "bewildered" and a loss of "passion to take sides." His nausea from "public horrors and private disenchantments" is apparent.

Two Roots of Judaism

Having grown up as a Jew in London's East End and partially assimilated into the British culture, Wesker and his family have followed the worn route of some Anglo-Jewry who migrate to London, then leave the ghetto one generation later to find homes in non-Jewish neighborhoods elsewhere in Britain, maintaining limited ties to Judaism through the bar mitzvah and important religious ceremonies that mark life's passages.

Like most secular Jews within the Jewish community, Wesker has had to negotiate the way between the opposing factions of Jewish fundamentalism, which feels oppressive to him, and total assimilation into the British culture, which would erase his Jewish identity. On the one extreme are those whose lives center on the synagogue and maintain strict standards of orthodox observance and belief; on the other are those who have taken steps to "pass" entirely into the British culture. In the middle are those who chose between what Wesker calls in his essay "The Two Roots of Judaism," the "ritualists" and the "rationalists" (*Distinctions*, 253). These rationalists are those Jews who are working out the tension between faith and skepticism, between obeisance and searching. The ritualists are the "practicing orthodox," those who keep alive the daily practices of Judaism, protect the status quo, subscribe to Maimonides's Thirteen Principles of the Jewish Faith, and believe in the divinity of the

Torah. The rationalists are "practicing moralists," Jews who may or may not believe in God but who seek out "a return to the original principles of righteousness, justice and mercy" (*Distinctions*, 253–54).

Wesker defines himself as a rationalist. For him, being Jewish means an ethnic identification with a people as well as with centuries of ideals—namely, a humanitarian search for truth through scholarship and a "reverence for, and greater preoccupation with, man and his ways" (*Distinctions*, 255). Indeed, Wesker places a deep trust in the ratiocinative processes as a means to "control man's more destructive passions, illuminate his bewilderment, calm his fears, reassure him of dignity, of his place in the scheme of things" and the sanctity of the human being created in God's image. Wesker has more confidence in what he knows about humanity than about God, whom he regards more as a human than a divine being (*Distinctions*, 254). He believes that Abraham conceived of the highest ideal possible and called it God; then "Moses took back for *man* the qualities Abraham gave *God*" (*Distinctions*, 254). "It was as though Abraham had conceived of God in order to give anarchic and arrogant mankind a direction and a sense of humility, to make him bend at the knee, in the first stage; and then Moses recognized the need for a second stage to restore dignity: 'You are created in the image of God,' he told them. 'Stand up! Be proud!'" (254).

While Wesker's understanding of Judaism is not a mainstream approach, even for a secular Jew, it is not unique either. The ideas of Liebman Hersch (1882–1955), also a socialist Jew from Eastern Europe, a Bundist, an agnostic, and a broad-minded thinker, help to situate some of Wesker's arguments. In *Mein Yiddishkeit* Hersch wrote that all religion is a "social product," meaning that people create their definition for God, their ethic and law, morality, and pattern of living out of the historical conditions of their existence.[2] According to Hersch, the concept of Judaism as a socially constructed "national" religion—in contrast to the "universal" character of Christianity, for example—has shaped its holy writings (the Old Testament and the Torah) around its history, its ritual laws and holidays. Its social and legal contracts, too, have determined much about the faith. Hersch concludes, "Not God created man according to His image, but man creates his God according to his own image. It is not God who chose the people of Israel, but Israel selected its God, fashioned its conception about the world and life and its rules of practical conduct." Although Wesker was not directly influenced by Hersch, Hersch seems to be describing a line of thinking in Jewish secularism that links Wesker to European intellectual thought.

Jews believe that, through the Abrahamic covenant, God charged humankind with the responsibility of preserving truth and justice, which in turn leads to a strong sense among Jews of social and moral responsibility. The rationalist translates this charge into social action on behalf of human need, into a high value placed on human endeavor and the sanctity of human life and furthermore feels compelled to conduct a lifelong search for truth and human understanding. Illustrating what it means to be a humanitarian scholar, a "fixer," and morally wise Jewish man is largely what Wesker had in mind when he drew up his Shylock, one of his best developed characters.

Shylock

Originally titled *The Merchant* (written in 1977), *Shylock* taps many of the stories that Shakespeare drew on for the *Merchant of Venice*. Wesker conceived of the first draft in 1973, while watching Sir Laurence Olivier's interpretation of Shylock that exaggerated many anti-Semitic stereotypes—stinginess, greed, and an irrational compulsion for revenge. Wesker wrote about Shakespeare's version:

> Here was a play which, despite the poetic genius of its author or who knows, perhaps because of it!—could emerge as nothing other than a confirmation of the Jew as bloodsucker. Worse, the so-called defence of Shylock the Jew—"If you prick us, do we not bleed"—was so powerful that it dignified the anti-Semitism. An audience, it seemed to me on that night, could come away with its prejudices about the Jew confirmed but held with an easy conscience because they thought they'd heard a noble plea for extenuating circumstances. (*Distinctions*, 156)

Wesker took his interest in writing his own play about Shylock to Boulder, Colorado, where he was slated in 1974 to teach a course in contemporary drama. There he turned the idea over to the class for their help. One of the graduate students, Lois Bueler, discovered through her research that Venetians of the sixteenth century could not transact business with a Jew without a contract. She also unearthed other Venetian laws that treated Jews unfairly. *Shylock* has been dedicated to Bueler's research, which helped Wesker make a breakthrough in his thinking.

Since the idea's inception, the play has gone through nine drafts, and partly because, as a favorite choice for the O-level exams, it has had more exposure in the classroom than in the theater. Unfortunately, *Shylock* was another one of those jinxed productions of the 1970s that plagued Wesker's efforts to stage his works. At first its future seemed quite promising. While Wesker was still looking to mount the play at the National Theatre, he bumped into his old collaborator and director of the first five plays, John Dexter. Dexter embraced Wesker and volunteered that he had read *The Merchant* and liked it very much. Dexter then agreed to direct it, but not at the National Theatre, partly because the then-director Peter Hall had already vetoed the play for being too wordy and because Dexter did not want to work at the National for personal reasons.

So they turned to New York City with Zero Mostel, the star of the recent hit *Fiddler on the Roof*, playing Shylock. But those plans were never realized either. Mostel died suddenly of an aneurism after the opening preview night in Philadelphia. When *The Merchant* had premiered in Stockholm one year earlier (8 October 1976), Wesker received word that his mother had died, and Mostel's death seemed too much. He movingly writes about this dark period in "Extracts from a New York Journal": "My play had killed him. He dieted for it and was under pressure for it and silly bugger! he overdid it! Oh Zero, Zero, Zero! Now I'm crying for you. You were so rested, you were like a plum pudding!" (*Distinctions*, 91).

In Shakespeare's *Merchant of Venice* Antonio needs to borrow 3,000 ducats to lend to his friend Bassanio so that Bassanio might have the means to woo the fair and rich Portia. Antonio turns to the Jew for a loan, even though he is viciously anti-Semitic. Although Shylock wants to be friends with Antonio and tells him so, Antonio's prejudices anger Shylock and make him so vengeful that he demands a pound of flesh as collateral from his enemy. Shylock's daughter, Jessica, shows us yet more evidence of his spiteful nature when she tries to win his approval for her marriage to the Gentile Lorenzo.

Momentarily everything turns sour when Shakespeare's Shylock hears that his daughter has eloped with Lorenzo and, out of humiliation and rage, he threatens to collect the pound of flesh from Antonio, who cannot repay the debt on time. In disguise as a young judge, Portia saves the day when she wisely awards Shylock his pound of flesh but refuses him a single drop of Antonio's blood. Since he cannot collect the flesh without spilling the blood, he loses out altogether. Indeed, he is the only character to experience defeat. Eventually Antonio's ships do come in, Bassanio wins Portia's hand in marriage, and all of Shylock's worldly goods are gifted to Lorenzo and his daughter as part of his sentence. To add to the insult, Shylock is ordered to convert to Christianity.

Wesker's Shylock Kolner more closely reflects the qualities that Wesker thinks the old Jew, born of the 'compassionate sons of the compassionate' in the Abrahamic line of descent, was likely to have exemplified. Though a mere "loan-banker," his Shylock is also deeply learned, spending more hours every day with his books than his business. As a rationalist, he obeys the laws in Venice that restrict Jews when he must, but he also undermines them whenever possible. Not the least of their restrictions is that Jews must practice banking—the borrowing and lending of money—because other professions were closed to them. Moreover, Jews had to live in the *Ghetto Nuevo*, which in Venetian dialect means "new iron foundry," apparently a Venetian place where the Jews were corralled when curfew began at nightfall. These restrictions on their movement after dark of course were meant to cripple the Jews's chances of financial success and social integration by limiting their personal contacts. When Antonio finds himself benighted at the Jew's home, he is forced to remain illegally in the ghetto overnight.

Unquestionably the most galling laws in Venetian history were those that allowed Venice to profit by charging Jews substantial sums for their apartments, which provided little more than forced imprisonment at night on Foundry island, where they were also harassed by Christian guards.[3] Even after many Jews had moved away to Holland they had to continue to pay rent on vacated housing because the leases obligated them to nearly a lifetime of debt on these places. Furthermore, Jews were not allowed to own land or vote, even though they were taxed heavily. And Jews were also forced to keep bank accounts and businesses open long after they proved profitable, because the Jewish owners were not allowed to sell out or declare bankruptcy. These laws remained on the books until Venice had to admit that the Jewish community had been bled dry. When Antonio and Shylock draw up a contract in Wesker's play, they do so only because they are mandated by the Venetian law to record all dealings between Jews and Gentiles. Wesker's Shylock loves Antonio as a brother and believes the law anti-Semitic and barbarous. Together, therefore, they conspire to make a mockery of it by choosing to contract a pound of flesh as collateral. The aristocratic Bassanio and Lorenzo reveal themselves as the real gold diggers for wanting to marry women they believe are wealthy, even though Jessica does not abscond with her father's money in Wesker's version and Portia's fortune has long since been dissipated.

When it happens that Antonio cannot repay his debt, Portia steps in and saves him, just as she does in *The Merchant of Venice*, and the Doge of *Shylock* strips Shylock mercilessly of his belongings—in this case his books that have religious and cultural significance for him. The scene poignantly comments on the cruelties in Shakespeare's "comic" ending. Unlike Shakespeare's Shylock, however, Wesker's Shylock is tremendously relieved that he does not have to collect a pound of flesh from his friend to satisfy the bogus contract.

But that is just about the only note of joy at the end of Wesker's play. Doubt is cast over the future marriages of Portia and Jessica, who are justifiably disillusioned with Bassanio and Lorenzo. Not even Antonio will live happily ever after, because there is no reversal of misfortune in this play. Wesker makes no pretense at an artificially happy ending because the real tragedy, after all, lies in the institutionalized injustices of the Venetian laws that contaminate human interaction in both versions. Antonio freely spits on Shylock in Shakespeare's play, and Wesker's magnanimous Shylock cannot, by law, be permitted to act on the generosity that is a part of his nature. The women, too, bound by marriage laws and customs that victimize them, can foresee that their potential for creativity and intelligent living could be crushed.

Although the historical facts about Venice fascinated Wesker, his primary purpose for writing *Shylock* was to develop a more plausible image of the enlightened, free-spirited Jew. Kindhearted, tolerant, and a seeker of knowledge like Boomy in *The Old Ones*, Wesker's Shylock is the sort of person that he believes Judaism encourages. He is moral and committed to his principles and this commitment is reinforced by his readings and studies in Jewish thought. Shylock comes out of the Jewish tradition of prophecy—one that augurs "criticism, chastisement, warning" rather than the more dire Messianic teaching. Having the capacity to seek the truth and teach, he has the training, even though self-taught, to use language with respect. He uses it to educate, to explain, to enlighten. When Shylock gives his word, he considers it binding, a teaching from the Torah. High regard for ethic and education are the bases of Wesker's course for a more just society; this is almost wish-fulfillment for a man who was not able to go beyond the eleventh year in school. In 1979 he wrote, "If education means anything it means essentially this: the upholding of language as man's greatest creation. It means a constant freshening, a constant guarding against abuse by demagogues, bureaucrats and copy-writers, whether political or commercial" (*Distinctions*, 214). On one level, words are dangerous because they can "confuse, distort, oversimplify, mislead, mean different things for different people"; but they can also be taught, analyzed, understood as a possible defense against oppression, intimidation, hysteria (*Distinctions*, 171). As a way of assuring understanding, words and education build bridges between people. Wesker has been insisting on the peace-making capacity of language since *Roots*. And yet he recognizes that his is largely a "Jewish reverence" for the pursuit of knowledge and the power of language and intellect, and he is proud of the heritage.[4]

But Shylock is not without flaws. Like Joshua (*When God Wanted a Son*), he has his abrasive moments. He and Jessica clash wills. He is, moreover, edgy and arrogant with the other women of his household, dismissive of those who work for him, and prideful. His dignity intact, Shylock explodes at his own defense attorney for the patronizing arguments. His outrage expresses much of what Wesker himself feels about this familiar section in Shakespeare's play:

LORENZO: The bond is inhuman, not the man. No one doubts the Jew is human. After all, has not a Jew eyes?

SHYLOCK: What is *that* fool attempting now?

LORENZO: Has not a Jew hands?

SHYLOCK: Is he presuming explanations on *my* behalf?

LORENZO: Has not a Jew organs, dimensions, senses, affections, passions?

SHYLOCK: Oh no! . . . No, no, NO! I will not have it. I do not want apologies for my humanity. Plead for me no special pleas. I will not have my humanity mocked and apologized for. If I am unexceptionally like any man then I need not exceptional portraiture. I merit no special pleas, no special cautions, no special gratitudes. My humanity is my right, not your bestowed and gracious privilege. (4: 254–55)

Of all the women, Shylock's sister Rivka best understands his moral indignation and impatience, but she scolds him for defying Gentile law, for wanting to be the scholar he is not, for believing in a better world, for daring to challenge authority. She fancies herself the realist who knows how to protect herself through appeasement. Unlike his sister, Shylock will not bow to his enemies. He is the visionary who believes that someday Jews will be accorded respect and dignity, as is their due; he holds the sort of wisdom that fuels "the spirit of justice and tolerance, and the Jewish energy for action" (*Distinctions*, 255). Shylock is a man with a still center who recognizes the existence of bigots and knows that, because he stands out as a free spirit, he becomes their target. Nevertheless, as one who refuses to accept things as they are, he will not be intimidated.

Everything Shylock represents clashes with the moral character of most Christians in the play—Bassanio, Lorenzo, Graziano—who are bigoted, provincial, small-minded, and ignorant. Lorenzo is especially loathsome because while he romanticizes the working classes he disparages Jews and does it all in the name of virtue that, for him, lies in "simplicity, suffering, renunciation" (4: 261). It is the kind of self-sacrifice that frightens Wesker. Hiding behind a veneer of humility and discipline, Lorenzo is the sort of person who terrifies Jews because he uses the excuse of an ideological cause to bully and intimidate others. He is the sort of leader to require sacrifice in the ranks to achieve his political ends.

Wesker has no charity for intimidators, especially the bigot who threatens others for the sake of race, religion, or politics. He identifies in that person "the special quality of spiritual fixation, a quality made chillingly sharp by values once human but now hardened by written dogma. A scripture, political or religious, simplified out of all reason and logic, informs, protects and petrifies the lucid juices of his intelligence. He is calm because he is protected from the belief that opposition is possible. He *seems* intelligent because he listens to opposition with the thoughtful patience of one who *must* know, with absolute certainty, all opponents are wrong" (*Distinctions*, 17). Indeed, closed mindedness in any form, including religious ardor, frightens Wesker. This accounts for his rejection of extremism in religion—any religion—that gives undue importance to a credo over the spirit of joy, gladness and celebration of life. For this reason he speaks out against fanaticism among Muslims, Jews, and Christians alike and finds in Shylock a man who represents the best impulses of Judaism, with its "freedom from the darkness of superstition and fear into the light of Genesis where all was explained: the world was created out of love and for all mankind AND in the image of the God who created it" (*Distinctions*, 259). To battle the darkness, Shylock embraces life with all its responsibilities. The credo of the anchoress Christine in the play *Caritas*, by contrast, represents the religious tradition Wesker rejects: a complete surrendering of self, ignorance of the world, withdrawal from social responsibility and familial attachment, acute awareness of alienation from God, and painful desire for union.

Caritas

Like *Shylock, Caritas* (written in 1980) was the result of an idea Wesker got at the University of Colorado—this time as a suggestion from Paul Levitt who urged Wesker to look into the anchorite tradition.[5] Wesker based his play on the true story of Christine Carpenter who, in 1329, was voluntarily immured and three years later left the convent only to be persuaded to return by the religious community.

Christine enters the convent against the wishes of her mother, her father, and Robert, her ex-fiancé. As an anchorite, she is not completely cloistered, so she is allowed contact with people who come to her cell with food, local news, and need for religious consultation. Her family visits her repeatedly trying to get her to leave. She ignores that advice until she realizes that she still loves Robert and cannot rid herself of the deadly sins by running away from life, nor can she experience a religious vision by limiting human contact. Once she changes her mind, however, she finds that the rector of the church, in accord with the lord bishop of Norwich, will not release her. Their joint decision reveals the pernicious collusion between church and the feudal estate that was in its last stages of power at this time. It also produces an unbearably claustrophobic atmosphere when it becomes clear that she has no hope of leaving.

Wesker's focus of attack here is not the Catholic Church but the insidious effects of dogma in any faith that entraps individuals and reduces them to mere mouthpieces for the institution. He draws a parallel between the dogma that destroys Christine and the ideology of the peasants that destroys human life when "in the process they became intoxicated with blood-letting, and perpetrated other injustices" (6: 61). Wesker continues, "All dogma is anti-human because it presumes the way life *must* be lived, which kills spontaneous creativity. The human spirit must be given room to grow, enjoy, to innovate. Anything that suppresses this spirit, whether it is a capitalist or socialist or religious dogma, is anti-human" (6: 61).

Wesker is similarly suspicious of the Lollards and other radical protestant religions that rose up against the established order in the fourteenth and fifteen centuries. Even though these sects meant religious freedom for many who were oppressed by the corruption of the Catholic Church and its entrenched wealth, he is horrified by the emotional excesses that were promoted by these small Christian movements. Nevertheless, he has no intention in *Caritas* of attacking contemplative movements per se. Christine only serves as a metaphor for the destructiveness of unquestioning obedience in religion. The subtext to both situations in *Caritas*—the Peasants' Revolt and the "entombment" of Christine—is his warning to the next generation "that they should not be subject to the single tyranny of one regime, one kind of education, one anything" (Bigsby 1977).

Wesker is also averse to the zealot whose fanaticism perverts rationalism and rejects other human beings out of religious bigotry. He writes,

> The test of your beliefs, whatever they may be, is in how you treat me. The zealot is foreign to such thinking. The zealot helped carve up many a dissenting saint, placed the faggots on the fire that burned poor Joan, stood by knitting as the guillotine lopped off the heads of the innocent as well as the guilty . . . marched Jews to the gas chambers . . . built homes on the West Bank of the Jordan, burnt a book in Bradford, offered £3 million for the head of its author. We are here dealing with a special mentality which cannot bear deviation from its own perceptions and beliefs.[6]

In a way, Wesker's objections here are aimed at the sort of mindless lynch-mob mentality that has always been a concern for him, but more than that, he fears that blind faith is at the root of much of this destructive rage—a blind faith that should be condemned by any thinking individual.

Against the background of Christine's story is the turmoil of the Peasants' Revolt of 1381. The rebellion takes place at the time of the Black Death that took the lives of about half England's population, leaving an extreme labor shortage. On some manors this shortage was met by whipping the peasants into higher production, as we see in the case of Robert Lonle's father. But most peasants realized that the law of supply and demand for workers favored them, so they could ask for more equitable wages and a fairer system of management on the manor, as well as lower poll taxes. The trigger for the uprising was the poll tax that regressively hurt the poor more than the rich. Fomented by the preaching of John Ball, the rebels invaded the manor houses and abbeys, at first burning the documents that registered their property for purposes of taxation and later murdering unpopular leaders. One group even marched on London, where they were met at Mile End Road in the East End and returned home, satisfied their cause had won. Most socialists have hailed the spirit of this rebellion for the boost it gave to personal freedom and the demise of serfdom in England, but not Wesker. Concerned about peasants resorting to violence, disorder, and terrorism as a way to improve the conditions of living, Wesker could not condone the peasants' tactics, even though they realized more personal freedom in the long run. Wesker's solutions to the deplorable exploitation that marked the life of a fourteenth century peasant are saving money to buy freedom, seeing to it that their children are educated, and staging peaceable protests against inequitable taxes. Some historians agree with him since, in the short run, many of the peasants suffered even more loss when they were forced from the land once serfdom collapsed.

Anti-authoritarianism

Although identification with Judaism has afforded Wesker a tradition where he belongs and a basis for action according to individual conscience, he nevertheless insists on an unfettered freedom of religious choice, even from the dictates of his own faith. Thus he has established his own level of independence from other Jews and asserted his right to maintain a disputatious stance that questions just about everything, including God and Judaism. He demonstrates what this sort of disputatious character is like in Joshua (*When God Wanted a Son*). He underscores his identification with this sort of insufferable character in an article written for the *Independent*, "The Fundamental Right to Give Offense," in which he defends Salman Rushdie's right to blaspheme, to question sacred beliefs. Fortunately, this argumentative mode of showing doubt is also a healthy part of the Jewish tradition, and so he is proud that his own religious leaders would not threaten his life for expressing his doubts.

As Wesker explains it, lacking respect for historical imperatives, Jews tackle the Scriptures to wrestle meaning out of them. In this manner of verbal sparring, "Jews invented God." Through argumentation, debate, rage, fancy, and individual interpretation, "He was theirs. They possessed him, not he them. Of course the Jewish proclivity for God-making and doubting has infected much of Western culture [by encouraging an anti-authoritarian posture], though not enough for my peace of mind. The free spirit cannot be claimed an exclusive Jewish trait but I do suggest it is the one identifying mark" (Hollander, 500). Although Wesker talks about a number of humanist values he inherited through the Jewish tradition, he is most enthusiastic about Judaism's "twin virtues of questioning and incredulity," maintaining a rational doubt about authority and freeing the spirit from any shackles whatsoever. Although he protests, as ever, the ravages of inequality and injustice, he also insists on his right to interrogate Judaism, the source of his moral inspiration, and any other religious or political philosophy. What seems like insubordination continues to be, he will admit, a source of irritation to others. One such moment came in 1969, when Wesker was named to the Queen's Honor List with the prestigious Commander of the British Empire (CBE), and he turned it down to make a point about Centre 42.

When God Wanted a Son

One of the best examples of this form of argumentation—but by no means the only character who shows this—is Joshua's aggressiveness in Wesker's play *When God Wanted a Son*, written in 1986. Here Wesker demonstrates what happens when the opinionated Joshua impetuously challenges the most revered ideas, even his own, and the irritating effect he has on everyone around him, particularly his Gentile ex-wife, Martha. Their offspring Connie, having inherited traits from both parents, is a self-deprecating stand-up comedian with her father's temerity and her mother's sensitivity to how this brashness can be grating. So she tells a cheeky joke and then yells at herself as though she were a heckler in the audience.

The two-act play contains 30 short scenes—some with only a few words or no lines at all—that fall into a rhythm of exchanges between Connie and one or the other parent that are then followed by slices of comedy from Connie's nightclub act. Joshua does not appear until act 2, but when he does the scenes ignite with antagonism between him and Martha.

Although they are divorced, Joshua is trying once again to win Martha's affections, partly because he needs some of the money she has earned as a stockbroker, partly because he seems to love her in his own way. A onetime college professor fired for philandering, Joshua believes he has invented a hypocrisy machine, a way of detecting hidden intentions—demagoguery, arrogance, seduction, mockery, intimidation, among others—by registering the lilt and intonation of the speaker's voice. He needs Martha's financial backing to promote the idea.

Martha stubbornly refuses all of Joshua's requests. She reacts largely out of a confessed anti-Semitism, which she has felt so guilty about since they were first married that she struggled to mask it. Years hence, she openly resents the fact that he is "Jer-" (Jewish) and cannot bear his "air-, air-" (arrogance) for requesting money of her. In her outrage, she literally gags on the words "Jewish" and "arrogance," and she rants about his irreverence—his disrespect for martyrs', his contempt for clever educators, and his impertinence. She is furious that Joshua has written the Pope about "the creation of a Jewish ecumenical council to decide whether to forgive the Christians" after the Catholics voted to forgive the Jews for the Crucifixion (6: 166–67).

Furthermore, Martha and Joshua cannot agree on the subject of money. She is a capitalist who goes around repeating to herself "money is worth twice its value" (if invested); he is an open-handed spendthrift who believes money is to be enjoyed and shared. At the peak of their conflict over her money, he calls her a "mean, thin-lipped, tight-arsed, unimaginative, sanctimonious, hypocritical, gold-plated bitch" (6: 173).

Joshua knows that she is easily irritated by him, but he dismisses it because he is proud of being rebellious. Like Uncle Martin in "Said the Old Man to the Young Man," Joshua is very blunt: he means "no harm, but if there's something [he's] got to say then [he has] got to say it" (*SOM*, 40). Whereas Martha describes him as "shrill self-serving" and "guttural, strident, ostentatious," Joshua egotistically uses words like "enthusiasm, appetite, energy, ideas, touch, loud laughter, generosity" to describe himself. He tries to laugh at himself, but he is too earnest and admittedly egotistical. Nevertheless, he refuses to apologize for his irreverence and insolence toward others—a strategy that has enabled his ancestors to survive centuries of deep suffering. He deliberately keeps his distance from an affiliation with country, family, political movement, or any other group identity because he wants to be free to act out of his own conscience.

Connie is torn by her parents' incompatibility. She shares with Joshua a sense of humor that knows how to deflate pomposity, debunk myths, and ridicule foolish, self-defeating behavior—even by Jews. Indeed, most of her jokes are aimed at Jews who, like her father, indulge in behavior that hurts them in the long run:

> Two Jews, two Jews. About to be executed. The Nazi captain, a civilized man, sensitive, a lover of Wagner virtue heroes children dogs and the Alps, not being without pity, and mindful of tradition, asked the Jews if they had a last request before being shot. The first Jew asked for a cigarette and was given one. The second Jew thought a second and then—spat in the captain's face. At which the first Jew spluttered, choked on his cigarette, went pale and whispered, "Hymie, Hymie, do me a favor, don't make trouble." (6: 165)

Joshua understands the source of Connie's self-deprecating humor better even than she does, and with deep pride he tries to tell her about the stubbornness, the self-confidence, the dignity, and skepticism that characterize Jewish humor. His argument closely follows Wesker's own arguments elsewhere: "Laughter comes from the Jews. Why the Jews? Because we're a nervous people. When you invent God you make people uneasy. When you then say he's chosen you to bear witness to the beauty of his creation and to guard justice you make people feel indignant. . . .

When you've invented God no other authority can really be taken seriously. . . . [The Jew] even questions the authority he claimed was unquestionable. . . . And they write funny books about it all" (6: 176–77).

Connie is less than persuaded by Joshua's argument, largely because her father has ignored the liabilities of being a woman in what seems to her a patriarchal religion. She fears she has somehow disappointed her father by not being a son; as a Jewish woman in the male world of nightclub entertainment, she is even more out of place, "A lynch mob, a lynch mob! That's my problem, I'm telling jokes to a lynch mob!" (6: 178). Her father urges her to assert her independence to protect herself from prejudice. Being a woman and not even fully Jewish, not fully capable of identifying with his tradition, she lacks the confidence to take his advice.

In the end Martha tries to make amends for her anti-Semitic guilt by serving up a special tea, but the occasion is spoiled by another one of Joshua's insufferable remarks—this time a flippant comment about a passage from Ecclesiastes. Martha snaps and screams. Joshua realizes, "almost as if it had never occurred to him before" that "she will never have any peace" (6: 187).

When God Wanted a Son makes a discomforting and complex statement about what it is like to be a Diasporan Jew, especially one who is not protected by a Jewish community or supported within a synagogue. The play explores Connie's uncertainty about her identity that is entangled both by gender and by Jewish and Gentile family relationships. Her situation is made all the more poignant when she must face a father who stubbornly brings his intellect to bear against received opinion and challenges authority in a non-Jewish community. Although the decision to speak out is one of premeditated choice and individual conscience, *When God Wanted a Son* illustrates how such a decision is unavoidable for many Jews, even if speaking out becomes problematic for themselves and others.

For all I have said about the extent to which Judaism has shaped Arnold Wesker's politics and his spirituality, and therefore his writing, there is a danger of overemphasizing his identification with the Jewish faith. As a secular Jew he has been long resistant to the label of a religious playwright. He is also chary of allowing any label that might stereotype him: "I do not want it imagined . . . that everything I've written has been specifically about Jews and things Jewish. I would like to think I've interestingly tackled many themes, many natures—from ideals and disillusionment to love and sexual appetite, from ageing and death to the celebration of self-discovery" (*Distinctions*, 261). Certainly Wesker has successfully explored these secular themes and more, but when he speaks about other matters through his Jewish heritage—when he acknowledges it and brings it to bear on his writings—he seems to speak from a more authoritative voice and his works are the richer for it. Although he is not preoccupied with Judaism and is certainly not a religious man in the traditional sense, it is through the working-class and Jewish contexts that he finds his truth.

Chapter Six
The Women in Wesker's Writing

In 1981 Arnold Wesker noted with some pride and astonishment that more of the central parts in his plays were written for women than for men. In the short piece "The Women in My Writing: Notes for a Reading" he pointed to 22 roles for women that, taken together, created a mosaic or pastiche of the extraordinary woman: "I didn't plan my life's work that way, that's the way it happened. Out of eight long short-stories five have central or major female characters" (*Distinctions*, 150–51). In this count Wesker probably had in mind "Love Letters on Blue Paper," "The Visit," "Six Sundays in January," "Pools," and "A Time of Dying." The women he represents are very different in age, background, and temperament. Since that time, nearly three-quarters of his major works contain significant roles for women. Among the ranks are unforgettable characters like Betty Lemon, Annie Wobbler, Connie in *When God Wanted a Son*, Samantha in *The Mistress*, and Rosie in *Lady Othello*, all challenging and complex personalities with a wide range of emotions. Moreover, his women are unusually plucky, self-confident, free-spirited, warm, intelligent, compassionate, and persevering—qualities that actors most enjoy portraying. Indeed, Wesker has probably done more to provide a fresh supply of enduring and varied roles for female characters than any of his male contemporaries writing for the British stage today.

Wesker's interest in strong parts for women began with the earliest plays, which drew heavily on the influence of his mother for the values she taught him about people—to care for one another and to share whatever there is. She passed on to her son the "very Jewish" and humanist values of reaching out to help people in need. She is, in effect, the one who taught him to be a "fixer"—that is, "someone who cared about a society in which human beings realised their potential"—and she taught him that each individual is worthy because of that potential (Clare, 53). Leah Wesker also taught him the more basic qualities of individual strength, which he perceived as unwavering determination, an unconditional love for family, strong conviction, and a good sense of humor. Ironically, it is in these simple lessons that Arnold discovered the conflicting values of communal responsibility and individual will. The contradiction did not bother Leah because she knew her own mind. Arnold once noted that "they used to call my mother a spitfire. Still is. *She* kept the family together, not my father—everyone just loved him" ("Miniautobiography," 243). It is ironic because of his mother's belief in the importance of the individual that Wesker adamantly dreads any institution, political or otherwise, that exploits or diminishes the vitality of a person, and yet he also reproaches himself when he retreats too far from the community and its needs, a sense of duty to others that she taught him out of her communist value system.

Leah Wesker is best portrayed in the trilogy, where her character, Sarah Kahn, represents a mélange of quintessentially female traits. Feminist critic Michelene Wandor calls her a "mixture of earth-mother, Jewish matriarch and socialist-realist heroine."[1] At once she is an articulate and feisty spokesperson for her political principles; a dedicated mother who sits tirelessly by her children's side when she is needed; an impatient, sometimes nagging wife of a misdirected but gentle tailor; and a woman who is disliked by her son-in-law, though we never really know why.

Because Wesker loved his mother deeply, he developed many roles for women out of a love for her, but he also recognized her character flaws (Clare, 58). He therefore felt quite uncomfortable about her embarrassment when seeing herself in the trilogy, especially in the scenes with family fights and the suggestion in *Chicken Soup with Barley* that Sarah's confrontations provoked Harry's stroke. These scenes cut so deeply and so distressed his mother that Wesker has since become very reticent about including intimate details of his family in his plays and even reluctant to discuss any of his family publicly. His decision to discontinue portraying his family, at least in recognizable form, must have been quite awkward because he admittedly writes best out of his own experiences, and that would entail stories supplied by his immediate family and friends.

In any case, his sometimes harsh treatment of the characters that represent his mother seems nevertheless honest and real, the addition of detail offered by a loving son who recognizes all the manifold aspects of a human being, flattering and unflattering. A good example of this is his mother's death, a scene described intimately in his story "Love Letters on Blue Paper" ("Miniautobiography," 243). The scene is related by Maurice, who details his mother's physical disintegration of mind and body with disturbing yet poignant realism. Wesker records the monologue tenderly as he tries to work out his own feelings about his loss in October 1976.

"Pools"

"Pools" is an early story based perhaps on a family member, possibly an "aunty" or a favorite neighborhood character. The clue is that she lived at 43 Flower and Dean Street, the address of two of Wesker's aunts. Every week without success Mrs. Hyams plays the football pools. Feeling sorry for her, Mrs. Hyams's neighbors collect £20 in donations to send her on holiday. Unfortunately the pleasure of the trip never really sets in because she continues to be totally preoccupied with her hopes of winning that week's pool.

When Sunday comes, she panics because she cannot find a newspaper with the scores that would tell her whether she has won the pool. Her mounting frustration forces her back to London where she becomes disoriented and lost in a state of confusion. Eventually she discovers the results, only to be disappointed. This bittersweet story gives us another picture of a foolish but lovable woman: her ridiculous obsession with winning £75,000 is outweighed by her grit in the face of loneliness and defeat.

A touching insight into a mother's (and possibly Wesker's) feelings about his daughter is revealed in *Letter to a Daughter*, an unpublished play in five parts with songs (written in 1991). As she writes to her daughter, Melanie acknowledges that her own life is a mess, she nevertheless offers 10 pieces of advice: "Wear tight skirts, but achieve . . . everything you do has a consequence for others and yourself . . . select your friends . . . beware of emotions . . . don't let anyone abuse you . . . don't blame others for what goes wrong in your life . . . realize that love makes no sense . . . use reason, but don't expect it from others . . . choose your men by the three qualities that are most important to you . . . men are products of their mothers and don't forget it." The play reveals as much about Wesker and the hard-knocks lessons he has learned in life as it does about the relationship between a mother and her daughter.

Wesker also portrays his sister Della (Saltiel) in his earlier works. He fondly recalls Della as the one who protected him from parental quarreling while he was young. Eight years older, Della understood more than Arnold about the reasons for disagreements between their parents and tried to shield her brother from the hurt of their parents' fighting. Even so, neither her character (Ada) nor her mother's (Sarah) is treated entirely sympathetically in the trilogy. Ada is somewhat short-tempered and sharp-tongued with her family, and Sarah's nagging and complaints at Harry's ineptness do not leave a favorable impression of either woman.

Still more influential than Della in Wesker's writing has been his wife, Dusty, the subject of several plays and short stories. He indicates in an autobiographical essay for the *Contemporary Authors Series* that she could well have been Sonia, the adoring author of "Love Letters on Blue Paper," the joyous Deborah in *Four Portraits*, and the nurturing Maddeau in "The Visit," as well as the irrepressible Beatie in *Roots*. All four of these women are generous and warm, nurturing, full of energy and vitality. Each exemplifies love, confidence, and self-fulfillment. Of these characters, the one most fully flattering to his wife is probably Maddeau in "The Visit." Nevertheless, the wife as subject of his plays in the 1960s and 1970s makes way for the mistress who gets this attention in the plays of the 1980s. In his later plays—particularly *When God Wanted a Son*, *The Mistress*, *One More Ride on the Merry-Go-Round*, and *Lady Othello*—the spouse becomes a dull, unimaginative but reliable person to love in contrast to the mistress who is a fascinating and unpredictable lover. In the plays of the 1980s and 1990s the themes about marriage are bitter and full of doubt.

Although Wesker generally idealizes the role of the wife in those early plays as one who makes "a place no one ever wants to leave . . . a treasure house full of little goodies in cupboards," and makes a comfortable nest for everyone, including strangers, he writes also about an acquisitive wife who "marries a man in order to have something to attach to herself, a possession" whom Dobson describes in *I'm Talking about Jerusalem*. Dobson continues, "The man provides a home—bang! She's got another possession. *Her* furniture, *her* saucepans, *her* kitchen—bang! bang! bang! And then she has a baby—bang again! All possessions! And this is the way she grows. She grows and she grows and she grows and she takes from a man all the things she once loved him for—so that no one else can have them. Because you see, the more she grows, ah! the more she needs to protect herself" (1: 184). Dobson's attack on women as monstrously voracious parasites is clearly extreme and unfounded, but more than that it is a one-sided argument that goes unanswered. Unfortunately the woman's silence is too often the case in Wesker's works. Rarely do any of his women have the opportunity to reply to charges brought against them, to explain themselves, or to retaliate. And that silence is the very problem that Wesker has in portraying women.

Despite women's high visibility in Wesker's plays, their inmost desires are too often underrepresented. The characters rarely offer genuine insight into a woman's private self. Despite her many opportunities to speak from the heart, for example, Sonia's character in *Love Letters on Blue*

Paper is denied by the author any real ironic distance from her mate—perhaps a bitter disappointment in the quality of his companionship, or to express a desire for deeper sex, or a need to talk freely about her sexual insecurities. She is certainly never given an open and frank monologue to talk about her sexuality like Molly Bloom in Joyce's *Ulysses* or Mary Hooligan in Edna O'Brien's *Night*. In fact, few of the married women are sexually aggressive or have yearnings and fantasies that would surprise their husbands. Mischa in *Three Women Talking* and Nita in *One More Ride on the Merry-Go-Round* are exceptions to this. Most of the women in Wesker's plays who want erotic pleasure for its sake or more control over their sexual choices are young and unmarried. But more than the absence of sexual issues, these women seem lost to themselves. They almost never explore their own personal authority—the identity that sets them apart from anyone else—and they rarely set out on a quest for a secure self-concept that allows them to break away from relationships within which old identities have been embedded. In short, they define themselves and are defined primarily in the context of the males in their lives.

These women—mothers, sisters, wives, mistresses—wait to be given significance by the males they serve. As subordinates, their role is often oversimplified and their characters are, more often than not, relegated to cultural stereotypes out of a received male tradition of theater. Wesker portrays dedicated wives, loving mothers, saucy mistresses, and embittered single women—all of whom appear somewhat two-dimensional and could have become much more interesting if their author had afforded them some complexity and expression. Because these women are almost entirely realized through and on account of their relationships with men, it is difficult to see them as fully rounded people with needs of their own and a drive to exercise real control over their own futures.

Although nearly three-quarters of Wesker's plays cast major roles for women, these are plays only incidentally about women because their stories are too often circumscribed by the male sensibility. In some of these stories, for example, the woman is rarely given the opportunity to speak for herself since the male, totally absent in some instances, overshadows her presence. Furthermore, her decisions tend to devolve to the male as she routinely defers, more frequently than one would expect, to a man's lead. These are indeed romantic views of the ideal woman. There are Deborah (*Four Portraits*), whose whole being centers on her household duties that she finds satisfying; Beatie (*Roots*), who believes she would know nothing if she had not met Ronnie; Samantha (*The Mistress*), who, though accomplished in a profession outside the home, shapes her schedule around a phone call from *him*; and Stephanie (*Yardsale*), Ruth, and Naomi (*Four Portraits*), who cannot help but feel at a loss without a man to love and care for them.

Love Letters on Blue Paper

Another case in point is Sonia in the one-act play *Love Letters on Blue Paper* (1977),[2] told almost entirely through the eyes of Victor, a trade union leader dying of cancer, and the narrator, Maurice, who visits him regularly during his final weeks. The bulk of the play centers on the conversations between the two men that are more important for the friendship they generate than for their content. There is something of an old-boy camaraderie here as they laugh about aggressive women together ("bitch goddesses") and discuss philosophy, art, and politics. Their discussions—with the exception of some remarks about death—seem to lead nowhere and are easily forgotten as soon as Victor's wife, Sonia, reads her letters in an offstage voice-over. They come through the post on blue paper and are never signed—mysterious and sensual interludes in the otherwise pointless discussions. Because the letters are personal and loving, they lie at the center of the play's tension.

Although they read like diary entries, too intimate to share with anyone, the letters reveal remarkably little about Sonia. She chooses instead to speak about her moments with Victor: the bet she won from him about their vegetable garden, driving lessons (on his insistence), the time she had to host the Italian delegation without his help. She continues, "When you first went abroad for a fortnight and I carried my affairs and your affairs along without you that was a landmark. When you first put your head between my legs that was a landmark" (3: 219). Sonia recalls with affection and pride many of their unforgettable experiences together, like the time he taught the family a round to sing atop a peak they had climbed together. More often than not, her reminiscences become a living testament to *him* as a family man—his achievements, his wit, his importance to the family—and a validation of *his* life.

Not only do the letters offer precious little about her inner desires, wishes, and dreams, they seem to express a male's version of what the ideal woman might think. She is everything he wants her to be and nothing without him. Sonia's sixth letter describes Victor's Pygmalion-like accomplishment of making her what she is today. Incredibly, Sonia confirms this notion as well: "You took me and you shaped me and you gave me form. Not a form I couldn't be but the form I was meant to be.

You needed only to be in the house and I felt my life and the lives of the children I cherished could never go wrong. It was so . . . I've been a white sheet, a large white canvas and you've drawn the world upon me, given outline to what was mysterious and frightening in me" (3: 231). She appears content to have little or no identity without him, although it is difficult to believe that any woman would find total satisfaction in becoming the person someone else wants her to be.

Their relationship is thus a curious one. Why she feels more comfortable writing to Victor than speaking to him in person is unclear. We never see them discuss anything with each other directly, not even the business of the household. Then, too, Victor behaves as though she knows nothing about his impending death and Maurice never disabuses him of that delusion, even though he knows Sonia is clearly aware of everything. Her devoted nursing alone should signal Victor that she knows the full truth. And yet they both allow this unspoken truth to impose a wall between them.

Just as puzzling, Sonia seems to be two different people to Victor: warm, tender, loving, and playful to him when they are alone; and aloof to the point of being rude to outsiders. Why she is not better integrated as a person, we can only guess. She might be socially shy, or possessive of Victor's attentions, or protective, or she may not have been allowed to grow into a mature and sociable person. Whatever the case, Maurice eventually wins her trust and friendship, and that is as it should be, since Victor has shared the most personal letters with him. Maurice has even stolen a glance at one letter that Victor never had the opportunity to read. It is an oddly blinded relationship when the husband shares with his friend feelings that he cannot discuss with his wife, even though she saves her most tender moments exclusively for him.

Despite her dual personality, we like Sonia and want to know more about her. Her soft, sensuous voice fills the theater when she reads her letters, giving the impression that she has more presence than she does. Because of the play's structure, however, her presence is almost an absence because when she does appear on stage, she is reduced to pantomime. Then, too, her character is often mediated through the men's descriptions of her as though she were an object, someone deaf or far away. Add to that the play's dual themes—Victor's imminent struggle with the fact of death and her love for him—and we get a Sonia whose needs as the one beloved are greatly underplayed, particularly since we have only limited access to her private thoughts about him and almost no expression of his love for her.

Wesker does not see these competing tensions as a problem. To him the two halves of the play converge in a story about a loving relationship in which she "instinctively finds the right thing to do—to write him these beautiful letters" (Leeming, 139). *Love Letters on Blue Paper* represents for Wesker the perfect marriage in which each partner is so sensitive to the other that the wants of both are satisfied without direct communication. His concept, although compelling, is compromised by a disproportionate emphasis on the husband and his impending death. It is difficult to know why Wesker lent so much weight to the charismatic figure of Victor Marsden except that he probably could not get the idea of premature death off his mind. His onetime friend Robert Copping had just died at a young age, and Copping had written letters shortly before he died to his wife, Valerie, who shared some of them with Wesker. Then, too, is the "macabre coincidence" that Vic Feather, the former general secretary of the Trades Union Congress and friend of Wesker, coincidentally died of leukemia about the same time, even though Wesker was unaware of Feather's grave illness when he was writing. Finally, the play is based on a short story written two years earlier (in 1975), at a time when Wesker feared his own premature death in London's theatrical industry.

Whatever Happened to Betty Lemon?

Although most of Wesker's women passionately articulate their need for men, occasionally someone declares her independence and does so proudly. The title character from *Whatever Happened to Betty Lemon?* (written in 1986) is a notable example of this sort of individuality. Even so, she is not depicted as a woman who enjoys taking care of herself.

Betty Lemon, the widow of a Labour party peer, is confined to a wheelchair and lives alone. As she circles her efficiency apartment, she growls at the inconvenience of her situation: "I didn't fucking plan it this way" (5: 36). Talking mostly to herself and to inanimate objects, she scorns the Handicapper of the Year award that has been offered to her, ridiculing a recognition she has done nothing to achieve. She hates the awardmakers' pity and their ignorant gesture, done more out of their collective guilt than out of any real appreciation for her, and she wonders about who the recipients *should* have been. Sardonically she begins listing the truly handicapped—those with impoverished imaginations, those who are stunted by their ignorance or bigotry, those whose lives are ruined by "demagogues, charlatans, charismatic politicians" (5: 31).

As she speaks, we can hear Wesker talking through her, and this becomes all the more evident as she tells stories about her own (and Wesker's) past. She talks about how she was never a joiner, how she "never really liked the majority" (5: 30). She laughs about moments in her childhood, then she speaks poignantly about her loneliness as she shouts into her daughter's telephone answering machine: "Hello, machine. And how are *you* today? Can't talk? Not feeling well? Feeling depressed? Well, one thing you'll never have to endure: speaking into the fucking void" (5: 35).

At the time this play was written, 16 years had passed since the collapse of Centre 42 and almost that many years since the critical disasters of Wesker's last major productions—*The Old Ones, The Four Seasons*, and *The Journalists*. It had been 23 years since he had written a hit. His livelihood since those failures had depended almost totally on overseas productions. Longing for a box office blockbuster in Britain—a play that would turn into a lucrative film contract or a best-seller—Wesker often cast his feelings into roles of abandoned women who, although isolated by circumstances beyond their control, doggedly refuse to surrender.

Most of them speak as thinly disguised mouthpieces for Wesker's disappointments, frustrations, fears about failure, and anger. Many of Betty Lemon's fears of inadequacy reflect a terror about speaking into the void, and her resilience and defiance reveal a great deal about the determination it took to sustain Wesker during this period. *Betty Lemon* encapsulates the plight of a writer who has no one to befriend and no one to blame. While raging about her condition Betty Lemon accidentally falls out of her wheelchair, and it turns against her as though it had joined ranks with all the others. During much of the play she spends trying to lasso the wheelchair and talking to her noose. Although humor and courage offset the pathos here, her bitterness leaves an unsettled mood at the end, where nothing is resolved except that we know Betty will not speak this candidly at the awards ceremony. The play tells us more about Wesker than about female courage.

Yardsale

Yardsale (written in 1984) is another one-act written at a time when Wesker was feeling the depths of his isolation from mainstream British theater, but this brief play seems a more honest attempt at exploring the female condition than *Betty Lemon*, and it does so quite successfully.

Stephanie has just received the painful news that her husband has left her. Although she is a spirited and warm woman, involved in the world around her and concerned about her family, her husband writes that he wants something new, "Curiosity gone, nerve-ends dead, mechanical. We are boring. I need to be able to surprise someone" (5: 13). He has another woman in mind, no doubt. Without any other information, his actions seem totally reprehensible. For one, he and Stephanie appear to have a great deal in common: she is a primary school teacher; he is a secondary school teacher. Furthermore, it is difficult to imagine her as dull—Stephanie's bright chatter in the opening scene indicates a compassionate, caring, and entertaining woman. She is surely capable of being delighted by something new and returning the favor, if her mate were willing to excite those qualities.

Her response to his letter is naturally one of grief, then anger, and in her anger Stephanie offers one of Wesker's best arguments in defense of the undervalued woman: "I've invested in you my youth, my womanhood, the secrets of my body, my fund of love, friendship, wisdom and patience, and my investments should be showing a return, damn it! I should be plucking the profits by now! But you have taken them. Run off with them. Snatched them from under my nose to share with someone else" (5: 14–15). Gradually she realizes, perhaps by way of rationalization, that she has never really loved him, and much about him annoys her: "And then he'd leap on to the bed in his altogether and start jumping up and down so's his shlong and spheroids flip-flapped about his thighs and I'd have to join him and bounce alongside of him so's my titties went flip-flap too and we made such a right old slap-smacking sound that I'm certain all the neighbors could hear. . . . He had the sensuality of a rhino stuck in mud, of a crocodile with false teeth, of a baboon full of fleas" (5: 16). Even though their match was not perfect, she remains nevertheless hurt by his rejection. She tries to travel, to go out to museums, theaters, restaurants, but she is consumed by her loneliness. Nothing satisfies her anymore.

As a result of her loneliness, her wit—once an assault weapon against her husband—becomes acrid as she turns it against herself. No longer expressing the self-protective indignation of a woman who knows her own worth, she begins to cast herself as a has-been, a woman with no future. This anger aimed inward is prompted by her trip to New York City's Barnes and Noble bookstore, where she characterizes herself as a "remainder among remainders," a book that sells below cost because there is no call for it.

Her most self-destructive revelation finally occurs at a garage sale where she compares herself to other personal belongings that people readily discard. Spotting a photo album full of pictures marking special occasions, she asks, "What kind of people throw away their relatives?" (5: 19). Sadly she recognizes herself as an object that has been used up and dumped, stripped of any future worth. Although it has a ring of truth for women, Stephanie's situation also echoes Wesker's own story—his fears of having the best parts of his writing consumed then remaindered, of being exploited by Britain's commercial trends in theater, then discarded even though his writing still has meaning and vitality. Indeed, he is writing more tightly structured and wiser plays than ever, yet few producers in major theater circles are willing to give him a chance. *Yardsale*, for example, has played in New York City, but has not been taken to full production in London. Critics, producers, and actors prefer new lovers/playwrights, perhaps for their own cheap thrill of surprise.

Four Portraits—of Mothers

Written for a Tokyo festival and a culture with fairly conservative views about gender roles, *Four Portraits—of Mothers* (1982) presents four rather conventional images of women—the single parent; the barren woman who wishes she had been a mother; the dark, brooding mother; and Wesker's version of the earth mother—each defined more in terms of the child (or absence of one) than the woman herself. It is an interesting concept, but the scenes are so short that they render only light character sketches of each person.

Instead of four different people, as Wesker intended, they could be construed as a composite of one person at four different phases in her life. There is the mother who, raising a child on her own, feels solely responsible for it, the mother who is thoroughly content with her duties, the mother who fears she has made mistakes, and the mother who is left alone in her old age as though she had born no children at all. Since these mothers all have Old Testament, or traditionally Jewish names, Wesker possibly had fragments of his mother in mind as he wrote the play.

Although the original Hebrew translation for these names seems to have little direct relevance to this play, their Jewish origins and stories resonate throughout the scenes. Ruth and her mother-in-law, Naomi, from the Book of Ruth are long-suffering widows who have to eke out their livelihood through persistent hard work, drive, and familial loyalty until Ruth is "rescued" by a man who wants to marry her. Deborah in the Book of Judges is the poet who sings verses about Jael, a courageous woman who slays a tyrant over the Jews by luring him into her tent, then driving a tent peg through his temple. And Miriam is the sister of Moses and Aaron of the Levites who is not guaranteed any claims to the wealth that is being apportioned to the men, since the laws of inheritance and property rights were decided patrilinearly, a system that effectively disenfranchised the woman's claim both materially and tribally.

In *Four Portraits* Ruth is a struggling single mother completely devoted to her child. Though she never married, she has her "divine brat," a teenage daughter she hopes will grow up to be fully independent of men. Ruth speaks freely about her daughter's father, who sounds as though he was an irresponsible mismatch for her. Her daughter, sitting offstage, is never heard or seen. At first Ruth's one-sided dialogue with her daughter runs headstrong and tough. "Yes, I know, fathers are important. But lesson number one: no one is indispensable. Lesson number two: face reality: don't succumb to it. And lesson number three: girls who cry miss planes" (5: 40). Then her thoughts turn to self-deprecating pity. After admitting she hates playing both father and mother to her daughter, she says, "Full of consolation, masculine protectiveness, and suppressed fantasies. God! I hate them! (*Pause.*) God! I need them. (*Pause.*) God! I hate myself for needing them!" (5: 40). By scene's end, Ruth has turned against herself entirely, "Who would've wanted to marry me? Plain, graceless, difficult, clever. Impossible combination for a man to accept" (5: 42). Why she believes that plain and clever women do not marry cannot be told, but we sense that she is nevertheless likely to marry, though possibly late in life, if she still believes then that marriage is important.

This slide in conversation from a flippant bravado to self-degrading and self-abusing comments is a familiar Weskerian topos used by female characters in several earlier works, including in *Yardsale* and *Love Letters*, and in later works—namely, *The Mistress* and *When God Wanted a Son*. Although in each case the woman initially defies the claim of any man to have a hold on her, she ends up wishing she had the love and security that some relationships with males can offer. Almost every woman has that double consciousness—one that acknowledges her desire for a man, and one that wishes she does not need him. Now and again she self-consciously hates herself for not being independent, but never do we see a Weskerian female who is content as a fully self-contained and inner-directed person, at home in a predominantly woman's world, satisfied with the security of sisterhood. Wesker surely knows women who do not need the intimacy of men for happiness—his own aunties could probably have provided him with these models—but such women are not to be found in his plays.

Never having married or given birth to a child, Naomi finds herself living alone and wishing for a different life. Like Ruth, the woman who could have been her daughter or daughter-in-law, she complains about her loneliness, but her lament shows more sign of bitterness and self-defeat: "My childhood was terrible, my youth was terrible, I missed a married life, which I knew some people would say was not so terrible but I'd like to have decided for myself, and here I am. No one in the middle of nowhere with no more chances. Nothing good to remember, nothing good to miss" (5: 45).

Though she is less spirited than Betty Lemon, Naomi has something of the same sharp-tongued humor and social consciousness. In this case she rails about insensitivity toward older people, especially when some euphemistically refer to them as senior citizens, "Do you call your children junior citizens? Young is young, and old is old.... Don't insult me!" (5: 47). Her type also appears as Sophie in *Menace* and as Gerda in *The Old Ones*.

Miriam is the dedicated mother who feels she has failed. We are not certain what has happened, but she tells her psychiatrist that she should have given her daughters more "space." In a moment of insight that recollects Harry in the trilogy, she blames herself that she did not "allow their father to be what he is ... didn't give him his space" (5: 50). Finally, in a moment of desperation Miriam admits to having assumed a subordinated role—an admission that very few of Wesker's women make: "My whole life is just an echo of someone else's echo whose life was an echo of someone else's echo, whose life was an echo of an echo of an echo of an echo of an echo of an echo." With hints of dissolution, even madness, Miriam embodies many mysteries of the Dark, Terrible Mother.

In contrast to the others, Deborah seems to share none of their disappointment or neuroses since she believes she has experienced a life full of joy and delight. Here is a woman who has, by choice, devoted her entire existence to her family but has no regrets about being confined by her duties; indeed, she feels entirely fulfilled in the role: "Me a prisoner? Never! Those poor men, tied to their jobs, tied to their hours, caught in a rush to a top they'll never reach in a thousand years—they're the prisoners, they're the slaves! But not me! I enjoy the freedom of my home too much!" (5: 50–51). Clearly Wesker's idealized version of Dusty Wesker, Deborah loves to shop, to organize the household, budget, plan ahead. Her pleasures lie in providing for others: "snacks in the fridge, crisp sheets on the bed once a week, different soaps, copper shining on the walls, shelves and leather dusted and smelling of pine, always a clean shirt, a fresh hot towel, a home-cooked meal" (5: 52). Although her monologue is enthusiastic and sincere, Deborah's ardor is undercut by what has been left unsaid. What would she like others to give her? Nothing? We never know.

Annie Wobbler

Like *Four Portraits, Annie Wobbler* (written in 1981) requires a solo actress who plays multiple characters. This dramatic structure allows Wesker the economy of working with a minimum of players in small venues, important to a playwright who has not been able to mount major productions. Moreover, he was able to feature at its opening one of his favorite actresses, Nichola McAuliffe, for whom the part of Anna was added in 1983. The vignettes are absorbing but undeveloped (one critic called it "doodling"), and each part is only tangentially related to the others. If these three women have anything in common, it is their sassy speech and defiance. The instrument therefore works more to feature the talents of a consummate actress or even to serve as character studies for later roles rather than offer fresh insight into the female psyche.

The title character of *Annie Wobbler* as "part-time tramp, part-time cleaning woman" is based on several personalities of singularly gingery women who lived in Wesker's childhood neighborhood in the East End. The "little master," as Annie Wobbler describes him in her monologue, reflects a bit of the way Wesker sees himself and contains a compliment to his sister: "He upsets everyone sooner or later. But they all love him! That's the funny part of it! They all love him but no one can control him. 'Cept his sister. She controls him. He listens to her. Very clever girl she is. Talks posh. . . . She's noble. She's noble but he's bonkers!" (5: 90).

Then Annie Wobbler strips her heavy, old-fashioned clothing, and she becomes the scantily clad Anna, a lusty intellectual whose salty language and heavy makeup mock the conventional behavior of her Cambridge colleagues in French. As she dresses for her date, it becomes clear that he is not her match. Too conditioned by what others might think of him, her date will not enjoy Anna, a woman who is full of herself and flaunts a "don't give a damn" attitude. Anna is another one of those rare Wesker women (like Deborah) who refuses to apologize for her behavior because she is fully satisfied with the person she has become, and we like her for it. We only wonder why she is wasting her time with this arrogant and pretentious male, even if she does enjoy dallying with his affections.

In the last moments of her preparations, Anna pulls off her dress and adds a wig to become the tweedy Annabella Wharton. Annabella is a middle-aged writer who so loathes interviews that she decides to give out conflicting impressions of herself so the articles will cancel each other out. In the first interview she pretends to be somewhat scattered and diffident; in the second she is assaultive and poised; once alone, however, she turns on herself trying to be as honest as she can. There she betrays her insecurities and her sadness about the vagaries of her profession. More than the others, Annabella is Wesker's alter ego. She concludes with an anecdote: "My father used to have a 78 record of a song called 'Ah! Sweet Mystery of Life' and he'd put it on and it would get stuck at the 'myst.' (*Gently sings it.*) 'Ah sweet myst- sweet myst- sweet myst-' And then he'd push it and you'd get to 'life.' Well, I'm a bit like that. Stuck in the 'myst'" (5: 111). Not surprisingly, Wesker recognizes something of himself in every phase of *Annie Wobbler*. Although he is unusually generous and patient with interviewers, he hates going through the motions of answering obvious and repetitive questions, and he resists peeling down to the quick for just any journalist or writer, especially since he has had to learn the art of self-protection. Perhaps because something of these characters named Anna touch the Wesker of the present, their initials match even, he sometimes takes all the parts himself in a stage reading.

The Mistress

Of all the plays in the series of one-acts about lonely and abandoned women, *The Mistress* (1988) is the most fully conceived and explored. Like *Four Portraits* and *Annie Wobbler*, this play has multiple characters played by one person, but the various facets are better integrated with the story. Like Ruth (*Four Portraits*) or Stephanie (*Yardsale*), its sole figure is a cheery, energetic, imaginative woman who nevertheless suffers rejection. But Samantha is more fully realized as a character than the others; consequently, the play has a stronger center in the theme of guilt and the "cursi" metaphor.

Samantha is a dress designer, successful enough to be the target of many charities seeking donations. She is also a politically involved and caring woman with concerns for the "Colombian Volcano Appeal . . . Gay Sweatshop Theatre Company . . . Campaign Against Censorship . . . Marie Curie Memorial Foundation . . . Survival International . . . for the rights of threatened people" (5: 70). As she pores through her mail, however, she begins to admit that she is the one who should be crying out for help. For reasons that never seem adequately explained, she has been stood up by her lover and has possibly been spurned altogether. Although she feels guilty that he is a married man and she is the other woman, she suffers knowing that she ranks second in his life.

What she desires above all is an intense and exclusive relationship—one in which she and her lover connect on a profound level. She knows such a relationship could exist by the ecstasy and the real joy she feels when she is with him, but it is never fully realized on any permanent basis. She has rejected the idea of romance, the lesser version. It is "cursi," a term taught her by her father. He always enjoyed telling about a bourgeois Venezuelan father with three daughters who unthinkingly express cheap sentiments. "Oh, look at the moon, how it moves my soul," says one and "I love music, it makes me weep," says another. "Cursi," says the father, a word that is an anagram of the town's name, Sicur. Soon many adopt his epithet. When one of the girls exclaims, "Oh, how mysterious the nights are," another townsperson replies, "Oh my God, another cursi!" It was their way of decrying "kitsch of the heart," clichés that substitute for the fully lived and emotionally significant experience (5: 69).

For Samantha, her affair is anything but "kitsch of the heart." It is "real joy, real happiness," the ferocious passion in love that is rare and fleeting, but the exhilaration of love, in this case, is not without guilt. Unfortunately, her lover's wife is her good friend—indeed, a person Samantha admires—so the guilt becomes an overwhelming obstacle to her being able to welcome her lover openly. She debates the situation with herself in the persona of her clothes dummy, Ninotchka, who says, trying to make Samantha face up to her ethical dilemma, "Let me tell you about virtue and the ease with which one is devious and expects virtue from others." When she gets no reply from Samantha, Ninotchka continues with her side of the argument, "You may never be given another chance. Virtue, betrayal, loyalty, guilt, all pale, fade, are as nothing to that ecstasy which may never come again. Imagine! To live only once and never, never taste that ecstasy! Imagine!" (5: 68). Samantha tries to deny her moral responsibility by explaining to Ninotchka that she has no ethical duty if she has no faith in God. That line of debate does not convince anyone, including herself.

In the end she is thrown back on a question that Ninotchka asks, reversing roles: how can Samantha justify her treatment of his wife when she knows how much it hurts to be abandoned? How would she be able to justify her choice to "love a man who betrays his wife"? And so at the end of the play Samantha is again reading through her mail requests for donations, and, as she considers those tragic appeals, she realizes that their possible dissolution of his marriage could be, like adversity in the Third World, another one of those "horrors that cry out for help" and she would be wrong to ignore her responsibility.

The Mistress is a little jewel among Wesker's one-act plays: it is tightly constructed, limits the emotional discourse, and interweaves theme and metaphor without a skip. Furthermore, Wesker uses a smooth blend of personal experience, particularly in the theme of rejection, and other material to produce a credible female character. He affords her the latitude to choose between perpetuating an affair in which she will always be the victim or assuming responsibility for her own happiness and perhaps even demonstrating that she cares about the well being of those around her. Although none of her choices is going to make her happy, *she* has the option of deciding about her future. The moral dilemma is all the more interesting when placed under her care. Written in 1988, *The Mistress* has undergone some changes made after rehearsals in preparation for its world premiere in a festival of one-act plays in Rome in November 1991. It was also, at the time of this writing, being considered as the book for an opera in Italy.

Lady Othello

In many ways *The Mistress* could have been the prototype for *Lady Othello* (written in 1987). Like Samantha, Rosie Swanson, a Jamaican American with Barbra Streisand–like serendipity, is about to be deserted by her pretentious lover, the redoubtable handsome professor of American literature at a British university, Stanton Myers. Nevertheless, he has flown from Britain to have one last fling before he tells her good-bye. In flight he hears his wife's voice giving him permission to make a decision about their marriage. Judith's soft submissiveness recalls the devotion and loyalty of Sonia and her anxiety of loss in *Love Letters on Blue Paper*.

In contrast to the sedate and old-fashioned marriage of *Love Letters*, however, Rosie and Stanton's relationship is lusty and electric, open, and so uninhibited that their sexually charged intimacy casts doubt on the staying power of the love they declare for one another. As Stanton's friend Julie says, "It's passion—passion lasts six months then it's over, done" (6: 207).

At the heart of the play is Wesker's contrast of two women—Stanton's wife, who is "harmless, loving, wise, playful, faithful," and his mistress, who is brassy, crude, spontaneous, sensuous, young and self-centered.

Judith is, moreover, fastidious, well-organized and self-sacrificing, while Rosie is messy, aggressively independent, and "devouring." Despite Wesker's flirtation here with some pernicious racist stereotypes about the mythical sensuality of African-American women and the selfish looseness of American women, Rosie is a more fully realized and complex person than any of the others in this series of plays about women. But Rosie is difficult for us to admire, partly because Wesker undercuts what could be intriguing female qualities by calling her Lady Othello.

Associating her with Shakespeare's Othello, partly because of her African origins, Wesker is also drawing on his dislike for the Shakespearean character's blind jealousy. In Stanton's (and Wesker's) estimation, Rosie has no right to ask about Judith and his other women. Her possessive emotionalism is strangling to him. Furthermore, her casual acceptance of everyday violence in New York City life and her volcanic moods remind him of the raging Othello, a soldier who too easily finds solutions in violence. At one point she thinks nothing of pulling a gun from under her pillow to tease Stanton. And yet the coddled and stuffy professor admires the way her streetwise toughness rescues them both during a riot.

Rosie accepts Stanton's characterization of her because she admires Othello. She defends the Moor's desire to dedicate himself utterly to Desdemona, and she praises his passion. Unmoved by Othello's "sob story" about being a slave and unimpressed by the dangers that this military officer might have faced, Stanton believes that Shakespeare made a fool of this character. He has no room for Othello's unmotivated temper tantrums and argues that any defense of him is unwarranted. Stanton is further convinced that Othello never really loved Desdemona, but since the Moor has bargained for her, he protects her as one might guard any purchase, any chattel. In short, Stanton's reference to "Lady Othello" is meant only ironically as a term of endearment, revealing an underlying fear and mistrust of Rosie's passion and rage.

In the end Stanton leaves Rosie, probably forever. The turning point for him is her jealous attack on his wife. He finds her outburst vulgar— not only because she raises a taboo subject but also because she creates a scene in public. Rosie has no chance for an appeal. The outcome of their relationship is dictated entirely by his rules. She begs him repeatedly to stay and desperately asks over and over what she will do without him. Even her roommate, Stella-Bella, pleads to him: Rosie has never before been in this state. Somehow untouched by their entreaties, Stanton tells Rosie in the end that *he* will be the one to suffer:

> I know exactly what it'll be like when I get back. *You'll* be all right but *I'll* grieve. You'll meet your friends, make your sunny jokes, pursue your degree studies, hide it all inside. Not me. I'm transparent. That's how the family knew. I came back from the seminar last time and all I did was keep playing your music. Jesus! How could they *not* know. Grieve. Sit shivah. Know what "shivah" is? After a death the Jews insist on a week in which you do nothing. Everyone who isn't family does it for you. I'll sit shivah. Grieve. (6: 257)

Perhaps because Rosie is a woman, perhaps because she is a free spirit sexually, perhaps because she is young and self-absorbed, perhaps because she has a potential for violence he cannot understand, Stanton mistakenly feels she is incapable of loving him as much as she swears she does, and so he leaves her—having rationalized his departure—with a cool detachment born of a clear conscience that she will not suffer. He may feel he has done the right thing; still, the signs point to the abandoned Rosie's being as miserable as Stephanie in *Yardsale* or Samantha in *The Mistress* in his absence.

One More Ride on the Merry-Go-Round

In *The Mistress* and *Lady Othello*, the errant husband eventually leaves his mistress to return to his wife. The male lead in *One More Ride on the Merry-Go-Round* (written and performed in 1978) is an exception to that pattern, but many of the other elements remain fairly much the same. In all three plays there is the middle-aged man who pairs off with a younger woman, usually someone in her twenties. She is unusually intelligent, employed in an interesting capacity, and alive to her body's pleasures. He has left at home a woman who is also somehow remarkable—more nurturing, more generous, more patient, more self-effacing than most women. As a result, he feels some sort of guilt and finds himself trying to choose between right behavior and his desires.

Like the male leads in *The Mistress* and *Lady Othello*, Jason is middle aged, "on the verge of fifty," and swept away by the delights of the wild and insatiable Monica, who is doing her best to make him forget his aches and pains. As though freed from imprisonment, he has quit his job as an academic and left his wife. He says he wants to travel and "go somewhere where the only pressure put upon you is to decide between orange and grapefruit juice" (6: 54), but he does not seem up to it physically. Monica likes the idea and is ready to go. Jason's academic friends, on the other hand, make every effort to dissuade him from his choice.

Jason's wife, ironically enough, seems to have found more happiness than Jason since their divorce. As an administrator of an international fundraiser for the Third World, Nita not only handles her job with brilliance and imagination but also manages a young lover with an insatiability of his own. Unlike any other woman in Wesker's plays, she claims to be pleased not to have her old mate around anymore, and unlike other women her age, she has the restored energy and verve for a new sex life. Here is one play in which the female could outshine her mate. She seems to have everything going for her—beauty, talent, self-confidence—and yet her potential is never explored in the play. *One More Ride* is more about *their* relationship than about her possibilities for new connections and new beginnings.

The reasons they have separated, however, remain unclear and unjustified. Jason claims that Nita "numbed" him because she was too "dutiful" and "silent" during sex. Nita claims that he was "a good man, even competent, but there was no—no—no urgency, no passion!" He lacked a "wild gaiety"; he never understood how to seduce her slowly, "to play games of exposure and innocence, or how to ravish her with his eyes and his tongue" (6: 40). In short, they seemed to have been working at cross purposes to each other. With a little bit of communication between them, they could well have been more compatible. In fact, Jason's description of Nita is, on balance, quite positive: he calls her "hare-brained," which he contradicts with an account of her profession, and then he brags about her plan to raise money, a concept that he judges "not dull and dowdy at all!" (6: 13). Although Nita is much less complimentary of Jason, she clearly enjoys sparring verbally with him (something she calls "besting"), and she has a better match in him intellectually—despite his desire to avoid academic life—than she has in her lover, Mat, who seems more of a convenience than a companion.

So the question remains: What does Jason really want from his divorce? Too much is left open to doubt at the end of the play. He contends that he wants freedom, but his languor belies his alleged desire to travel or entertain a young girlfriend. He has got too many health problems to keep up with her enthusiasm and plans for the future. More than anything, he seems tired of family responsibility—a lethargic and sharp-tongued daughter, a successful and competent wife, and an illegitimate son who turns up out of nowhere. Peter Hall, onetime director of Britain's National Theatre, observed that the play is "not centred"—meaning that it seems to pursue two ideas at once. Wesker understood what Hall must have meant and explained that he set out to write a comical play when two darker themes emerged—"the demise of the work ethic" and "the way in which a couple blossom into what each wants the other to be only when they have separated" (Leeming, 152).

Taken by itself, *One More Ride* does seem to drift and does seem pointless, but in the context of *Lady Othello* and *The Mistress*, it takes shape with several familiar and identifiable themes about individual responsibility. The theme of the work ethic, which Peter Hall objects to as distracting, explores the conflict between duty and the need to satisfy personal will: that is, Should one have to work or stay married out of obligation? Or should one pursue real happiness through following one's heart in work or marriage? The second theme concerning the couples who seem happier once they separate speculates about what freedom from a responsible marriage might be like in the best of circumstances. We have seen these ideas rehearsed elsewhere—in *The Mistress*, of course, but also in a large number of plays going back to *The Kitchen*. Although *One More Ride on the Merry-Go-Round* appears at first glance to be scattered in theme and a significant departure from the earlier plays, it is not. A closer look at this play and others about infidelity indicates Wesker's continued involvement in many of the same issues: How much must a person shoulder for the general good? Where does duty end and neglect begin? When should one follow one's heart at the expense of others? Jason's dilemma is yet another of Wesker's attempts to weigh individual against communal values. Would Jason have a more satisfying family life by staying with Nita and working out their problems? Or is he better off satisfying his fantasies with a new lover? Is she better off? As before, the questions about responsibility go unresolved.

Three Women Talking

In an unusual attempt to explore the subject of female friendship and women's responsibility to communal values, *Three Women Talking* (unpublished, written 1991–92) revolves around the conversation of two rejected women and one who has walked out on her husband.[3] They have come together for food, drink, and conversation—especially to excoriate their mates—and sisterly comfort. Each has brought a special wine and dish to share—Mischa has brought an hors d'oeuvres made from a recipe she collected in Lebanon, Minerva has brought a fondue made with special sauces, and Claire has brought a cake made from the recipe of a Jewish woman who was the sole survivor in her family from the gas chambers at Auschwitz.

As the evening progresses, and they eat and drink, each woman tells her story about the man who used to be a part of her life. The Jewish Mischa has left her husband, a dull suburbanite who sees no meaning in life without her. He is "faithful, loyal, dependable," but he has no zest for life, no burning desire—either for her or for something he would secretly like to do himself. Montcrieff has left his wife, Minerva, for similar reasons. Like Mischa, he wants to break away from someone who had made him the center of her life because he needs a mate who will be more his equal, and he yearns for more spice in his life. Unlike Mischa, who seems to be level-headed and rational about what she hopes to find in a future relationship, Montcrieff's reasons are muddled—something about "broody longings for immortality," something about being "wild, full of appetites and divine discontent"—and sound like an ill-defined mid-life crisis. Claire and Vincent have been having an affair, even though he is married. Now that Vincent is running for prime minister, he wants to break it off even though they have shared years of deep, loving, and spiritual moments. Claire is clearly distraught about the matter and refuses to talk about it much except to describe a trip they had taken together to a Japanese temple.

In the end all three males come together, a tricky stage maneuver since they are played by the same male actor, but it serves as a visual reminder of Minerva's observation, "Men! They're all the same! Interchangeable!" Leo, the dull husband, is on the phone to Montcrieff threatening to commit suicide. Montcrieff is in his study watching Vincent's interview with barracuda journalists on television. As it turns out, Claire has been agitated because she anticipates trouble at the end of Vincent's television interview. She has voluntarily spilled everything to the press about their affair and she knows he will surely be grilled about it. She also knows that it will destroy his chances for winning public office.

When the women discover what Claire has done, they are horrified. Minerva defends her as a woman in love; Mischa calls it treachery. In her quiet, thoughtful manner Mischa explains, "I question the nature of a love that wants to destroy because love is withdrawn." Perhaps thinking about her own choice to leave Leo, Mischa elaborates, "It is no crime to choose a new direction in life. That's everyone's right. If my new love wakes up one morning and decides to move out I will hurt to the core of my being but I *would* not, *could* not find it in me to punish him." Minerva fires back angrily that Claire was used by this selfish politician, but Mischa disagrees. Claire had benefited from his love, and besides, Minerva insists, "Love is a vow, in or out of marriage, it's a commitment.

A woman who loves surrenders herself totally, completely, utterly. It can't be treated lightly." Perhaps bitterly remembering Montcrieff's desertion of her, Minerva replies, "Used is what's left when loving stops."

Claire stops their wrangling by telling her side of the story. She is still in love with Vincent, but the man she betrayed is not that man, "The man who rejected me couldn't be the man I loved or who loved me. . . . He was somebody else. What I did, I did to somebody else. I talked to the television researchers about somebody else." She would not have hurt the man she loves, she repeats.

All the voices in *Three Women Talking* are, one way or another, Wesker arguing with himself. Here again—just as we have seen in *One More Ride on the Merry-Go-Round*, *The Mistress*, and *The Journalists*—is the conflict between honoring one's own, sometimes selfish desire against the ethical consideration of what impact these self-serving decisions might have on others. At one point in the evening Minerva reveals that she had a fling with an American physicist who explained to her the "butterfly effect." It is "the notion that a butterfly stirring the air today in Peking can transform storm systems next month in New York," even though the origin of these later storms cannot be determined. The smallest stir in the universe can have an unpredictably significant rippling effect on some other part of the universe. This use of a central metaphor to clarify human relationships is one of Wesker's favorite techniques. By analogy, he is saying that each member of these couples has had a tremendous influence on the other, and whatever they decide to do, they will continue to affect not only their mates but many others for some time to come.

Wesker stops short, however, of explicitly prescribing his values about duty and responsibility. As earlier, he does not tell us which characters are the selfish fools and what should be done to punish them. What continues to be uppermost in importance is the question, Wherein lies personal responsibility and how far must one go to meet our commitment to others? For all the mistakes these people have made in their lives, Wesker's answer is philosophical. Mouthing what might be Wesker's own thoughts on the matter, Minerva quotes some of his favorite lines about human error from Ruskin, "All things are literally better, lovelier, and more beloved for the imperfections which have been divinely appointed, that the law of human life may be effort, and the law of human judgement, mercy."

Played off against the frictions of these three couples is the issue of male/female discord and what lies at the basis of it. Wesker is not interested in assessing which gender is most to blame in these relationships.

He can assign plenty of mistakes made on both sides: the women in this play are manipulative, and the men are bullies; the women have no principles when it comes to wooing their mates, and the men are blind fools thinking that women only want "thick pricks and thick heads." Vincent says that "women seem not to want to behave as equals"; Claire says that Vincent talked about equality, talked like one who believed himself her equal. But he seemed incapable of behaving like one. Wesker does not want to arbitrate this typical list of accusations but to explore what it is that men and women fail to understand about each other: What can a woman add to a man's understanding of himself? For one, there is the process of giving birth: Montcrieff is jealous that he cannot know that experience. Second, women know about practical matters that men overlook. Minerva believes men are immature creatures who do not know reality when they see it: "They hover. Have you noticed? Men hover, like birds before a window-pane, fluttering their poor wings at reflections instead of the real world. No comprehension of what they're looking at." Leo concurs, "The real difference between men and women is that women have the perceptive powers to recognise paradise when they see it, and the emotional capacity to hang onto it. Men are never certain it's paradise they see." Montcrieff resents women's freedom and flexibility. As his analogy he uses the queen on a chess board: "She can move where she likes—diagonally, horizontally, back and forth. . . . Why do you think the queen was chosen to be aggressive, defensive and free-wheeling, while the king creeps crippled across the board one step at a time?"

Montcrieff's complaint reflects the thoughts Wesker expressed in his essay "Queen Moves to Protect King," in which he contends that "men are quintessentially moral and women quintessentially amoral" ("Aftenposten," no. 3). What he has in mind is the popularly held theory that a man generally adheres to a social code and bases his decisions on that ethical framework, but a woman reacts situationally. Her basis of action is more pragmatic, based on considerations of self-protection and the survival of her family and community. She will do what works to defend "King and family." Wesker writes with both respect and reservation: "It is for this reason women are both feared and depended upon: they will do the dirty work without shame, the man will plead guilty and keep his hands clean." Of course, his narrow understanding of women grows strictly out of his personal experiences. Although he does not speak for women with any real comprehensive understanding, he can speak for himself when he says that men are largely suspicious of what women know, and he calls on Eve's story as evidence. He swears, even so, that he enjoys the intriguing quality of women who keep him on edge by what they know: "I am more comfortable with the uncertainties induced by knowledge than the certitudes of innocence—warm though I do to the power of the metaphor of paradise lost." For all their prerogative and authority, the men in *Three Women Talking* echo Wesker's suspicion and fear that they have lost control over women for a lack of understanding. They believe that women have the keys to a fuller life—one that, for an absence of a larger wisdom, will always be denied to men. Mischa explains the mistrust between the sexes as one in which "Eve, being a woman with an instinct for the good things in life, and having more courage than her male companion, bit, and got pregnant with learning and lost paradise." Like the Jews, she says, women have been hated "for knowing too much."

Wild Spring

Even though Wesker is quite proud of the long list of roles he has written for women and the many complex issues he has raised about male/female relationships, it becomes clear that these plays are much less an exploration of women in all their possible contexts than a narrowly defined view of them as objects of desire. The women in Wesker's plays are, have been, or would like to have been someone's playmate. They are perceived almost exclusively as the condition of unfulfilled desire in the male subject and they are rarely viewed outside the male context; as such, they have become the objects of action, rather than the initiators, even when they are the sole figures on stage.

Like her predecessors, Gertrude Matthews in *Wild Spring* (1992) is surrounded by males who love her, and yet she comes closest to defining herself, to constructing a sense of who she is independent of and in opposition to those others. In act 1 this 44-year-old actress seduces a black 19-year-old car park attendant, Sam. During the course of their affair, she talks and he listens. She tries to construct a concept of herself by reminiscing about her mother and father, examining her love for her mongol son, Tom, and analyzing the source of her acting successes.

In act 2 Gertie repeats the obviously failed steps of her earlier attempt to understand herself. This time, however, it is 15 years later, she is 59, and Tom has died of leukemia. But the man she wants as her lover is a 30-year-old black man also in a position subordinate to her as the theater company manager, also someone who listens patiently. In this case, however, he is largely waiting to tell her that the company is not renewing her contract. She struggles not only to know who she is by the definitions others have supplied about her as an aging actress but to recover her self-respect.

Gertie's character is especially interesting because we see in her an honest attempt to find her voice and articulate her differentiated self; nevertheless, the development of this character has many of the markings of women in earlier monologues. She is not forward-looking or positive, she seems stuck in relationships that entrap her, and she is uncannily dependent on the males in her life. There is also something of Wesker's own person speaking through Gertie. He began writing this play at the age of 59 when he too was still struggling to survive an identity crisis and the fear that he was somehow redundant.

While Wesker's characters in these plays do little to illuminate the alienation and mistrust that *women* feel, or *their* frustrations, or *their* role in the moral community, we do gain insight into the human condition. What Wesker tells us about disillusionment and abandonment has a universal truth to it. Moreover, he is clearly fascinated by women and a bit awed by them, so he never seems to tire of exploring the battle of the sexes and their need for each other. He complained in his "London Diary for Stockholm" (1969) that no one had given him full recognition for the "emotional truth" of his characters, particularly his women, who emerge stronger and more sympathetic than his male characters (*SS*, 162). Even if he is probably correct about his women being strong, they still exist almost exclusively as extensions and reflections of his own experience. He seems incapable of giving them full rein to be themselves. In the plays of the 1970s he cloned female versions of himself, isolated and very much the rebellious victim, deliberately silenced by others and vulnerable. In later plays many of the females become an excuse for talking about the burden of moral accountability, particularly for the male who is tired of bearing up the responsibility of husband and father.

Although these topics are interesting, Wesker's agenda does little to develop women as full-bodied and active subjects in his plays, largely because they are too often governed by limited, patriarchal stereotypes of "mother, wife, mistress, devourer, survivor, victim, daughter." Too often, for example, Wesker's women are judged by their attractiveness, and the "plain, graceless, and clever women" lead unfulfilled lives. The women in these plays with unconventional family relationships similarly lack complexity, breadth, or real interest as people.

Chapter Seven
A Sense of What Should Follow

Benedict Nightengale, now theater critic for London's *Independent* newspaper, conceded in a 1986 interview with me that Arnold Wesker has rarely received the praise that he deserves in reviews. Nightengale confessed that even his own columns did not give Wesker sufficient credit for his achievements as a playwright.[1] Certainly the history of relations between London's critics and Arnold Wesker has been difficult. Almost from the start of Wesker's campaign to provide affordable drama to the working classes the press began its attack, and the London theatrical establishment took a long, skeptical look at who Wesker was and what he was trying to accomplish. Although he won friendly coverage as the voice of the "proles," he was rarely accorded full respect for his work as a serious artist, possibly because, as an uneducated, working-class playwright, reviewers only grudgingly accorded him status beyond the season's novelty. Furthermore, as a Jew, a gadfly, a didactic playwright, and an old-fashioned humanist, Wesker was clearly different from the rest of the leftist playwrights of the 1960s, so critics have always found it difficult to read his plays in some sort of context familiar to them.

Even so, with his role as a spokesperson for Centre 42, Wesker was allowed to take full advantage of the press's forum. He wrote letters to the editor, generously granted many interviews to journalists, and sent out dozens of his own articles for publication—all practices he has kept to this day. When he was a young turk with trendy and fashionable new ideas, producers welcomed his plays. Once saturated with Wesker's fervent notions about Labour and the arts, the theater world (which includes the press) quickly tired of his sometimes strident rhetoric and moved on to the next new fashion in theater, leaving him to wonder what happened. Part of Wesker's difficulty since the 1960s may have been overexposure, since his letters to the editor continue to be published, but it was largely the depth and intensity of his convictions that seemed naively idealistic that drove critics to their typewriters with a vengeance.

Initially in the 1960s he goodnaturedly took knocks against Centre 42 by paying them back in kind. He would chastise critics and scold opponents, then he would take up the banner again to push for more reform. When their attacks persisted, however, particularly in reviews about his plays in the early 1970s, at a time when he was feeling most defeated, he began to reply more angrily. What concerned him was that many critics reviewed these plays not on the work's merit but on other, more personal considerations. In some instances his intuition was accurate, but the antipathy that Wesker sensed was also of his own making.

In the early 1970s he published a series of articles beginning with "Casual Condemnations" in *Theatre Quarterly* in which he attacked John Russell Taylor and Ronald Bryden, even though Bryden had been particularly kind to him in earlier reviews. Wesker had grown tired of "spit and run" journalism. He was battle weary from the collapse of Centre 42 and the setback of a lukewarm response to *Their Very Own and Golden City*. Mostly Wesker was protesting reviews of *The Friends*, but he lumped Taylor and Bryden with other reviewers that he had not been able to forget: a snide article by T. C. Worsley that ridiculed "prole" playwrights, McGrath's *Black Dwarf* review of *The Friends*, and Penelope Gilliatt's review of *The Four Seasons*. His complaints are numerous, many of them justified. In "Casual Condemnations" he protested "making the playwright victim of private hates and thus distorting meaning, sacrificing fact to feeble humour; disarming through self-abasement; criticizing on the basis of misquotation; boldly stating opinions without attempting to substantiate them; and failure to listen to the play" (*Distinctions*, 292). In some of his grievances—distortion of meaning, misquotations, and failure to listen to the play—Wesker was quite right to be angry. He has produced a litany of evidence that these critics misquoted and misread sections of his plays after forming false assumptions about the plays even before they had viewed them. He was able to document many examples of this sort of sloppy writing and could have cited many more examples if he had had the space. Reviewers under deadline often take a cursory glance at a play and sometimes do not even sit through to its end before they begin writing their columns. And yet it is on these careless viewings that a playwright's future can be determined. Word-of-mouth praise cannot outweigh a bad review in London or New York, especially when the columnist is well known. To counter the possibility of being misunderstood, Wesker has tried sending the script to reviewers to read before they attend a performance to avoid "misreadings," but few critics have been interested in reading a new play before they see it.

Wesker has also decried the press's "casual condemnations," their "Lilliputian" efforts "to bring down giants" as soon as their success is apparent.[2] He allowed them their foibles if their motivation did not appear malicious or self-serving. He made this point repeatedly: "The argument is *not*, repeat *not* about criticism versus praise; it is about the superficiality of peevish, journalistic comment which has the power to fold or encourage a certain category of play, and which too frequently appears instead of an authoritative comment contributing to the understanding of a writer's work" (*Distinctions* 348). He had the least patience with the sneering tone that is written primarily to get a snicker. In this series of articles, which were reprinted in *Distinctions*, the fed-up Wesker struck back with a vengeance of his own. He told his "Cretinue of Critics" that they do not set the aesthetic standards, the artist does. Moreover, he chided the powerful critic of the *Sunday Times*, Harold Hobson, for his "patronizing flattery so transparent as to be sickening."

Wesker recognized a vicious streak among certain reviewers who prided themselves in witty put-downs and self-consciously clever sarcasm. One unsigned *Times* review had this reaction to *Roots*, for example: "Amid a lot of sentimentalizing about the value of family ties, the importance of keeping close contact with our origins, and the awful consequences of a rootless society, in bursts Mr. Wesker to point out the unpopular (but surely undeniable?) truth that many people lead brainless, pointless, ignoble lives, and that if these are our roots, the sooner we sever all connexion the better" (1 July 1959). Bound by convention and seduced by the need to show off their "pyrotechnic insults" (Wesker's term), too many critics seem to be straining to produce glitzy copy. To that point he accused John Russell Taylor of a "carping style" and concluded with a choice of words that demonstrates he was nigh choking with anger: "But the awful truth is that this wretched noise of sour and done-for complaint cancerously permeates most of journalism's jaundiced review columns, unctuously assuming it has the public's confidence, talking to it as though on intimate terms" (*Distinctions*, 336).

With many of these charges Wesker justified his outrage. Most of the reviewers he named in this series of articles were indeed guilty of cheap shots in the name of wit and superiority. In some cases, however—instances where the critic has stated his opinion without substantiating it—Wesker has since learned to accept that these are reviews and not scholarly papers and so critics enjoy the prerogative of saying what they think without producing evidence for every expressed opinion.

Although Wesker has put his finger on crucial problems with the critics, he has not made sufficient allowance for the integrity of their individual tastes or personal construction. In "Unhappy Poisons," for instance, Wesker took John Russell Taylor to task for saying, "In all his plays there is this feeling that the characters are not there as people, with an independent existence of their own, constantly struggling to be free of the pattern the playwrights wants to fit them into, but as mouthpieces, spokesmen for various attitudes and points of view" (*Distinctions*, 337). Taylor's criticism is justified, and Wesker should have granted him his reasoned response.

Benedict Nightengale reflected some of his own discomfort in a *New Statesman* review of *The Friends*: "One has to admire Wesker, for his crusading passion, his contempt for petty-mindedness and his determination to embarrass us out of it. Men ridicule him but he doesn't wither. He returns and returns, to blast his playwright's trumpet in our wilderness. Anyone who resists him, as I find myself doing, would do well to admit that he does so for largely despicable reasons. And yet . . ." (Nightengale, 780). Nightengale's hesitation with his "and yet . . ." is followed by "and yet *The Friends* . . . isn't a very good play." Certainly *The Friends* and *The Four Seasons* have elicited more comments like this than any other Wesker plays. Reviewers like Nightengale squirmed with lines such as "I have a golden eagle for a lover" (*The Four Seasons*) and "When Esther suffers pain so will I, that's how I'll know—it'll come to me also; that's what being an aesthete means" (*The Friends*). What makes Nightengale uncomfortable is the heavy pathos and pretentiousness in those lines—too rhapsodic, too swollen for an Englishman's tastes. Unfortunately, Wesker could not grant the legitimacy of Nightengale's personal reactions.

Wesker's retort to reviewers who, like Nightengale, cannot stomach sappiness is Manfred's speech from *The Friends*: "I despise the Englishman. His beliefs embarrass him. . . . Belief demands passion and passion exposes him so he believes in nothing. He's not afraid of action. Action, battles, defeats—they're easy for him. No, it's ridicule. Passion invites ridicule. . . . Listen to an Englishman talk, there's no real sweetness there, is there? No simplicity, only sneers" (3: 97). Well aware of an element of truth in Manfred's speech, Nightengale was self-conscious about his distaste for the play, and yet he still could not praise what he did not enjoy. Wesker's attack on Englishmen, a statement that reflects his own sensitivity about the British culture, lacks forbearance. It was gestures like that that made some in the West End wonder why Wesker was committing this sort of professional suicide.

Are the reviewer's objections ever valid? Reluctantly Wesker will concede a critic's right, even responsibility, to point out structural weaknesses or other such problems in a given play, and he is appreciative when the criticism is constructive. He also acknowledges, to some extent, the influences of history and cultural bias on the viewer. Wesker recognizes that each age holds its own paradigms for religious, political, and scientific theory, and these influence the way audiences, directors, and actors understand and respond to a given text over time, so theater classics have inevitably been subjected to a variety of innovative interpretations with each new era "whether the play *demands* a fresh view or not, *that* is what must inevitably happen, like it or not."[3] He is loath to concede, however, that multiple responses inevitably arise out of *every* audience and that these many reactions are a legitimate and natural part of the process. John McGrath's review of *The Friends*, for example, however hurtful it might have been to Wesker, was meant more as a statement about his own political position and philosophical approach to play production than an explication of Wesker's play.

Although he does not deny that drama is open to many possible interpretations, Wesker will not accept the theory that meaning is always individually constructed and largely conferred on a work of art by the viewer rather than extracted from it. He would prefer to believe that there is one and only one true interpretation to a piece. Holding to the one right answer to the question, "What is this play about?" Wesker cavils as though variant readings were willful departures from the author's intent—departures that obstinately ignore *the* meaning of the text. The author's intended meaning emerges more strongly than any other construction, as far as Wesker is concerned, so that any separation in approach between the author and reader/viewer is obvious and must be conscientiously delineated by the reader. Overriding the author's message has to be an intentional and deliberate attempt on the reader or viewer's part to subvert the text to one's own purposes (*Journalists*, 11).

"Interpretation—to Impose or Explain"

Wesker discusses the personal imprint that directors and actors bring to a play's text in "Interpretation—to Impose or Explain." Here he differentiates between a director's *comprehension* of a play, in which some attempt is made to understand the work at a most basic level of authorial "meaning and intention," and *interpretation*, which should mean "to render clear, to elucidate, to explain" but more often amounts to an imposition of the director's own meaning. Suggesting that individualized readings are either the result of poor comprehension or stubborn attempts to assert one's own viewpoint, Wesker concludes, "In short, there do not exist different interpretations of meaning, there only exist different levels of talent and intelligence attempting to comprehend meaning." He therefore believes that an alternative understanding of the work—particularly if it is a director's "concept" that will shape the entire production—should be saved for presenting some other play, one that better reflects that peculiar viewpoint. Wesker believes that a reader, director, or critic who has a different idea should withhold discussing it out of deference to the art form and the author's intentions. Nightengale regards many of Wesker's objections to reviewers as "contempt for the practical realities of sublunary existence" and fears that he is "too uncompromising for everyday life on an everyday planet."[4] That may be the case. Certainly honest, unmalicious misprision has been widely accepted as legitimate in the profession—indeed, it is the stuff that drives the entire literary industry.

Because the playwright must depend on intermediaries like directors, actors, academics, and theater reviewers to address audiences, Wesker devotes a great deal of energy to their handling of his plays. They are the only access the public has to his unknown works, so their role compared with the playwright's is greatly exaggerated. He has complained about actors and academics from time to time, but he especially chafes at the elevated power that some directors have assumed while mounting plays: "The playwright's vision of the human condition has become secondary to the director's bombastic striving for personal impact; his text, his visual concepts, his rhythmic arrangement of scenes, his emotional tensions, his perceptions of human behavior, his unfolding of narrative action are cut, re-arranged, distorted, or ignored by the director and sometimes by the actors" ("Interpretation," 63).

Although actors and directors have rights to their own—and possibly more interesting—perceptions, Wesker believes their first obligation is to represent the playwright's conceptions rather than build their reputations by distorting what has been written. But "little humility exists among the interpreters," laments Wesker. "So extreme is this development that directors are refusing to direct plays which are tightly constructed, leaving no room for them to impose their concepts" ("Interpretation," 66). He recognizes, of course, that the world's greatest directors are those who have taken possession of the original script. He also concedes that some directors like John Dexter have been good for his work; he even dedicated *Chips* to Dexter for helping him "understand the theatre of [his] plays" and for directing them "when most others said they would fail" (3: 10). Still, he fumes when he recalls Dexter's tyranny as a director, and he continues to resent any director who has undue influence over the outcome of the production, especially on new plays that rely on the director's insights to interpret them for the public.

Wesker most resents the director who too often receives credit without having to risk the terror and humiliation that comes with the artistic creation. Wesker explains what insulates the director: "You do not know anything about his private life, his fears or self-doubts, you do not know the quality of his thought, the poetic power of his perceptions. He has not committed or risked his ambivalence, his uncertainties, he has not articulated views which go against the cant in vogue, you do not know in detail what he thinks about sex, politics, human beings in the way you know what a writer thinks and feels after he has written a play" ("Interpretation," 64). The director should respect the author's vulnerability. If the playwright is the only one in the process who must expose raw and intimate emotion as well as the darkest side of the imagination (since all great art is in some way confessional), then no one else should take the liberties to exploit the material. Wesker feels much the same about actors who have little to risk in a failed production: "If every living dramatist stopped writing plays for the next fifty years the work of director and actor could continue. Damn their efforts over one play and they move on to another; for them there are many houses after the storm. For an author the house must be built again, and his raw materials are not so easily come by as those of the actor and director" (*Distinctions*, 349).

The danger of such authorial attacks on the theater industry, of course, is that they emphasize Wesker's ongoing marginality and hold him hostage as an outsider. Like Salman Rushdie, a writer with whom Wesker is empathic because Rushdie too has been imprisoned for his candor—Wesker remains quarantined by London's theater circles. Insulting the director's power runs the risk that the rights to new plays might not be purchased and the works ignored. Even the possibility that he might direct his own plays seems remote since he encounters similar resistance from London's producers when that is proposed. He would like to direct more of his own productions, but few venues trust authors to be "objective" about their works, even when playwrights like Wesker have learned a great deal over the years about directing. Either way—by being forced to withhold opinions or by assailing directors and foregoing future opportunity—playwrights have become silenced by an industry that treats its artists as expendable.

The Journalists

Wesker first used the sobriquet "Lilliputianism" in the early 1970s to refer to the journalist mentality that seemed to him bent on trivializing or destroying others through witty scorn. To prove his point, Wesker spent six weeks observing the activities of the *Sunday Times*, and out of a journal kept during that time he wrote the play *The Journalists* in 1971.

By Wesker's own account, the play is not about journalism but "the poisonous human need to cut better men down to our size," so it becomes his definitive response to the hazards of being the topic of media coverage (*Journalists*, 11–12). Like Jonathan Swift, Wesker assails petty, small-minded people who turn their limited power more toward getting even with others "to indulge resentments or pay off private scores than to arrive at real justice" (*Journalists*, 12).

At the heart of the play is the journalist Mary, whose self-righteous outrage takes her after two stories—one about a female gynecologist who has refused on moral grounds a young patient seeking an abortion and one about a terrorist gang who work their underground tactics through a highly placed government official. With the instincts of a stalker, Mary pushes her team of reporters to expose the gynecologist's private life, "I want this woman hung, drawn and quartered" (*Journalists*, 104). She drops that story, however, to pursue an inside contact with the Angry Brigade, youngsters caught up in ideological warfare, robbing supermarkets, and planning bombings. Mary returns triumphantly to the *Times* with her story on the extremists, but it is killed by her editor, Harry, who has discovered at the last minute, without Mary's knowing it, that Mary's own children are among the terrorists. This story eerily foreshadows parts of the Patty Hearst story that broke three years after Wesker wrote *The Journalists*.[5]

Mary is the most dangerous sort of reporter because she "possesses [herself] of a fantasy and lures the truth towards it" (*Journalists*, 133). Making up her mind about the gynecologist or the terrorist long before she has garnered the facts, she practically has the story written before the interview. She decides peremptorily to diminish the stature of a new, popular socialist M.P., "Well, *I'm* not intimidated by working-class haloes—the pain of poverty has never blinded me to its product of ignorance, and underprivilege was never a guarantee against charlatanism and *that's* the function of journalism—to protect society from shabby little charlatans like him" (*Journalists*, 48). In the play Wesker is less concerned about the fact that Mary might be right about some of her judgments—like those about the gynecologist or the terrorists—than he is about her assuming "the self-righteous responsibility of interfering to protect society against others" based on her own possibly mistaken judgment (*Journalists*, 285). She not only chooses her stories by the opportunities that allow her to "name the guilty" but shapes her findings as though they speak the whole truth. Without hesitation she assumes that she is in possession of the truth with fact, even though facts are almost always selective and in need of interpretation and even though the process may be compromised by human fallibility. Ironically, as a playwright Wesker has also been accused of selecting journalists as a topic so that he too could "name the guilty" and use them to vent his spleen about critics. He insists, however, that he begins with events and characters and builds his plays out of their experiences.

As Wesker sees it, if they are not fractiously tearing after adversaries, the press corps generally treat their subject matter with fashionable condescension and detachment. What Wesker wants in the profession is some sense of humanity in the reporting, but what he finds are reporters who either remain so detached from the news that they write in absence of principle or commitment or human concern, or they are so blinded by their own ambition that they use ideology as an excuse to exploit others for their own gain. It is difficult to say which among them Wesker despises the most—those who are witty, fast talking, clever, and seemingly unreflective, or those who become self-important and pompous with their own sense of mission. Because they are often able to remain detached from the tragedies they witness, he wonders if their wit could possibly be a "safety valve against the world's horrors or against suspicions of their impotence to do anything about them" (*Journalists*, 199). But he cannot tell what they actually feel since reporters seem suspicious of all the information they gather and believe little of it. Furthermore, earnest reporters invite mockery from their peers; the most seasoned among them mask whatever feelings they might have. Stripped of caring for their subjects, they are left with little more than cynical arrogance and a fascination for novelty.

Countering the jadedness of the media machine are a few journalists with integrity. There is Harvey, the editor who tries to maintain some perspective by warning Mary against vindictiveness, "because each 'god' you topple chips away at your own self-respect" (*Journalists*, 121). And there are several journalists who express some self-doubts about their profession. Even Mary has her moments of hesitation when she stops to realize that she is paying a price with her children and herself when she behaves so aggressively. A particularly poignant scene is one in which she tries to justify her career to her children as someone who, in trying to "create order out of chaos," has acted out of a deeply human impulse more than a bourgeois need for luxury. In Mary's speeches we also get some sense of a person who is conscious of toppling a few giants and feels conflicted by it. Although her profession demands it, she would rather not be in that position.

The sets for *The Journalists*, as Wesker has imagined them, are stacked boxes that form a cutaway view of the offices' interiors. Action is suggested by the shifts in focus from box to box, each representing activity in one of the newspaper's eight departments—In Depth, Business, Political, Women's Page, Sports, Foreign Department, Arts Pages, Editor's Office. Action outside the offices takes place on a raised platform center stage that may be retracted when not in use. Even while the focus is on one of the newspaper's departments, activity continues in all the others with the background din of machines, telephones, and conversation. Like *The Kitchen*, the pace of these scenes speeds up as the deadline approaches for putting the *Sunday Times* to bed and the subtheme tells us that these people are exploited as much as they exploit others' tragedies.

For all its topicality and originality of form, this play has been performed only in a community theater in Great Britain. It was slated for production in 1972 by the Royal Shakespeare Company, but then one of the oddest events in theater history occurred: the actors revolted and refused the script. Their reasons are still not clear. Wesker eventually sued the Royal Shakespeare Company, winning the paltry settlement of £4,250 in 1980 to compensate a £25,000 loss of royalties and £2,400 in legal fees, but he continues to question what happened in those years that locked him out of London's best-known theaters. Particularly difficult to swallow was the fact that Howard Brenton and David Hare opened *Pravda: A Fleet Street Comedy* in 1985 on the same subject. They generously credit Wesker with some of their ideas.

One of the most important contributions of *The Journalists* are the notes that Wesker kept during his writing of the play because of the valuable insider's view they give us into the creative processes of one playwright. Wesker produced the first draft in two weeks. He then spent the better part of the next four or five months revising it. He generally composes in long hand (even now that he has a word processor) because it allows him time to select the language carefully. Once the play is written down, he divides it into acts and, in the case of *The Journalists*, into parts.

The tedious and careful work comes with the balance of speeches within the scenes. Wesker adds new sections with some care about mood and emotional impact, but more than anything else he is listening for rhythm—the textures of the speeches, the music of the language, and the pacing. Months later, when he is still tinkering with the wording here and there, it is the rhythm that continues to weigh most heavily on him, so much so that the central theme is sometimes compromised by attention to it. Wesker retains the right to continue revising all of his plays whenever new ideas strike him, but he makes most of the changes during the play's first run. The most likely time for these revisions is during rehearsals of a new and untried play when he is readily open to actors' and directors' suggestions for changes. He listens carefully, evaluates their reasons, and will often have a new scene or speech ready for the next day's rehearsal.

Curiously enough, Wesker spends less time in anguish over character and plot. Ideas for the characters come to him long before he writes the plays. He will build a play around a character like Mary, taking into account her context within the play—the internal logic of her lines, the extent of her exposure, and her contributions to the theme. Plot concerns Wesker least of all, as he pointed out to Harold Hobson in "A Cretinue of Critics": "*Drama* not *plot* is essential to the theatre, and drama can be achieved by other methods of unfolding or slow revelation. There's nothing wrong with story telling but there is no rule which says every play must tell a story" (*Distinctions*, 343).

If pinned down, Wesker would have to say that the play's message is foremost among its elements, but he denies that he begins writing with the message in mind. It only emerges after he returns to the play with an analysis (*Distinctions*, 315). Ethically and philosophically committed to his ideas, he seems constitutionally incapable of writing something trivial just to get a hit. Although he would love to write that one work that sets him up financially for life, he cannot pander to audience tastes. He also takes risks structurally and thematically, refusing to go back over old territory when exploring ideas.

The Fixer

These plays are anything but an intellectual exercise for Wesker. He implicates and inscribes himself in every line. His forcefulness implies a certain amount of egotism, certainly, but it also indicates a profoundly committed writer. As a "fixer" he is compelled to do that which is just and right. Wesker uses his writing as his means for acting responsibly.

For this reason he defends the arts, especially playwriting, as a last resort to set things right by undermining injustices. Language is naturally vital to that mission—as a vehicle for being an adversary of ignorance and indifference, as a voice for life against tyranny and dehumanization, as a way to draw distinctions between creative solutions and destructive behavior. Freedom of speech is therefore so important to Wesker that he is willing to suffer anyone who wants to "mock and utter racist and genderist or any other 'ist' views that they like," because "to intimidate people into not expressing such views simply pushes them underground," and to silence them "relieves us of the responsibility for countering such views. It is easier to gag people than to educate them."[6]

As a committed social critic, Wesker launches missiles on anyone who would bully others into silence and pressures of all kinds that are placed on artists to conform to mainstream opinion. His remedy against the mean-spiritedness of lilliputians, credit-grabbers, and necrophiliacs (directors who "practice strange, often unnatural acts [upon the works of dead artists], without fear of protest") lies in the force of his writings.[7] He not only sallies out in raids on the enemy, but he does so in defense of the paralyzed, the marginalized, the abandoned.

At the center of Wesker's works is the primacy of the human being—flawed, warding off the twin evils of depression and chaos, disillusioned by inevitable failure, and every bit the individual. That individual—precious, because created in God's image—must have the right to speak out, to launch an assault on all authority (even God), and to be ideologically opposed to everyone else if necessary. No group of people—terrorists inside or outside institutions—should be allowed to remove the basic rights of that individual through intimidation or silencing. Wesker listed what is fundamental to him in a 1975 essay:

> Priorities based on values that have a long-fought-for and treasured history: socialist, humanist values founded in a society where the means of production are owned in common; where all men earn their living; where privacy and independence are respected in the form of each man's owning his own home; where every man is permitted his imperfection, since that is the nature of humanity; and where material possessions have their value measured by usefulness, personal association, and the individual's estimation of their beauty. Values based on a love and respect for and belief in art and knowledge.[8]

Being a "fixer," Wesker works to protect human freedom and dignity and to promote a life worth living. And although he identifies with many of the goals of socialism, he willingly subordinates his socialist principles of solidarity and communal cooperation to defend the rights of the individual if that person must necessarily choose between ideological coercion and personal conscience. In Wesker's estimation, no political or religious cause—not even Judaism or socialism—is worth the sacrifice of individual liberty.

Of course, choices are rarely that clear. Often the individual is a spoiler who would rather dismantle than preserve and reshape in some principled way. Above all, Wesker is concerned with the difference between destroyers who bring absolute ruin and revolutionaries who more constructively imagine inventions and establish institutions for human use that may displace the useless. Many of his plays thus ask again and again what it is to act ethically, to tend to ourselves and to fix the world without one act canceling the other. The possibility of failing to achieve both goals haunts him. As he points out, his plays are "filled with people who are victims of [making a mistake] and even doomed by it."[9]

Mistakes are tragic, but their effects are usually not irreversible. Offsetting selfish acts are children in racist neighborhoods welcoming the strangers, a mother who cares about others, even those who are not her children, and a beleaguered woman whose courage is indomitable. As Heiner O. Zimmermann has observed, the "conclusions of his plays . . . try to resolve the contradiction between failure and belief in an endeavor which acknowledges that the ideal is impossible to attain and yet, in spite of all, must not be abandoned" (Zimmermann, 192). Sometimes the solution, as weak as it may seem, is that merely attempting to achieve the ideal must be enough. Although his characters, like Wesker himself, never fully realize their dreams, they rarely yield to utter despair. The discrepancy between hopeful intentions of the first act and the reality of the final act engenders Wesker's "melancholy optimism" for human relationships (*Distinctions*, xiv).

As long as the potential for driving back the darkness is implied in the human spirit, these efforts are not so quixotic as it may seem. Wesker recognizes unfortunate absurdity in the act of drawing up architectural blueprints for golden cities, but, like Manny (*Old Ones*), his personal formula for survival rests on the attempt to imagine a better world; he no longer expects to achieve it. He wrote in a letter to critic Benedict Nightengale, "My plays are about people who, animated by ideas, allow those ideas to shape their lives—and fail. . . . They fail, make horrendous mistakes, are betrayed, grow to dislike themselves, grow old, face death and yet, it always amazes me, they go on, and often with grace. That has to be borne witness to."[10] Wesker has also had his own mistakes in mind—blunders that he has learned to accept with dignity as he grows older. Nigella Lawson of the *Sunday Times* points out that, for all Wesker's disappointments in himself and others, he is surprisingly not bitter: "His mood is not one of anger, but plangent obduracy." Unlike the Angry Young Man of the 1960s and the scrapper of the 1970s, Wesker is indeed more philosophical these days, a living spokesman for his "melancholy optimism." He told Lawson, "When you write you have, within you, two things: fear that you may be really mediocre and a kind of glow of confidence that what you've written has a value which will last. That glow kind of sustains me and shadows the despair."[11]

Notes and References

Chapter One

1. John Osborne, *Look Back in Anger* (1957; rpt., New York: Bantam Books, 1971), 2; hereafter cited in text.
2. *Political Writings of William Morris*, ed. A. L. Morton (New York: International Publishers, 1973); hereafter cited in text.
3. "The Modern Playwright, or 'O, Mother, is it worth it?,'" in *Fears of Fragmentation* (London: Jonathan Cape, 1970), 15–16; hereafter cited in the text as *FF*.
4. Interview with Anthony Clare, *In the Psychiatrist's Chair* (London: Hogarth Press, 1984), 53; hereafter cited in text.
5. John McGrath, "Friends and Enemies," *Black Dwarf*, 12 June 1970, 15; hereafter cited in text.
6. Catherine Itzin, *Stages in the Revolution: Political Theatre in Britain since 1968* (London: Eyre Methuen, 1980), xiv; hereafter cited in text.
7. TVS (Television South) interview with Richard Hoggart, "Writers on Writing," 7 March 1986; hereafter cited in text. Wesker made a similar observation to me in a 2 May 1985 interview at his home in London.
8. Much of the information from this section came from letters of 21 March 1990 to me from June Lewis and Arnold Wesker. Pieces of information were also added from Wesker's "Miniautobiography in Three Acts and a Prologue," *Contemporary Authors Autobiography Series* (Detroit: Gale Publishing, 1987), 7: 227–63.
9. "A Time of Dying: A Sort of Story," *Jewish Quarterly* 21 (1977–78): 134–43. This story was later reprinted as "A Time of Dying" in *Love Letters on Blue Paper* (New York: Harper & Row, 1975), 45–66. *Love Letters on Blue Paper* is hereafter cited in text as *LL*.
10. Letter to the author, 21 March 1990.
11. Much of the biographical information in this chapter is drawn from *Wesker on File*, comp. Glenda Leeming (London: Methuen, 1985); *Theatre Quarterly*'s *Theatrefacts* no. 14 (2 November 1977), ed. Rita Julian and Simon Trussler; and Wesker's letters to me.
12. Lloyd P. Gartner, *The Jewish Immigrant in England, 1870–1914* (Detroit: Wayne State University Press, 1960), 15–56.
13. James Parkes, "The History of the Anglo-Jewish Community," *A Minority in Britain: Social Studies of the Anglo-Jewish Community*, ed. Maurice Freedman (London: Vallentine, Mitchell & Co., 1955), 46.
14. Geoffrey Alderman, *The Jewish Community in British Politics* (Oxford: Clarendon Press, 1983), 118.

15. Alan Palmer, *The East End: Four Centuries of London Life* (London: John Murray, 1989), 134–35.
16. *Caritas* (London: Jonathan Cape, 1981), 58; hereafter cited in text.
17. "State-right Freedom, Birth-right Freedom," in *Distinctions* (London: Jonathan Cape, 1985), 223. *Distinctions* is hereafter cited in text.
18. C. W. E. Bigsby, "The Language of Crisis in British Theatre," in *Contemporary English Drama* (New York: Holmes & Meier, 1981), 20.
19. "The Visit," in *Said the Old Man to the Young Man* (London: Jonathan Cape, 1978), 178. *Said the Old Man* is hereafter cited in text as *SOM*.
20. Public relations leaflet published by Book Trust in conjunction with the British Council, 1988; hereafter cited in text as "British Council."
21. John Florance, "Arnold Wesker—the Radical Humanist," playbill, world premiere of *One More Ride on the Merry-Go-Round* at Phoenix Arts, Leicester, England, 25 April to 25 May 1985.
22. Michael Anderson, "Arnold Wesker: The Last Humanist," *New Theater Magazine* 3 (1968): 10–27.
23. Letter to the author, 23 August 1989.

Chapter Two

1. Ronald Hayman, *Contemporary Playwrights: Arnold Wesker* (London: Heinemann, 1970), 9; hereafter cited in text.
2. Emile Zola, *Oeuvres complètes* (Paris: 1927–31), 41: 95, as cited in Marvin Carlson's *Theories of the Theatre: A Historical and Critical Survey, from Greeks to the Present* (Ithaca, N.Y.: Cornell University Press, 1984), 274–75.
3. Eric Bentley, ed., *The Theory of the Modern Stage: An Introduction to Modern Theatre and Drama* (London: Penguin, 1968), 370.
4. Collected works in seven volumes (London: Penguin, 1990), 2: 9. Works hereafter cited in text by volume and page number.
5. Kenneth Tynan, review of *The Kitchen, Observer*, 2 July 1961.
6. Interview with the author, 2 May 1985.
7. "A Miniautobiography in Three Acts and a Prologue," 7: 249; hereafter cited in text as "Miniautobiography."
8. This passage marks one of Wesker's many additions and revisions to the plays for the Penguin edition.
9. Interview with C. W. E. Bigsby, sponsored by the British Council in association with Departments of English at British universities, 1977, and taped by the BBC on 4 March 1976 in Arnold Wesker's home in North London.
10. "London Diary for Stockholm," in *Six Sundays in January* (London: Jonathan Cape, 1971), 155. *Six Sundays in January* is hereafter cited in text as *SS*.
11. Kenneth Tynan, review of *Roots* (1960), in *A View of the English Stage* (London: Davis Poynter, 1975), 294–95; hereafter cited in text.
12. John Cunningham, "Arts: Wesker's Way with Women," *Guardian*, 15 June 1990, 35.

13. Harold U. Ribalow, *Arnold Wesker* (New York: Twayne, 1965), 53; hereafter cited in text.
14. John Russell Taylor, *The Angry Theatre: New British Drama*, rev. ed. (New York: Hill & Wang, 1969), 159.
15. Interview with Ronald Hayman, "Arnold Wesker and John Dexter," *Transatlantic Review* 48 (Winter 1973–74): 90-91.
16. Michael Leech, "John Dexter," *Plays and Players*, October 1972, 31–33.
17. "The Playwright as Director," *Plays and Players*, February 1974, 12.

Chapter Three

1. Clive Barker, "All at Sea," unpublished manuscript, 7.
2. Arnold Wesker and Bill Holdsworth, "The Modern Playwright, or 'O, Mother, is it worth it?'" and "Labour and the Arts: II, or 'What, then, is to be done?'" (London: Gemini, 1960). These two pieces were published together with the letters Wesker and Holdsworth wrote to the trade unions as one pamphlet. "The Modern Playwright" was later reprinted without "Labour and the Arts" and the letters as the first chapter of *Fears of Fragmentation*, Wesker's collection of articles about Centre 42.
3. Frank Stanley, "Centre 42," *Marxism Today*, March 1963, 77.
4. Frank Coppieters, "Arnold Wesker's Centre Forty-two: A Cultural Revolution Betrayed," *Theatre Quarterly* 18 (June–August 1975): 45. Much of this section on the history of Centre 42 is based on Coppieters's thorough and perspicacious research.
5. "Let Battle Commence," in *The Encore Reader: A Chronicle of the New Drama*, ed. Charles Marowitz, Tom Milne, and Owen Hale (London: Methuen, 1965), 96–103. This collection was later reprinted as *New Theatre Voices of the Fifties and Sixties: Selections from Encore Magazine, 1956–1963* (London: Methuen, 1981).
6. "From a Writer's Notebook," *Theatre Quarterly*, 6 (May–June 1972), 9; hereafter cited in text as "Notebook."
7. "Arnold Wesker on 42," *Observer*, Weekend Edition, 7 July 1963.
8. "Tarnished and Confused Manners," *Encounter*, November 1966; reprinted in *FF*, 63–81.
9. John Elsom, *Post-war British Theatre*, rev. ed. (London: Routledge & Kegan Paul, 1939), 137.
10. *The Nottingham Captain—A Moral for Narrator, Voices, and Orchestra*, in *SS*, 99–140.
11. Glenda Leeming, *Wesker: The Playwright* (London: Eyre Methuen, 1983), 154; hereafter cited in text.
12. "Art Is Not Enough," *Twentieth Century*, February 1961, 194.
13. Irving Wardle, *Observer*, as quoted in *Wesker on File*, 24.
14. Simon Trussler and Charles Marowitz, *Theatre at Work: Modern British Theatre* (New York: Hill & Wang, 1957), 91–92; hereafter cited in text. This article also appeared in *Tulane Drama Review* 11 (1966): 192–201.

15. Clive Barker, letter to Arnold Wesker, 6 May 1969.
16. Wesker to John McGrath, 4 October 1970.
17. Clive Barker, fundraising letter for Centre 42, 30 August 1961.
18. Andy Lavender, "Theatre in Crisis: Conference Report," *New Theatre Quarterly* 19 (August 1989): 210–16.

Chapter Four

1. From an unpublished collection of essays Wesker calls "Aftenposten," no. 4.
2. Gary O'Connor, "Arnold Wesker's *The Friends*," *Theatre Quarterly* 1 (April–June 1971): 78–92.
3. Leeming, *The Playwright*, 93. Leeming was quoting from the *Sunday Times*, Weekly Review, 30 August 1981.
4. Nigel Lewis, "Play Rights," *Guardian*, 18 June 1974, 12.
5. Margaret Drabble, "Profile 10: Arnold Wesker," *New Review* 1 (February 1975): 29.
6. Giles Gordon, "Arnold Wesker," *Transatlantic Review* 21 (Summer 1966): 17.
7. "The System and the Writer," *New Theatre Magazine* 9 (February 1971): 10.
8. Unpublished manuscript of *Beorhtel's Hill*. First performed 8 June 1989.
9. Michael Coveney, review of *Beorhtel's Hill* at the Towngate Theatre, Basildon, *Financial Times*, 9 June 1989.
10. Heinz Zimmermann, "Wesker and Utopia in the Sixties," *Modern Drama* 29 (June 1986): 192; hereafter cited in text.
11. Augustus Jessopp and Montague Rhodes James, *The Life and Miracles of William of Norwich by Thomas of Monmouth: Now First Edited from the Unique Manuscript with an Introduction, Translation, and Notes* (Cambridge: Cambridge University Press, 1896), 19–22.
12. M. D. Anderson, *A Saint at Stake: The Strange Death of William of Norwich, 1144* (London: Faber & Faber, 1964), 131.
13. Poland was secretly partitioned by Germany and the Soviet Union in August 1939, and Hitler reneged on that secret agreement by invading Poland on 1 September 1939.
14. Aharon Appelfeld, *Badenheim 1939*, trans. Dalya Bilu (Boston: David R. Godine, 1980).

Chapter Five

1. Harold Ribalow, "Wesker's Search for Identity," *Jewish Quarterly* 13 (Summer 1965): 5. Most of the information in these opening paragraphs is taken from that article and the chapter "Faith and Reason" from Wesker's unpublished autobiography *As Much as I Dare*; hereafter cited in test as *"Dare* MS."

2. Liebman Hersch, "My Jewishness," in *The Faith of Secular Jews*, ed. Samuel L. Goodman (New York: KTAV, 1976), 75–83. Hersch's article originally appeared in *Mein Yiddishkeit* (Geneva, 1944).

3. *The Merchant*, notes and commentary by Glenda Leeming (London: Methuen Student Edition, 1983), xiv–xvii.

4. John Hollander, "Hebrew and Yiddish Legacies—a Symposium," *Times Literary Supplement*, 3 May 1985, 500.

5. All the citations here are taken from the 1990 Penguin edition and not from the earlier edition of *Caritas* (London: Jonathan Cape, 1981). It should also be noted that there is a published opera libretto of *Caritas* that was first performed on 21 November 1991 at Wakefield Opera House with music by Robert Saxton.

6. "The Fundamental Right to Give Offense," *Independent*, 25 July 1989, 19.

Chapter Six

1. Michelene Wandor, *Carry On, Understudies: Theatre and Sexual Politics* (London: Routledge & Kegan Paul, 1981), 146.

2. This play first appeared in 1975 as a short story by the same name, 3–44.

3. Unpublished manuscript of *Three Women Talking*. The play had its world premiere in Chicago at the Northlight Theatre 15 January 1992 and has subsequently been revised with a new ending taken into account in this discussion.

Chapter Seven

1. Benedict Nightengale, "Wesker in the Wilderness," *New Statesman*, 29 May 1970, 780; hereafter cited in text.

2. *The Journalists: A Triptych* (London: Jonathan Cape, 1979), 100; hereafter cited in text.

3. "Interpretation—to Impose or Explain," *Performing Arts Journal* 32 (1988): 66; hereafter cited in text. It was revised in November 1990 and delivered as the first Raymond Williams Memorial lecture. Much of this discussion is based on the expanded form found in that lecture.

4. Benedict Nightengale, "Wesker among the Lilliputians," *New Statesman*, 23 October 1981, 26.

5. The wealthy daughter of newspaper magnate William Randolph Hearst, Patricia Hearst was kidnapped by a revolutionary group called the Symbionese Liberation Army in February 1974. Eventually she was converted to their cause and participated in a bank robbery on their behalf.

6. Letter to the author, 14 February 1992.

7. Unpublished essay, "The Necrophiliacs," 1991.

8. Autobiographical essay in *Voices for Life: Reflections on the Human Condition*, ed. Dom Moraes (New York: Praeger, 1975), 191. Parts of this essay

became "Words—as Definitions of Experience," a lecture given in Italy for the Associazione Culturale Italiana in 1975 and were published in *Distinctions* in 1985.

    9. "On Playwriting," interview with Robert Skloot, *Performing Arts Journal* 2 (Winter 1978): 44.

    10. Letter to Benedict Nightengale, published in "Wesker among the Lilliputians," 26.

    11. Nigella Lawson, "A Playwright Who Still Has Something to Shout About: Arnold Wesker," *Sunday Times*, 10 June 1990.

Selected Bibliography

PRIMARY WORKS
Collected Short Stories and Plays

Love Letters on Blue Paper. New York: Harper & Row, 1975.
Said the Old Man to the Young Man. London: Jonathan Cape, 1978.
Six Sundays in January. London: Jonathan Cape, 1971.

Collected Stage Plays

Volume 1: *Chicken Soup with Barley, Roots, I'm Talking about Jerusalem*. Middlesex: Penguin, 1990.
Volume 2: *The Kitchen, The Four Seasons, Their Very Own and Golden City*. Middlesex: Penguin, 1990.
Volume 3: *Chips with Everything, The Friends, The Old Ones, Love Letters on Blue Paper*. Middlesex: Penguin, 1990.
Volume 4: *Shylock, The Journalists, The Wedding Feast, The Merchant*. Middlesex: Penguin, 1990.
Volume 5: *Yardsale, Whatever Happened to Betty Lemon?, Four Portraits—of Mothers, The Mistress, Annie Wobbler*. Middlesex: Penguin, 1990.
Volume 6: *One More Ride on the Merry-Go-Round, Caritas, When God Wanted a Son, Lady Othello, Bluey*. Middlesex: Penguin, 1990.
Volume 7: *Three Women Talking, Blood Libel, Wild Spring, Beorhtel's Hill, Letter to a Daughter*. Middlesex: Penguin, forthcoming.

Miscellaneous

As Much as I Dare. Unpublished autobiography.
Caritas: An Opera in Two Acts without Interval. Chester, England: Chester Music Limited, 1981.
The Journalists: A Triptych. London: Jonathan Cape, 1979.
The Merchant. With commentary and notes by Glenda Leeming. London: Methuen, 1977.

Essays and Lectures

"Art—Therapy or Experience?" *Views* 4 (Spring 1964): 44–7.
"Art Is Not Enough." *Twentieth Century*, February 1961, 190–94.
Distinctions. London: Jonathan Cape, 1985.
Fears of Fragmentation. London: Jonathan Cape, 1970.

"From a Writer's Notebook." *Theatre Quarterly* 6 (May–June 1972): 8–13.
"Miniautobiography in Three Acts and a Prologue." Vol. 7. *Contemporary Authors Autobiography Series*, 227–63. Detroit: Gale Research, 1987.
"The Modern Playwright, or 'O, Mother, is it worth it?'" Co-authored with Bill Holdsworth. London: Gemini, 1960.
"The Fundamental Right to Give Offense." *Independent*, 29 July 1989, 19.
"Interpretation—to Impose or Explain." *Performing Arts Journal* 32 (1988): 62–76.
"The Playwright as Director." *Plays and Players*, February 1974, 10–12.
Words—as Definitions of Experience. With an Afterword by Richard Appignanesi. London: Writers and Readers Publishing Cooperative, 1976.
"Yiddish and Hebrew Legacies—a Symposium." Edited by John Hollander. *Times Literary Supplement*, 3 May 1985, 500.

Letters

Open Letter to T. C. Worsley. "Prole Playwright." *New Statesman*, 28 February 1959, 293.

SECONDARY WORKS
Interviews

Bigsby, Christopher. "In Conversation with Christopher Bigsby." Literature Study Aids, British Council, 4 March 1976.
Clare, Anthony. *In the Psychiatrist's Chair*, 47–61. London: Hogarth Press, 1984.
Gordon, Giles. "Arnold Wesker." *Transatlantic Review* 21 (Summer 1966): 15–25.
Hayman, Ronald. *Arnold Wesker*, 1–12, 92–102. 3d ed. London: Heinemann, 1979.
_____. "Arnold Wesker and John Dexter." *Transatlantic Review* 48 (Winter 1973–74): 89–99.
_____. "An Interview with Arnold Wesker: Centre 42." *Encore* 9 (May–June 1962): 39–44.
Hoggart, Simon. "Writers on Writing." TVS, 7 March 1986.
Itzin, Catherine, Glenda Leeming, and Simon Trussler. "A Sense of What Should Follow." *Theatre Quarterly* 28 (1977–78): 5–24. Reprinted in Simon Trussler, *New Theatre Voices of the 1970s*. London: Eyre Methuen, 1981.
Skloot, Robert. "On Playwriting: Interview with Arnold Wesker." *Performing Arts Journal* 2 (Winter 1978): 38–47.
Stoll, Karl-Heinz. "Interviews with Edward Bond and Arnold Wesker." *Twentieth-Century Literature: A Scholarly and Critical Journal* 22 (December 1976): 411–32.
"The System and the Writer," *New Theatre Magazine* 9 (February 1971): 8–11.

Trussler, Simon. "His Very Own and Golden City: An Interview with Arnold Wesker." *Tulane Drama Review* 11 (1966): 192–201. Later published as "Arnold Wesker." In *Theatre at Work: Playwrights and Productions in Modern British Theatre*, 78–95. New York: Hill & Wang, 1967.

Checklists

Julian, Ria, and Simon Trussler. *Theatrefacts*. TF 14. London: Theatre Quarter Publications, 1977. Out of print and a rare item, but still very useful for its play summaries and little-known facts about their productions.

Leeming, Glenda. *Wesker on File*. London: Methuen, 1985. The most comprehensive list to date.

Books

Craig, Sandy, ed. *Dreams and Deconstructions: Alternative Theatre in Britain*. Ambergate: Amber Lane Press, 1990. An energetic collection of articles on the various forms of alternative theater from a leftist perspective.

Dornan, Reade. *Arnold Wesker: A Casebook*. New York: Garland Press, forthcoming. A collection that emphasizes plays that have received little attention elsewhere and an assortment of critical approaches.

Innes, Christopher. *Modern British Drama, 1890–1990*, 113–21. Cambridge: Cambridge University Press, 1992. A general but comprehensive history that spans British drama, mainstream and alternative, from Shaw and the Fabians to the Marxists and feminists. Shows where Wesker fits in this period and identifies all the other major figures and movements.

Itzin, Catherine. *Stages in the Revolution: Political Theatre in Britain since 1968*. London: Eyre Methuen, 1980. An invaluable reference book on alternative theater in Britain from 1968 to 1978. This is the place to begin serious research of this period.

Leeming, Glenda. *Wesker: The Playwright*. London, Methuen, 1983. Discussions of the plays by a writer who knows Wesker. The plays are read through Wesker's biography, and her understanding is insightful and sensible.

——. *Arnold Wesker*. London: Longman Group for the British Council, 1972. A book-length essay that makes essentially the same points about Wesker and his plays of the 1960s as Leeming and Simon Trussler make in *The Plays of Arnold Wesker*, but she does not discuss the essays.

Leeming, Glenda, and Simon Trussler. *The Plays of Arnold Wesker: An Assessment*. London: Victor Gollancz, 1971. Important because it is written at the "watershed" of Wesker's career and covers the collection of essays on Centre 42, *Fears of Fragmentation*.

Marowitz, Charles, Tom Milne, and Owen Hale. *New Theatre Voices of the Fifties and Sixties: Selections from Encore Magazine, 1956–1963*. London: Eyre Methuen, 1965. A collection of articles that documents the insiders' debates in alternative theater during the 1960s.

Ribalow, Harold U. *Arnold Wesker*. New York: Twayne, 1965. The first book on Wesker discusses the trilogy, *Chips with Everything,* and other works through 1965. In the chapter "Wesker's Search for Identity" Ribalow speaks of "The Problem of Jewishness."

Taylor, John Russell. *Anger and After: A Guide to the New British Drama*. Revised and Expanded Edition. New York: Hill & Wang, 1969. Taylor recognized the significance of several key figures—John Osborne, John Arden, Shelagh Delaney, Peter Shaffer, and Ann Jellicoe—as early as 1962. This is a revision of that early book.

Tynan, Kenneth. *A View of the English Stage*. London: Davis-Poynter, 1975. Tynan was another rare critic who realized quite early the significance of this movement in alternative theater. His reviews of the trilogy are worth reading for their style and incisiveness.

Wandor, Michelene. *Look Back in Gender: Sexuality and the Family in Post-War British Drama*, 19–28. London: Methuen, 1987. A feminist take on the trilogy. Although Wandor can be satirical in her reviews, her discussion of Wesker's plays is quite straightforward.

Wilcher, Robert. *Understanding Arnold Wesker*. University of South Carolina Press, 1991. Brief but reliable textual readings of the plays. Wilcher's goal is to clarify rather than impose an interpretation on the works, and he gives them a close, reliable reading.

Articles and Parts of Books

Alter, Iskar. "'Barbaric Laws, Barbaric Bonds': Arnold Wesker's *The Merchant*." *Modern Drama* 31 (1988): 536–47. A well-researched article on the laws of Renaissance Venice, matched only by Leeming's introduction to the school edition of *The Merchant* and a closely argued discussion of the play now titled *Shylock*.

Anderson, Michael. "Arnold Wesker: The Last Humanist?" *New Theatre Magazine* 8 (Summer 1968): 10–27. One of the earliest writers to recognize the philosophical and political traditions that inform Wesker's sensibility.

Bigsby, C. W. E. "The Language of Crisis in British Theatre." In *Contemporary English Drama*. New York: Holmes & Meier, 1981. A clear and perceptive discussion of what happens to the language of political playwrights who find themselves caught between the desire to produce imaginative art and drama with a message.

Burrows, Jill. "Wesker's Angels." *Times Educational Supplement,* 26 May 1989, B5. Background information on the writing and directing of *Beorhtel's Hill*.

Coppieters, Frank. "Arnold Wesker's Centre Forty-two: A Cultural Revolution Betrayed." *Theatre Quarterly* 18 (June–August 1975): 37–54. There is no better history of the Centre 42 movement than this article. It is thoroughly researched and revealing about the direction(s) the movement took.

Dexter, John. "Chips and Devotion." *Plays and Players* 10 (December 1962): 32. "Working with Arnold." *Plays and Players* 10 (December 1962): 32. This pair of articles offers Dexter's own perspective of highlights in the early days of working on the trilogy and *Chips with Everything*.

Drabble, Margaret. "Profile 10: Arnold Wesker." *New Review* 11 (1975): 25–30. The most readable article ever written on Wesker. It describes Wesker's low period with compassion and honesty.

Evans, T. F. "Arnold Wesker." In *Dictionary of Literary Biography*. Vol. 13, part 2. *British Dramatists since World War II*, 539–58. Detroit: Gale Research, 1982. A quick overview of Wesker's achievements through 1982 with a basic discussion of the plays.

Griffiths, Malcolm. "Playwriting for the Seventies: Old Theatres, New Audiences, and the Politics of Revolution." *Theatre Quarterly* 24 (Winter 1976–77): 35–78. An excellent article for understanding the political climate of the 1970s through a roundtable discussion among 15 of the best-known British playwrights of that period; Wesker has some interesting comments.

Itzin, Catherine. "A Sense of Dread and Isolation." *Tribune*, 13 October 1978: 9. A brief review of the setbacks that depressed Wesker in the 1970s with a special emphasis on his feelings about his mother. Includes the epitaph he read at Leah Wesker's funeral.

McGrath, John. "Friends and Enemies." *Black Dwarf*, 12 June 1970: 15. The review that triggered the exchange of letters that debated the role of form and content in working-class theater.

Nightengale, Benedict. "Wesker among the Lilliputians." *New Statesman*, 23 October 1981, 25–26. "Wesker in the Wilderness." *New Statesman* 29 May 1970, 780. This pair of reviews is representative of Nightengale's responses to Wesker's plays. Nightengale shows Wesker a healthy respect but also draws the line with Wesker's sermonizing.

O'Connor, Garry. "Production Casebook No. 2: Arnold Wesker's *The Friends*." *Theatre Quarterly* 2 (April–June 1971): 78–92. A thorough and fascinating account of Wesker's history with the 1971 cast of *The Friends*. This story should certainly be considered when debating the pros and cons of author as director.

Zimmermann, Heiner O. "Wesker and Utopia in the Sixties." *Modern Drama* 29 (1986): 185–206. One of the best articles for re-evaluating Wesker's works 25 years after they were first staged because it understands both Wesker's compulsion to pursue his ideals and his lack of confidence in his ability to make a difference.

Index

actors' revolt, 9, 71–72, 73, 148
Allen, Walter, 3
Allio, Ron, 47
alternative theater, ix, x, 3–4, 5–8, 9, 42, 143–45; British Theatre in Crisis Conference, 67
Anderson, Lindsay, 15, 20
Anderson, M. D., 84–85
Annie Wobbler, 71
Angry Young Men, ix, 1–3, 16, 19, 152; Amis, Kingsley, 1; Braine, John, 1; Wilson, Colin, x, 1
Appelfeld, Aharon, 88
Arden, John, 1, 3, 9, 71–72
Ashcroft, Peggy, 45

Badenheim 1939, 80, 86–89
Barker, Clive, 42, 43, 46, 62, 65–67
Beckett, Samuel, 3, 4
Beorhtel's Hill, 48, 80–83, 86, 89
Bigsby, C. W. E, 17
Blake, William, 38
Blood Libel (*William of Norwich*), 80, 83–86
Bolt, Robert, 5, 45
Bond, Edward, 8
Brecht, Bertolt, 2, 48–49
Brenton, Howard, 148
British Arts Council, 47–48, 68
Bryden, Ronald, 140
Bueler, Lois, 100

Caritas, 16, 105–108
"Casual Condemnations," 140
Centre 42, ix, x, 6–7, 8, 19, 36–37, 44–49, 54, 57, 58–63, 64–68, 69–70, 79, 97, 108, 121, 139
Chicken Soup with Barley, ix, 1, 2–3, 4, 13, 15, 26, 27–31, 37, 39, 76, 83, 114
Chips with Everything, 9, 14, 41, 49–53, 74, 75, 76, 144
Coleman, Alec, 47
Copping, Robert, 120
"Cretinue of Critics," 141, 149
critics, and Wesker, x, 1, 3, 9, 139–43

Daldry, Stephen, 23
D'Arcy, Margaretta, 1, 9
Delaney, Shelagh, 1, 3, 42
Devine, George, 2–3, 15, 68
Dexter, John, 9, 23, 40–41, 71, 101, 144–45
"Distinctions, Intimidations, and Hysteria," 69, 98, 141
Drabble, Margaret, 76, 97

East End (of London), 10–11, 13–14, 27–28, 80, 98, 107, 126
Edgar, David, 8
Elsom, John, 3
Esslin, Martin, 64
Exton, Clive, 42, 45

family relationships, and Wesker's work, 113, 126–27
Feather, Victor, 120
Findlater, Richard, 3
Four Portraits—of Mothers, 15, 116, 117, 118, 123–26, 127
The Four Seasons, 8, 49, 53–55, 70, 121, 140, 142
The Friends, 7, 8, 58, 64–67, 70–71, 73, 76, 140, 142, 143
"The Fundamental Right to Give Offense," 108

Gaskill, William, 70
Gilliatt, Penelope, 140
Great Britain, post–World War II, ix, 1, 2, 3, 4–5, 14, 28–29, 37, 42–43, 81–82
Greene, Graham, 45
Greenwood, Walter, 42
Griffiths, Trevor, 8
Gulbenkian Foundation, 45

Hall, Peter, 101, 132–33
Hare, David, 148
Hayman, Ronald, 20
Henry, Victor, 71

165

Hersch, Liebman, 99
Hobson, Harold, 141, 149
Hoggart, Richard, 9–10, 19, 20, 33, 35
Holdsworth, Bill, 43–44

I'm Talking about Jerusalem, ix, 1, 2, 38–40, 116
Ionesco, Eugène, 2

The Journalists (play), 9, 71, 121, 146–49
The Journalists: A Triptych, 135
Joyce, James, 117

Kenny, Sean, 42
Kimura, Koichi, 23
The Kitchen, 2, 14, 15, 20, 22–26, 31, 37, 39–40, 41, 71, 76, 133, 148
Kops, Bernard, 1, 42
Kotcheff, Ted, 42

"Labour and the Arts: II, or 'What, then, is to be done?,'" 6, 43
Lady Othello, 56, 113, 116, 129–31, 133
Lawson, Nigella, 152
Leeming, Glenda, 48
Lessing, Doris, 42, 45
Letter to a Daughter, 115
Levitt, Paul, 105
Llewellyn, Richard, 42
"Love Letters on Blue Paper" (short story), 72, 113, 114, 116
Love Letters on Blue Paper (play), 71, 116–20, 124, 129

McAuliffe, Nichola, 126
McGrath, John, 6–8, 10, 36, 42, 45, 63, 66, 89, 140, 143
male–female relationships, and Wesker's work, 23, 54–57, 77, 91–93, 102–103, 109–12, 116–18, 118–20, 122–23, 126–27, 127–29, 129–31, 131–33, 133–37, 137–38
"The Man Who Became Afraid," 72–73
Maschler, Tom, 42, 62
Maxwell, Robert, 47
Menace, 49, 53, 54–55, 125
Miller, Arthur, 2, 4
Miniautobiography, xi

Mintz, Louis, 47
The Mistress, 56, 113, 116, 117, 124, 127–29, 131, 133, 135
Mnouchkine, Ariadne, 23
"The Modern Playwright, or 'O, Mother, is it worth it?,'" 6, 43
Morris, William, 5–6, 8, 10, 11, 18, 32, 36, 38, 40, 64
Mostel, Zero, 101
naturalism, and Wesker's work, 20–23, 53, 57

New Towns, 58–59, 80–81
Nightengale, Benedict, 139, 142, 144, 151
The Nottingham Captain, 48–49, 80

O'Brien, Edna, 117
Odets, Clifford, 42
The Old Ones, 9, 15, 41, 55, 71, 95–98, 103, 121, 125
Olivier, Sir Laurence, 45, 100
One More Ride on the Merry-Go-Round, 56, 116, 117, 131–33, 135
Osborne, John, ix, xii, 1–2, 3–4; *The Entertainer*, 71; *Look Back in Anger*, ix, 1–2, 3–4, 15, 54
Owen, Alun, 42, 45

Pinter, Harold, 13, 73
Plowright, Joan, 34, 40, 45
"Pools," 15, 113, 114
Priestley, J. B., 45

Rattigan, Terence, 45
Read, Herbert, 45
Redgrave, Vanessa, 45
Ribalow, Harold, 38
Roots, ix, 1, 2–3, 4, 15, 31–35, 103, 116, 117, 141
Round House, 47–48, 62–63, 64, 67, 70
Royal Court Theatre, ix, 2–3, 6, 15, 23, 27, 34, 41, 68, 71
Royal Shakespeare Company, 9, 20, 71, 148
Rudet, Jacqueline, 31
Rushdie, Salman, 9, 70, 108, 145
Russell, Sir Bertrand, x, 5

Index

"Said the Old Man to the Young Man," 15, 93–95
Saltiel, Della Wesker, 13, 28, 38, 115–16
Saltiel, Ralph, 38
Sandford, Jeremy, 42
Sellers, Peter, 45
Shakespeare, William: *The Merchant of Venice*, 101, 103; *The Merry Wives of Windsor*, 71; *Othello*, 130
Shaw, George Bernard, 16, 118
Shylock (*The Merchant*), 15, 100–105
Sillitoe, Alan, 45
"Six Sundays in January" (short story), 15, 91–93, 113
Six Sundays in January (story collection), 54
Snow, C. P., 45
socialist theater, ix, x, 4–10, 21, 24–26, 42–49, 54, 57
"State-right, Birth-right Freedom," 16, 79
Steiner, George, 22
Styron, William, 22
Swift, Jonathan, 146

Taylor, John Russell, 40, 140, 141, 142
Their Very Own and Golden City, 8, 57–63, 70, 71, 82, 140
Three Women Talking, xi, 117, 133–37
"A Time of Dying," 12, 15, 113
Trades Union Congress (TUC), 6, 43–44, 58–61, 120
"Two Roots of Judaism," 98–100
Tynan, Kenneth, 34, 40, 45, 71

"Unhappy Poisons," 141–42

Vandenbroucke, Russell, xi, 71
"The Visit," 17, 76–80, 113, 116

Wandor, Michelene, 114
Wardle, Irving, 52
The Wedding Feast, 15, 31, 72, 73–76
Wesker, Arnold: and aging, 54–55, 64, 67, 72, 81, 95–98, 120–21, 132; and anti-authoritarianism, 1–2, 33–34, 49–52, 74–76, 104–105, 106–108, 108–10, 120–21, 131, 146–48; and anti-Semitism and bigotry, 12, 13, 14, 70, 72, 74–76, 76–77, 79–80, 80–82, 83–86, 86–89, 91, 92–93, 93–94, 100–105, 109–12, 120–21, 150; and the arts, ix, 2, 5–6, 10, 32–34, 36–37, 42–47, 57, 62, 65–68, 70, 79–80, 89, 139; education of, 1, 3, 5, 9–10, 14–15, 32–34, 37, 44–46, 70, 89, 103–104, 106, 150; family history of, x, 3, 10–15, 17, 28–30, 73, 90, 95, 113–14, 115–16; as "fixer," 91, 100, 113, 149–52; and humanism, ix, x, xi, 2, 18–19, 20, 26, 51–52, 61, 77–80, 89, 90, 91, 94–95, 99–100, 103–105, 106–108, 113, 138, 139, 150–52; individualism vs. communal responsibility, 9–10, 15–17, 18–19, 25–26, 35, 37, 38–39, 40, 49–52, 61–63, 69, 75–76, 76–80, 104–105, 114, 118–20, 121, 125–26, 127–29, 131, 133, 134–35, 140–43, 146–48, 149–52; and Judaism, x, xi, xii, 3, 9, 10–18, 19, 25–26, 27, 31, 33, 69, 72, 77–80, 80–82, 85, 90–91, 95–97, 98–100, 103, 108, 111–12, 113, 123–24, 137, 139, 149–52; and "Lilliputians," 9, 70, 140, 146, 148, 150; "melancholy optimism" of, ix, 8, 31, 83, 97–98, 151–52; and popular culture, 36, 42, 45–46, 79–80; and pluralism, 67, 80–83, 105, 106–108; playwright-as-director, 41, 69–71, 73, 143–45; and revolution, 7–8, 63, 66–67, 77, 79, 81, 89, 106–107; and socialism, ix, x, xi, 2–18, 25–26, 27–30, 32, 37, 39–40, 42–47, 48–49, 57, 59, 61, 64–68, 69, 73–76, 77–80, 93, 94, 150–51
Wesker, Cecile (Leah) Perlmutter, 11–14, 27–30, 57, 113–14, 115
Wesker, Daniel, 31
Wesker, Doreen (Dusty) Bicker, 15, 31, 71, 76, 115–16, 118–20
Wesker, Joseph, 11–14, 27, 29, 30, 57, 114, 115
Wesker, Lindsay Joe, 31
Wesker, Tanya Jo, 31
Whatever Happened to Betty Lemon?, 71, 113, 120–21

When God Wanted a Son, 15, 104, 109–12, 113, 116, 124
Wild Spring, 137–38
Williams, Raymond, 45
Wilson, Harold, 4, 47
women, and Wesker's work, x, 39, 56, 69, 78, 103, 113–38, 150
"The Women in My Writing: Notes for a Reading," 113
working class, and Wesker's work, x, 2, 3–4, 5–10, 11, 20, 31–35, 36–37, 38–39, 42, 43–47, 48, 50–52, 59, 65–66, 73–75, 93–94, 112, 139; kitchen-sink dramatists, 3–4, 23
Worsley, T. C., 140

Yardsale, 71, 118, 121–23, 124, 127, 131
Young Communist League, 16

Zimmerman, Heiner O., 83, 151
Zionist Youth Movement, 16, 17, 90
Zola, Emile, 21–22

The Author

Reade W. Dornan received her A.B. from the University of Colorado and her M.A. and Ph.D. from Michigan State University. Currently teaching at the University of Michigan–Flint, she is the editor of *Arnold Wesker: A Casebook*, forthcoming from Garland Press, and *Preserving the Game: Gambling, Mining, Hunting and Conservation in the Vanishing West*, stories by J. R. Jones. She has published articles on Bertolt Brecht, Caryl Churchill, John McGrath, working-class writers of Victorian Britain, and American women playwrights.